Exploring Community Festivals and Events

The development of the festival and event industry has seen large scale growth and extensive government support as a result of objectives to enhance and project the image of place and leverage positive sponsorship and regeneration opportunities. As we move deeper into austerity measures prompted by economic recession, community festivals and events as a sacred or profane time of celebration can be considered more important than ever before.

This book for the first time explores the role and importance of 'community', 'culture' and its impact through festivals and events. Split into two distinct sections, the first introduces key themes and concepts, contextualises local traditions and culture, and investigates how festivals and events can act as a catalyst for tourism and create a sense of community. It then questions the social and political nature of festivals and community events through examining their ownership. The second section focuses on communities themselves, seeking to examine and discuss key emerging themes in community event studies such as; the role of diaspora, imagined communities, pride and identity, history, producing and consuming space and place, authenticity and multi-ethnic communities. Examples are drawn from Portugal, the Dominican Republic, the USA, Malaysia, Malta, Finland and Australia making this book truly international.

This significant volume will be valuable reading for students and academics across the fields of Event, Tourism and Hospitality studies as well as other social science disciplines.

Allan Jepson was awarded his PhD in 2009; which investigated community festival planning and decision making practices. He is currently a senior academic in Event Studies & Tourism, and researcher in communities and their events within the Marketing Insight Research Group (MIRU) at the University of Hertfordshire in the UK. Over the last decade he has developed undergraduate and postgraduate degree programmes, in Tourism, Hospitality and Event Management.

Alan Clarke works at the University of Pannonia in Veszprém in Hungary, where he helped to develop the English programmes at BA and Masters levels in tourism and hospitality. Since moving to Hungary he has continued his commitments in the UK and is a Visiting Professor at the University of Derby. His current research interests include religious tourism and finding the commonalities between wine tourism in Hungary and whisky trails in Scotland.

Routledge advances in event research series
Edited by Warwick Frost and Jennifer Laing
Department of Marketing, Tourism and Hospitality, La Trobe University, Australia

The Arts and Events
Hilary du Cros and Lee Jolliffe

Sports Events, Society and Culture
Edited by Katherine Dashper, Thomas Fletcher and Nicola McCullough

The Future of Events and Festivals
Edited by Ian Yeoman, Martin Robertson, Una McMahon-Beattie, Elisa Backer and Karen A. Smith

Exploring Community Events and Festivals
Edited by Allan Jepson and Alan Clarke

Event Design
Edited by Greg Richards, Lénia Marques and Karen Mein

Rituals and Traditional Events in the Modern World
Edited by Warwick Frost and Jennifer Laing

Forthcoming:
Events in the City
Using public spaces as event venues
Andrew Smith

Approaches and Methods in Events Studies
Tomas Pernecky

Exploring Community Festivals and Events

Edited by Allan Jepson and Alan Clarke

Routledge
Taylor & Francis Group

LONDON AND NEW YORK

First published 2015
by Routledge
2 Park Square, Milton Park, Abingdon, Oxon OX14 4RN

and by Routledge
711 Third Avenue, New York, NY 10017

Routledge is an imprint of the Taylor & Francis Group, an informa business

British Library Cataloguing in Publication Data
A catalogue record for this book is available from the British Library

Library of Congress Cataloging in Publication Data
A catalog record for this book has been requested

ISBN: 978-1-138-02328-4 (hbk)
ISBN: 978-1-315-77656-9 (ebk)

Typeset in Times New Roman
by Wearset Ltd, Boldon, Tyne and Wear

This book is dedicated to the supportive Jepson and Clarke families. Allan dedicates this book to his wife Joanna and his son Henry, and Alan to Team Clarke in Hungary and the UK.

Contents

PART II

Exploring and defining community festival and event communities 93

Contributors

Mohamed Azlan Ashaari is a full-time staff member of Universiti Sains Malaysia. He is currently finishing his Master of Business Administration, specialising in Tourism and Hospitality.

Vern Biaett is Assistant Professor, Nido R. Qubein School of Communication, High Point University, North Carolina. For over 30 years Vern worked as a leisure practitioner, the final 20 years producing major community festivals for the cities of Phoenix and Glendale, Arizona. During this period he was also involved with several mega events including the Phoenix Grand Prix, an NFL Super Bowl and the Albuquerque Balloon Fiesta. In 2003 Vern embarked on a new academic career that has included teaching events management courses as part of a special event certificate programme he co-created at Arizona State as well as pursuit of a doctoral degree in community resources and development, completed in 2013 with a dissertation focusing on attendee behaviour at community festivals using participant observation grounded theory method. Although a 'young' researcher, he has also authored and co-authored journal articles on a variety of topics including quantifying the triple bottom line in tourism, estimating attendance at parades, teaching students about the living wage and working poor, and a comparison of gathering marketing materials for special events while also continuing to investigate the subject of festivity and attendee experience. Vern served on the foundation board of the International Festivals & Events Association and was a co-founder and chairman of the Arizona Festivals & Events Association.

Cândida Cadavez is a Lecturer at the Estoril Higher Institute for Tourism and Hotel Studies, in Portugal. She has a Master's Degree in English Culture Studies with a thesis titled 'A Room With a View to the World: Tourism, Globalization and Culture' and a PhD in Literary and Culture Studies from the University of Lisbon with a thesis on tourism representations in the Portuguese *Estado Novo*, titled 'All for the Nation: Tourism Representations in Portugal from 1933 to 1940'. She has participated in several international congresses and published articles about her main academic research interests, which include tourism, popular culture, nation(alism)s, globalization and visual studies. Cândida is a member of the Research Center for Communication and

Culture (Portuguese Catholic University, Lisbon) and a researcher at Fundação António Quadros – Cultura e Pensamento.

Alan Clarke works at the University of Pannonia in Veszprém in Hungary, where he helped to develop the English programmes at BA and Master's levels in tourism and hospitality. His first ever teaching job was in community education and his work maintains this commitment to local communities. He has researched widely in the fields of cultures and heritages and published articles on authenticity, power and motivations in relation to festivals and events. Since moving to Hungary he has continued his commitments in the United Kingdom and is a Visiting Professor at the University of Derby. The shifts in regimes have been fascinating, especially in trying to understand the constructions and reconstructions of communities. His current research interests include religious tourism and finding the commonalities between wine tourism in Hungary and whisky trails in Scotland. Thanks to the joys of the Internet he still suffers in supporting Sheffield Wednesday – a football club founded on the local communities in Sheffield through the co-operative movement and the only professional club named after a day of the week. He will happily pass on the explanation of that to anyone who asks!

Reverend Ruth Dowson is a Senior Lecturer and the Course Leader of the BA Events Management course at the UK Centre for Events Management at Leeds Metropolitan University. With an extensive background as an events management practitioner, Ruth has considerable leadership expertise and over 30 years' experience in events, covering strategic development, management and delivery of events, conferences, seminars and exhibitions, in both public and private sectors in the United Kingdom. In that time, Ruth has managed thousands of events and developed high-performing event teams, as well as managing event venues. In 2007, Ruth moved into teaching events management and then took on course leadership at the UK Centre for Events Management in 2009. Ruth was ordained a priest in the Church of England in 2013, and is currently the only full-time events academic who can also officiate at weddings and funerals. Ruth's research interests focus on the role of events in the culture of church, the extended use of religious heritage buildings for events and the eventisation of religious heritage objects; they also include protest events and raves and the influence of personality on individuals and team development.

Michelle Duffy is a Senior Lecturer in Sociology at Federation University of Australia. Current research examines the role emotions and affect play in processes of place and community-making, and the significance of art practice – specifically that of sound, music and performance – in creating and/or challenging identity in public spaces and public events.

Jenny Flinn is a Lecturer in Events Management at Glasgow Caledonian University. She is the Programme Leader for the BA (Hons) International Events Management and also teaches on the MSc International Events Management and BA (Hons) International Sports Management. Jenny is the Secretary for the Association for Events Management Education, working closely with the events industry to raise the profile of events management education. Her research interests lie in the area of festivals and events, particularly in relation to the construction of identity at an individual, community, national and international level. Jenny is currently undertaking a PhD that examines the construction of identity within Mixed Martial Arts (MMA), one of the fastest growing sports in the world.

Jodie George is a Research Associate and Lecturer in Cultural Geography at the University of South Australia. Her research is concerned with the cultural meanings of place, examining how the discourses and practices of tourism and 'rurality' may impact upon the construction of particular locations, to better understand issues of belonging, community and sustainable practice. She has been a researcher on several projects examining identity and inclusion in regional areas and has published in a range of journals including *Continuum*, *Transnational Literature* and *Social Alternatives*.

Antti Haahti is Professor of Tourism at the University of Lapland, Multidimensional Tourism Institute. His fields of research are in entrepreneurship, strategy and marketing management, specifically of SMTEs.

Allan Jepson is a senior academic and researcher in event studies within the Marketing Insight Research Group (MIRU) at the University of Hertfordshire in the United Kingdom. He was awarded his PhD in 2009, which investigated community festival planning and decision-making practices under the supervision of Alan Clarke. Over the last decade he has developed undergraduate and postgraduate degree programmes in Tourism, Hospitality and Event Management. He also has extensive experience in festival and events praxis and research, and is currently developing networks locally, regionally and nationally to enhance the linkages between the events courses at the university and the practitioner communities within his role as Vice-chair of the Association of Events Management Education (AEME) in the UK. Allan's current research is exploring community engagement and inclusion within community festivals and events. Allan is also a proud supporter of Nottingham Forest Football Club.

Azilah Kasim is an Associate Professor of Tourism at Universiti Utara Malaysia. She earned her undergraduate degree from Brock University, Ontario, Master of Science from Michigan State University, USA and PhD in Tourism from the University of East Anglia, UK. She is currently a board member of the *International Journal of Culture in Tourism, Hospitality and Leisure* and an Advisory Board member of the *Asia-Pacific Journal of Innovation in Hospitality and Tourism* (APJIHT). She is an active ad hoc reviewer for many international journals including *Journal of Sustainable Tourism* and *International Journal of Contemporary Hospitality Management*. She researches extensively and publishes in many high index international journals. Her expertise is on sustainability issues, corporate social responsibility and marketing. She also writes books on tourism, recreation and qualitative research topics.

Maarit Kinnunen has a Master of Science in Computer Science from the University of Helsinki, and Master of Social Science in Tourism Research from the University of Lapland. Currently, she is working on her PhD on experiences of cultural event visitors.

Judith Mair is a Senior Lecturer in Event Management in the UQ Business School, University of Queensland, Australia. Her research interests include events and sustainability, particularly environmental and socio-cultural sustainability. Her recent research has examined the relationship between events and community, with a particular focus on the role of festivals in community building and community cohesion.

Kelley A. McClinchey received her PhD in Geography in 2011 specialising in cultural geography, urban tourism and festivals. Currently, she is a part-time Lecturer in the Department of Geography and Environmental Studies at Wilfrid Laurier University, Waterloo, Ontario. She has a Master's in Environmental Studies, also from Wilfrid Laurier University, specialising in resource management, sustainability and rural tourism. Her research interests include tourism mobilities, cultural globalisation, humanist and postmodern geographies, migration and multiculturalism, cultural festivals, place representation and literary tourism, and sense of place.

Jessica Pacella is currently in the late stages of her doctoral thesis at the University of South Australia, titled 'Trading Travellers' Tales: Performing Knowledge Exchange in Backpacker Hostels'. Her research focuses on youth hostels as sites for travellers to engage in understandings of cultural difference, sense of self and the importance of technology in the construction of 'mobile' homes. She has published in, and was a guest editor of, a special edition of *Social Alternatives* and is currently involved in a research project exploring issues of community identity and social inclusion at regional festivals.

Margherita Pedrana is Assistant Professor of Applied Economics at the European University of Rome. She was awarded her PhD in Economics of Communication in 2008 at IULM University in Milan and a MSc in Local Economic Development at the London School of Economics. She teaches enterprise's economy and local economic development. Her main research interests are economics of tourism, local development, regional economics and social capital.

Rosie Roberts is an interdisciplinary cultural studies scholar whose work focuses on the intersections of culture, place, equity and belonging. Her PhD research expanded upon labour-centred constructions of skilled migration, demonstrating the diverse mobility pathways and visa categories that migrants experience over time and through space. She was awarded a Maurice de Rohan International Scholarship to undertake part of her doctoral research in the UK and USA. Rosie is employed as a Lecturer in Aboriginal Education at the David Unaipon College of Indigenous Education and Research. She is currently engaged in research exploring issues of community identity in regional festivals as well as a project examining educational aspirations within low socio-economic status communities.

W. Gerard Ryan is a Senior Lecturer in Events Management based at The University of Derby Buxton Campus. Prior to teaching in HE, Gerard made a career in events for many years as a professional in a number of different areas. After many distinguished years as a musician, Gerard became the Development Manager at the Merseyside Music Development Agency (MMDA) where he developed a number of business services for the creative industries. He later became the event manager at the Cavern Club in Liverpool with numerous notable achievements during the period. While continuing to be involved in music-related events, Gerard's focus is for the most part academic with research interests in event management education and the effects events have on the local community.

Shahrul Aman Sabir Ahmad is attached to Tourism Malaysia (Kedah) and is in charge of marketing Kedah as a tourism destination. He is currently completing his Master of Business Administration (Tourism and Hospitality) at Universiti Utara Malaysia.

Daniel Turner is the Subject Leader for Events, Hospitality and Tourism within the Department of Communication, Marketing and Media of Robert Gordon University, Aberdeen. In addition, he acts as Course Leader for the BA (Hons) Events Management programme. Daniel's research and teaching interests lie in the field of events policy and the socio-cultural aspects of contemporary events. He teaches across these fields in modules such as Event Tourism: Legacy and Impact, Event Sponsorship and Fundraising and Lifestyle Consumption and Experience Economies. He also retains an active interest in the fields of sports studies and sports management.

Leanne White is a Senior Lecturer in the College of Business at Victoria University in Melbourne, Australia. Her research interests include: national identity, commercial nationalism, popular culture, advertising, destination marketing, events and cultural tourism. Leanne's PhD examined manifestations of official nationalism and commercial nationalism at the Sydney 2000 Olympic Games. She is the author of more than 40 book chapters and refereed journal articles, and co-editor of the Routledge research books: *Wine and Identity: Branding, Heritage, Terroir* (2014), *Dark Tourism and Place Identity: Managing and Interpreting Dark Places* (2013) and *Tourism and National Identities: An International Perspective* (2011). Leanne is a regular reviewer of journal articles, a doctoral thesis examiner and member of professional associations in tourism, marketing, leisure and sport.

Caroline Winter is a Senior Lecturer in the Faculty of Business at Federation University Australia where she teaches in tourism. Her main research concerns the Great War of 1914–1918 and the ways in which social memories are being rehearsed and reformed by current generations. She has conducted surveys relating to visitor motivations and experiences at several battlefield sites in Belgium and France including Fromelles, Ieper (Ypres), Villers-Bretonneux and the Passchendaele museum, and in Australia at the Shrine of Remembrance, Melbourne. Caroline is also interested in the visitation patterns at military cemeteries.

Nicholas Wise is Lecturer in Sport, Events and Tourism Management at Glasgow Caledonian University, Scotland. Trained as a geographer, much of his research focuses on image and place identity. Nick earned his PhD in 2012 from Kent State University, Ohio, and has published broadly on sport, events and tourism-related research focused on the Dominican Republic, Argentina, Croatia and Serbia.

Vincent Zammit, MA (Baroque Studies), BA (Mediterranean Studies), is currently the Head of the Tourism Studies Department and Lecturer at the Institute of Tourism Studies, Malta. He is also the coordinator of the Centre for Cultural and Heritage Studies. He has been involved in Maltese culture, heritage and tourism since 1978. Vincent has published a number of studies and books and has produced a number of radio and television programmes on Maltese history and culture. Vincent has also contributed papers and chapters in the sphere of religious tourism, events and tourism in general. A licensed tourist guide himself, Vincent has been responsible for the preparation of tourist guides for the last 20 years. He has attended a number of international conferences abroad where he presented papers about various aspects of tourism in Malta, as well as being the organiser of international conferences about religious tourism.

Acknowledgements

Thank you to Emma Travis, commissioning editor at Routledge, for believing in our original proposal. Thank you also to Professor Ross Brennan at the University of Hertfordshire for continuing to support ASJ's research time allocation. AC thanks the Head of Tourism for similar support. The majority of thanks are to all of our contributors who have worked on their chapters, to a tight schedule and came through for us. We hope they are pleased with how it has turned out.

1 Defining and exploring community festivals and events

Allan Jepson and Alan Clarke

Events are deeply embedded within society and culture and, as a result of this, events create and re-create their histories which generate community values, customs and particular types of behaviour. This book, unlike any other, explores the role and importance of 'community', 'culture' and their impact through festivals and events. The genealogy of this text begins in conversations between the editors back in the last days of the 1990s and the beginning of the 2000s. We were in what we considered to be a unique position to observe and participate in an attempt to develop a series of events, which was eventually branded a community festival, in our university city. The initial research was centred on a community cultural festival that was staged in Derby (UK) in the summer of 2002, the year of Queen Elizabeth II's Golden Jubilee celebrations. The festival was unique in the United Kingdom, as it tried to encapsulate three major celebrations under the umbrella of 'The Derby Jubilee Festival'. The City of Derby was celebrating 25 years since the Queen granted it city status in 1977, 50 years since the Queen acceded to the throne in 1952 and 75 years since Derby Cathedral was built in 1927 and the Church of England created the new Diocese of Derby, and with it 'Cathedral Status'.

The original concept of the Derby Jubilee Festival came from the Dean of Derby Cathedral, who had the idea when he met representatives from 20 music and choral groups in Derby that perform regularly at the cathedral. The idea was partly generated by the lack of an original festival in Derby; the last official festival of any kind in Derby had taken place in 1996, and had been predominantly concerned with the arts and classical music. The main problems identified with this festival stemmed from the narrow focus of the events and it being considered elitist, which resulted in a large proportion of the surrounding local community not attending any of the events. It was thus decided to widen the scope of the proposed festival by incorporating the three key celebrations (25, 50 and 75) into one programme celebrating the diverse and burgeoning cultures in Derby.

However, there were another six notable celebrations that, we would hold, were also significant within the City of Derby: the 25th anniversary of the opening of the Derby Assembly Rooms in 1977; the 25th CAMRA (Campaign for Real Ale) Beer Festival; 200 years since the death of Erasmus Darwin (1731–1802), grandfather of Charles Darwin; the 21st anniversary of 'Royal

Crown' Derby; and the 10th anniversaries of the Queen's Leisure Centre (opened by Queen Elizabeth II) and the Derby Heritage Centre. Although these events might be considered to be notable, they were to play little or no part in the formulation of the festival as the stakeholders focused on the 'big three' (Jepson & Clarke, 2005).

Our reading suggested that there were major issues surrounding the definition of culture and the types of culture that were approved as being worthy of inclusion. We also began to consider the nature of the 'community' that was being employed in the festival organisation. We moved to a position where we questioned both of the central terms. We had problems negotiating the imposition of a monocultural culture on a multicultural city by an elitist, middle-class, middle-aged minority. These reflections have led us to explore the complexities of both cultures and communities. We recognise that the discourses of identity are structured through those of gender, class and ethnicity and are fundamental to understanding the construction of the cultures and communities involved in the festivals and events that are often presented in their names.

It has been recognised that community festivals should be more than a series of loosely connected events, as can be seen in this definition provided by the Department of Culture, Arts and Leisure in Northern Ireland:

> A community festival is a series of events with a common theme and delivered within a defined time period. It is developed from within a community and should celebrate and positively promote what the community represents. Community festivals are about participation, involvement, and the creation of a sense of identity and are important in contributing to the social well being of a community. They must be initiated and led by a community organisation or a community-led partnership. It is not enough to run a festival for a community – the community must play a strong part in the development and delivery of the festival and have ownership of it.
>
> (Department of Culture, Arts and Leisure, 2007)

This definition calls into doubt the concept of development of community festivals, particularly when the power relations are considered. As we pointed out in one of our earlier articles (Clarke & Jepson, 2011, p. 8), political relations are significant to the creation of a festival because there are particular individuals who are the power-brokers of that community, 'those who hold direct power over the festival and its construction'. A community festival is therefore constituted out of a complex set of power relations that nonetheless serve to define notions of belonging.

Our work (Clarke & Jepson, 2009, 2010, 2011; Clarke, Jepson, & Wiltshier, 2008; Jepson, 2009; Jepson & Clarke, 2005, 2013; Jepson, Clarke & Ragsdell, 2012) has developed a focus on the way decisions are taken in and around community festivals. We found that none of the previous definitions referenced the conditions that create a community festival and therefore proposed a more critical and comprehensive definition that sees community festivals as a:

Themed and inclusive community event or series of events which have been created as the result of an inclusive community planning process to celebrate the particular way of life of people and groups in the local community with emphasis on particular space and time.

(Jepson & Clarke, 2013)

We hope that this genealogy helps to explain the range of the key themes introduced into this book's frame of reference, including: 'culture, authenticity and meaning of local community events'; 'the evolution and life cycle of local community events'; 'community events as tourist attractions'; 'the role and importance of community events'; and 'community hospitality, foods and wine'.

The development of the festival and event industry alongside the globalisation of major sports events has seen large-scale growth and extensive government support as a result of objectives to enhance and project the image of place and leverage positive sponsorship and regeneration opportunities, all with an overarching aim to ensure place competitiveness. As we move deeper into austerity measures as the result of worldwide economic recession, community festivals and events as 'a sacred or profane time of celebration' (Falassi, 1987, p. 2) can be considered even more important than ever. Particularly as festivals offer all stakeholders an opportunity to 'celebrate community values, ideologies, identity and continuity' (ibid.). As a social cultural phenomenon festivals can be seen as prime manifestations of the experience economy (Pine & Gilmore, 1999) as they entertain, educate, hold aesthetic value and provide the platform for escapism. Farber (1983, cited in Getz, 1991) investigated festivals and public celebrations and learned much about a community's symbolic, economic, political and social life. This book will be unique in the marketplace and has the possibility to take the lead in modules at undergraduate and postgraduate level where modules explore community involvement and importance within events. This edited collection aims to explore community festivals and events from various perspectives to elaborate their meanings.

Part I: Exploring and defining the *context* of community festivals and events

The 'explorations' section of the book introduces key themes and concepts that help to define community festivals and events. It seeks to explore and contextualise local traditions and culture and how community festivals and events can act as a catalyst for tourism, as well as create a sense of identity and community. This part also begins to question the social and political nature of festivals and community events through examining their ownership. The case studies in Part I are taken from community festivals and events in Australia, the United States, the United Kingdom, the Dominican Republic, Italy and Finland.

Part I begins with a fascinating study on the history and meanings of festivity by Vern Biaett (Chapter 2). There is no denying that community festivals have evolved into well planned and executed commercial organisms, but, Biaett asks, where is the fun and can there not be more? A riposte to this paradox suggests that while the physical, emotional and collaborative energy that goes into planning and producing the financial, marketing and operational aspects leads to expanded social capital for the organizers, the typical, mostly unimaginative, spectator aspects of community festival activity programming fail to adequately achieve similar results for their visitors. Real festivity is much more, having originated in the spiritualism of our distant ancestors, expressed in the performing and dramatic arts of rhythmic chanting and dancing to loud bass beats, as well as the visual art forms of costumes, masks and decoration, all combining to produce a sense of wild abandonment in the participants. It is these types of activities that get people out of their chairs and physically, emotionally and collaboratively engaged in social interaction; these types of activities that can develop and increase social capital; and these types of activities that event producers must acquire a deeper understanding and sensitivity about en route to luminal, authentic festivity. Event management must also have the aspiration and/or the knowledge to provide festivity.

Biaett also proposes that although a festival can be defined in context as a noun, a temporary happening or occurrence, he argues that it possesses a much more significant meaning as a verb, a word of action in the sense that it creates something, and part of that something could be social capital for attendees. Event producers who manage the economic, promotional and operations aspects of community festivals, however, with increased emphasis on programmed festivity also have the opportunity to manage larger social impacts.

This chapter is followed by Maarit Kinnunen and Antti Haahti in Chapter 3 offering insights into the experience of community festivals and events from Finnish summer festivals. The chapter focuses on two related questions: how do festival visitors perceive and experience the place and the locality of the venue of the festival? And, how do the local inhabitants view the festival taking place in their home community?

When visitors were asked to imagine an event that would be 'totally ruined', the key feature was the absence of residents and local characteristics of the community. It is the local people and the tastes and smells of local food that give the event its authenticity and the personal touch that makes it memorable.

The authors suggest three clusters within the experience. Young crowd-lovers like to hang out, seek to have fun in their rock festival and to share their experiences, mementos and feelings on social media. Active universalists are conscious consumers willing to spend more money than others, and much of it on local produce. Their choice of events is the most versatile of all the groups. Modest traditionalists are the oldest of the participants, and they favour both local and fair trade products. They are not interested in mobile, location-based or other technical services and they shun social media.

Chapter 4 sees Michelle Duffy and Judith Mair take us all the way to Australia in order to explore the issues surrounding festivals and the sense of community. They observe that many local councils have invested substantial resources into community events and festivals with the expectation that they will produce a range of social and economic benefits. Much of the research on festivals has begun with the underlying premise that such events sustain social benefits through their economic implications. However, recent work has begun to understand festivals as a way of 'performing' or 'doing' community. Festivals are inherently about celebrating community and are understood as community-building activities. Yet, these are complex, potentially divisive processes, and raise many issues, such as what is 'the community' being celebrated at festivals? Using a case study approach, the chapter focuses on the annual Yakkerboo Festival, held in Pakenham, a once-rural community near Melbourne that is now undergoing processes of rapid urbanisation.

In Chapter 5, Margherita Pedrana draws our attention to continental Europe, as her examination deals with the combinations of new and old traditions in the construction of the experiences of the Skieda, in Livigno, Italy. Community events are often based on traditions and on the social need to be interconnected with each other, creating and maintaining the sense of ownership of a community or a place. However, community events may also have other functions. The local community in Livigno is strongly connected to tourism, which is the main economic resource along with retail (it is also a duty-free area). The event is a full week of festivals based on the telemark style of skiing. Telemark is based on a traditional skiing technique, and is also how the old Livigno inhabitants used to ski, with a free heel. The success of the discipline and of the event thus depends on the local community, which started to understand how the old traditions may also be important in the future and give the community a competitive advantage in attracting new tourists.

Chapter 6, by Jodie George, Rosie Roberts and Jessica Pacella, asks 'Whose Festival?' They explore questions of participation, access and ownership in regional festivals. They begin from a recognition that much of the literature within tourism and event studies highlights the important contribution of regional festivals to local communities in terms of social cohesion, regional identity and fiscal viability (Bell & Jayne, 2010; Brennan-Horley, Connell & Gibson, 2007; Getz & Andersson, 2008; Gibson & Stewart, 2009; Gibson, Waitt, Walmsley & Connell, 2010; Gorman-Murray et al., 2008). These questions sit within a context where government bodies in particular have adopted an instrumentalist approach, prompting rural communities to develop economic self-sufficiency, in part through the promotion of festivals as a tourist space. The resulting commodification of community events as a space of consumption may have problematic outcomes in practice, raising questions about whose versions of 'community' are recognised, legitimated and institutionalised through the discourses of event tourism. This chapter extends critical tourism and event studies literature by further unpacking the emergence of competing discourses of 'place' in regional and rural areas, disentangling the ways in which rurality is constructed, experienced and legitimated. Through participants' diverse stories of 'place', the authors' research reveals the complex ways in which festivals construct local cultures for both residents and visitors and how these individuals in turn contribute to shaping festivals through their own participatory practices.

Part II: Exploring and defining community festival and event communities

This part builds on the first by focusing on the communities themselves. It seeks to examine and discuss key emerging themes in community event studies such as: the role of diaspora, imagined communities, pride and identity, history, producing and consuming space and place, authenticity, multi-ethnic communities. Examples are drawn internationally from Portugal, the Dominican Republic, the United States, Malaysia, Malta and Australia, making this book truly international.

In this second part, we present chapters that develop the specificities of local communities. In Chapter 7, Jenny Flinn and Daniel Turner critically explore the construction and consumption of the Scottish diaspora in the United States. Their chapter examines the manner in which the diasporic Scottish community in North America uses events such as traditional Scottish Highland Games as a tool for the creation of a distinct community identity. Drawing upon a case study of the Long Island Highland Games in New York, the chapter highlights the roles that cultural events play in the creation and articulation of community identity. Crucially, the chapter will highlight the complexity of lived identities in contemporary society, highlighting how such traditional events not only enable the diaspora to forge a link back to their homeland but also, through the production of such traditional festivity, position themselves within their new community. With their title 'Wha's Like Us?', they specifically posit the argument that the key role of the Long Island Games is to position the diaspora as a fundamentally American community first and foremost but via the signs and symbolism of Scottish events.

As editors and serious football supporters, we were fascinated by Nicholas Wise's study on 'Football on the Weekend: Rural Events and the Haitian Imagined Community in the Dominican Republic' (Chapter 8). Although there has been much research written on sporting events and community identity, here Wise represents a need to focus on the sense of community in rural locales and how 'common' locally organised weekend sporting events foster social cohesion among transnational groups. This research contributes to this particular understanding by focusing on rural Haitian communities in the northern Puerto Plata province of the Dominican Republic. While much research concerning sport and the Dominican Republic has focused on the national sport of baseball, Wise's chapter reflects on how Haitians use sports and events to reinforce their place and ethnic identity. In situations similar to those experienced by many transnational groups around the world, Haitians residing in rural locales in the Dominican Republic often meet with difficulties and prejudices, often regarded as 'others'. In this regard, the sport of football represents an activity that can encourage social interactions with other Haitian communities. It was not uncommon for Haitian community football teams to travel several hours to visit another Haitian community on a Saturday or Sunday afternoon, reinforcing their collective passion for their national sport. It has been noted that football has become a distraction from feared social inequalities, and allows Haitians to retain links with communities across the northern region.

Vincent Zammit, in Chapter 9, offers valuable insights into three of the central concepts involved in community festivals by reflecting on pride, identity and authenticity in Malta. He notes how community events have become an important and integral part of the tourism product. In recent years there has been a number of such events being organised, first by the National Tourism Authority and subsequently by many different local and communal organisations. These have provided the organisers with the possibility of participating in a niche tourism market, where they can feel part of an important industry in the local economy, attracting tourists to their events and localities, and at the same time giving an identity to their own community. Some of the events have taken on the aspect of providing the authenticity of the local community and at the same time there has been an impetus to revive lost traditions. These festivals are influenced by the highly successful religious feasts that have been organised by the various localities for decades. These feasts are a source of pride and identity for the local community.

A historical approach is introduced by Cândida Cadavez in Chapter 10 with her investigation of 'The Importance of Community Events in Nationalist Oriented Political Environments', as she focuses on the case of the Portuguese *Estado Novo* (1926–1974). Particularly in the first years of this new paradigm, it was of the utmost importance to explain the rules and creeds that should shape the new nation. As in similar contemporaneous regimes, propaganda was a valid tool to plan and implement the most effective strategies to introduce leaders and systems of belief so that the population would become acquainted with the recent way of understanding Portugal.

The focus of the analysis is what Cadavez identifies as *the* event of the regime: the Exhibition of the Portuguese World, which took place in 1940. This was the most important happening in a year that celebrated the birth of Portugal (1140) and its independence from Spain (1640), echoing on a national scale what we had experienced in Derby. The purpose of this major event was to praise the regime of Oliveira Salazar and exhibit the uniqueness of a nation that had miraculously been kept out of the Second World War. The Bureau of National Propaganda, headed by António Ferro, played a key role in an a priori success and managed to engage the whole Portuguese community in this six-month event. At the end, the official voices claimed that the national and foreign visitors to the exhibition had learnt about the essential and authentic core of the new nation.

Little is known about community cultural festivals in multi-ethnic urban areas (Getz, 2007) and cross-cultural differences have not been studied systematically (Getz, 2010). There are various motivations for becoming involved in a festival, whether in the interests of profit, charity, raising money for organizations, cultural information or community information (Lee & Arcodia, 2011). Chapter 11 by Kelley A. McClinchey addresses these issues by presenting her research on the multi-ethnic 'Narratives of Sense of Place at a Community Multicultural

Festival'. The chapter examines the sense of place perceptions of multi-ethnic not-for-profit festival exhibitors involved in a community multicultural festival.

Festival exhibitors had a sense of place for places they experienced as an insider and identified with places both socially and physically (Hidalgo & Hernandez, 2001). Relph (1976) described insiders as feeling at one with a place and having deep experiences with place as well as the intangible essences of a place. Festival exhibitors also found meaningful places that were not extraordinary but were where they had strong feelings of belonging, identity and attachment (Manzo, 2005).

'Home' emerged as an important theme, but in two very different contexts. In one context, home was perceived as having a sense of place for one's origins, roots and being 'back home' in the country of origin. In the other, it is perceived as a sense of place for somewhere that is comfortable, a place in which to be rooted for a long time or with family and friends, being 'home'.

In these particular narratives, exhibitors described having a sense of place for two places: one, the country of origin and two, where they live currently; thus there was a dual sense of identity or a duality of place. Festival exhibitor narratives demonstrated that festivals contribute to a sense of place by allowing them to value their own ethnic identity, maintain cultural traditions and increase the awareness of their culture, thus contributing to more positive place perceptions.

The results of this research have demonstrated that the multicultural festival has contributed to varying conceptualizations of sense of place. The festival connects multi-ethnic festival exhibitors with their own interpretations of place whether it is within the city itself or somewhere else far away. The presence of the festival may also conjure up nostalgia and memories or reconfirm the pride, identity and attachment one has for any place.

Community events are known to be laden with traditional and cultural elements. However, in some parts of the globe, community events are fast losing those essential elements due to modernisation and the acceptance of new life values. The chapter by Azilah Kasim, Mohamed Azlan Ashaari and Shahrul Aman Sabir Ahmad provides a perspective from Malaysia on the issue of whether or not professional food catering in *kenduri*, or open-house events, can destroy local culture and traditions. It looks at weddings and *Hari Raya Aidilfitri* to compare the traditional open-house concept where food preparation is considered a personal affair (involving only the family and local community members) with the modern open-house concept, where professional food caterers are hired to serve guests.

The concept of open house is something quite unique to Malaysia. It is a tradition practised by Malaysians of all races, an act of 'opening one's door' to receive people in your house, to welcome friends, family and neighbours or guests from everywhere and all walks of life to help one celebrate a traditional event. In the Malay tradition, for example, *kenduri* refers to traditional and cultural practices for special occasions such as circumcisions, completed study and understanding the Qur'an, instruction in *silat* (Malaysian martial arts) or some other discipline, and at religious celebrations like *Hari Raya Aidilfitri* and

AidilAdha (major Muslim religious celebrations for the Malay community in Malaysia). As for weddings, or *kenduri kahwin*, the open house is more than just a manifestation of joy for the wedding couple and their relatives, as it also functions to invite the community to join the happiness of the newlyweds and their families. This gives substantial standing and meaning in the people's living principle. It also provides a community framework or platform of ethnic traditions, customs, practices, norms and culture.

The typology of community events and festivals would be incomplete without some reference to the role religion plays, both within the local community and in building a community of its own. In Chapter 13, Ruth Dowson addresses these issues by examining the roles that churches and their associated events play within a specific community, whether in a specific geographic location or more widespread. An aim of most mainstream religions is to engage with and include a wider community. Church members contribute 23.2 million hours every month in volunteering outside church activities within their own communities, more than for any other organisation.

While connections between church and 'events' may not initially be apparent, in addition to the range of projects and services within local communities, many churches' energies are focused on events, from fetes to community days, to music events and to conferences for clergy and laity. Such events, whether for church members or the wider community, may be held within the church buildings, and may include involvement in community-led events and the provision of resources – such as venues – for use by the local community for their events. In her chapter, Dowson argues that the use of events by churches enables the development of a sense of community, whether within their own locality, within their church, or in a community connected to the church and its ethos or interests.

Chapter 14 sees Jessica Pacella, Jodie George and Rosie Roberts writing about understanding constructions of regional identity through community festivals. The importance of regional festivals as an aspect of regional identity and economic sustainability has gained significant research interest over the last decade (Bell & Jayne, 2010; Brennan-Horley et al., 2007; Gorman-Murray et al., 2008). While these studies have articulated the importance of rural festivals in the construction of place-identity, this research extends this by addressing the significant negotiations of 'taste' that take place during festivals, which is both sensory and demonstrative of class conventions. In particular, this research discusses the symbiosis between taste and class at regional festivals to better understand what we identify as 'festival capital', in which all the different elements of the festival combine to brand itself to particular audiences and communities.

Specifically, the chapter focuses primarily on the Gorgeous Festival, an event held over one day/evening, celebrating the food, wine and music of the South Australia region. Given South Australia's position as a global stakeholder in wine production, and the importance of McLaren Vale's brand image as one of the premiere wine regions in the country, this festival provided a rich space in which to examine the impacts these identity-driven events have on community members and the tourists who attend. As festival spaces may be understood to promote multiple dimensions of community identity, this chapter seeks to examine how and why the Gorgeous Festival provides a carefully cultivated and singular version of the region's complex identity and the impacts this may have on the wider community.

In particular, the participants' consumption of gourmet foods and premium wines at this festival and the cultivated aesthetic of the festival itself allowed for understandings of 'taste' both in terms of being a festival of 'the senses' and a space for providing particular understandings of class. Through a discursive analysis of participant responses, promotional materials and observations, the chapter examines the complex ways festivals help manage regional community identity and construct particular understandings of 'taste' through 'the senses'.

Another perspective on rural community festivals is offered in Chapter 15, by Leanne White, with her examination of Swiss and Italian identities in the 'Swiss and Italian Festa' and associated traditions in the popular tourist towns of Daylesford and Hepburn Springs in Central Victoria, Australia. The chapter particularly ties in with key areas identified in this book such as 'culture, authenticity and meaning of local community events'; the evolution and life cycle of local community events'; 'community events as tourist attractions', 'the role and importance of community events'; and 'community hospitality, foods and wine'.

The Festa incorporates a variety of activities such as music, food, wine, the arts, heritage displays, street parades and sporting events. The Swiss and Italian Festa has become the largest celebration of the region's cultural heritage 'probably because it is a highly unusual heritage in Australian terms', which must 'surely rank among the best uses of stories from local history in Australia' (Mulligan et al., 2006, pp. 106–123). Of the many festivals held each year in the towns of Daylesford and Hepburn Springs, a 2006 report focusing on community celebrations and well-being found the festival to be the most interesting as it has 'revived interest in the unique Swiss-Italian heritage of Hepburn Springs' (Mulligan et al., 2006, p. 88). Like many community festivals, it relies on the good will and commitment of a small group of volunteers.

In Chapter 16, Caroline Winter looks at a complex construction of Australian identities. She focuses on the Pozières Son et Lumière (Sound and Light Show) and its representations of peace and memory after the Great War. The small village of Pozières in northern France was the site of deadly battles in the First World War (1914–1918). The village was eventually captured by the Australians in July 1916 and they held the ridge, but at terrible cost: 23,000 casualties were incurred in a 6-week period. So intense was the conflict that the village and the men who fought were blasted from the face of the earth. The landscape is therefore difficult to interpret unless one has undertaken a significant amount of background reading. Despite the best efforts of some historians, Pozières' place in the history of the war has been somewhat forgotten by Australians.

The chapter describes the way in which the Son et Lumière offers opportunities to create and re-create memories of the war that for various reasons have faded over the past century. It examines the different communities involved and the memories that are being renewed, and situates Pozières in the broader context of the First World War centenary.

In 2006, on the 90th anniversary of the war, volunteers from the area around Pozières organised a Son et Lumière, which they performed on the site of the old Tramway Trench. The performance was designed to commemorate the war and those who had fought, to educate young people and to welcome citizens from all nations. Each year up to 80 people from the local area give up their time to rehearse for the two-hour-long performance, in July, with a range of other activities and entertainments accompanying the show. The unique offerings of the Pozières Son et Lumière are the unpretentious village setting, the traditional village-green atmosphere, the generosity of local people and the opportunity these offer for friendship and goodwill. In addition to contributing to the local community, a global community of remembrance is also attracted to the event – British, French, Australian, Canadian and German visitors are gradually finding their way to Pozières.

The final contribution in Chapter 17 from Gerard Ryan takes us to the end of the rainbow by looking at the role of community festivals in Liverpool. The genealogy of the chapter works through the organisation and performance of the Liverpool Community Festival that was originally planned to continue bi-annually, but disappeared the following year after a structural review of the Liverpool Arts & Culture Unit.

The findings presented suggest that while the city has progressed in recent years and the number of community-facing events have increased, the communities for whom the events are meant have little influence on the decision-making process due to a lack of consultation. Moreover, some communities are actually being marginalised and are granted no input whatsoever. At the same time, the process that organisers of community-facing events have to go through is creating further problems and barriers to the events' continuing existence.

A sense of community is considered an invisible yet critical part of a healthy community (Derrett, 2003) and, as such, is the responsibility of community members themselves to maintain its well-being. Furthermore, a community identity suggests that individuals affiliate themselves with or are categorised by others as belonging to a certain identity-based social group (Vigurs, 2009). So it could be argued that one way of assessing Derrett's healthy communities is through the events the members of these communities adopt.

Welcome! We hope that this brief introduction has tempted you to spend more time with us and that you will accept our invitation to join us in the land of community festivals and events. It is a complex landscape worthy of our careful attention. You will finds maps through questions of identity, senses of place, different visions of home, accounts of nationality, ethnicity, gender and social class. You will even meet the bunyip, but you will definitely have to keep reading to discover the answer to that particular one! We have found that the tasks involved in bringing this book into the world have reinforced our own sense of community, as we have been amazed by the insights and observations that our colleagues have brought to the project. We also hope that it is the beginning of a closer community as we hope that the contributors will stay in touch with us.

References

Bell, D. & Jayne, M. (2010). The creative countryside: Policy and practice in the UK rural cultural economy. *Journal of Rural Studies, 26*, 209–218.

Brennan-Horley, C., Connell, J. & Gibson, C. (2007). The Parkes Elvis Revival Festival: Economic development and contested place identities in rural Australia. *Geographical Research, 45*(1), 71–84.

Clarke, A. & Jepson, A. (2009). Cultural festivals and cultures of communities. In C. Cooper (ed.), *Proceedings of the EUTO Conference 2008 'Attractions and Events as Catalysts for Regeneration and Social Change'* (pp. 68–88). Christel DeHaan Tourism and Travel Research Institute, University of Nottingham and the Centre for Tourism and Cultural Change, Leeds Metropolitan University, September 2008.

Clarke, A. & Jepson, A. (2010). *Power, hegemony and relationships within the festival planning and construction process.* Paper presented at the 2010 Global Events Congress IV, Leeds, 14–16 July 2010.

Clarke, A. & Jepson, A. (2011). Power and hegemony in a community festival. *International Journal of Events and Festival Management, 2*(1) 7–19.

Clarke, A., Jepson, A. & Wiltshier, P. (2008). Community festivals: Involvement and inclusion. In *CHME 2008 Hospitality, Tourism and Leisure: Promoting excellence in research, teaching and learning.* Conference proceedings of the 17th Annual CHME Research Conference.

Department of Culture, Arts and Leisure. (2007). *Community festival fund: Policy and guidance framework.* Retrieved from www.dcalni.gov.uk/index/arts_and_creativity/community_festivals_fund_revised_policy_document.

Derrett, R. (2003). Making sense of how festivals demonstrate a community's sense of place. *Event Management, 8*, 49–58.

Falassi, A. (1987). Festival: Definition and morphology. In A. Falassi (ed.), *Time out of time: Essays on the festival* (pp. 1–10). Albuquerque: University of New Mexico Press.

Getz, D. (1991). *Festivals, special events, and tourism.* New York: Van Nostrand Reinhold.

Getz, D. (2007). *Event studies: Theory, research and policy for planned events.* Oxford: Butterworth-Heinemann.

Getz, D. (2010). The nature and scope of festival studies. *International Journal of Event Management Research, 5*(1), 1–47.

Getz, D. & Andersson, T.D. (2008). Sustainable festivals: On becoming an institution. *Event Management, 12*, 1–17.

Gibson, C. & Stewart, A. (2009). *Reinventing rural places: The extent and impact of festivals in rural and regional Australia.* Wollongong: University of Wollongong.

Gibson, C., Waitt, G., Walmsley, J. & Connell, J. (2010). Cultural festivals and economic development in nonmetropolitan Australia. *Journal of Planning Education and Research, 29*, 280–293.

Gorman-Murray, A., Darian-Smith, K. & Gibson, C. (2008), Scaling the rural: Reflections on rural cultural studies. *Australian Humanities Review, 45*, 37–52.

Hidalgo, M.C. & Hernandez, B. (2001). Place attachment: Conceptual and empirical questions. *Journal of Environmental Psychology, 21*, 273–281.

Jepson, A.S. (2009). *Investigating cultural relationships within the festival planning and construction process in a local community festival context.* Published doctoral thesis, University of Derby.

Jepson, A.S. & Clarke, A. (2005). *The Jubilee Festival in Derby: Involving the local community.* Paper presented at the 3rd DeHann Tourism Management Conference: 'The Impact and Management of Tourism Related Events', Nottingham University Business School.

Jepson, A.S. & Clarke, A. (2013). Events and community development. In R. Finkel, D. McGillivray, G. McPherson & P. Robinson (eds), *Research themes for events* (pp. 6–17). Wallingford: CABI.

Jepson, A.S., Clarke, A. & Ragsdell, G. (2012). *Investigating the use of the Motivation-Opportunity-Ability (MOA) model to reveal the factors which facilitate or inhibit inclusive engagement within local community festivals.* Global Events Congress: Conference Proceedings, Stavanger, Norway, 13–15 June 2012.

Lee, I. & Arcodia, C. (2011). The role of regional food festivals for destination branding. *International Journal of Tourism Research, 13*(4), 355–367.

Manzo, L.C. (2005). For better or worse: Exploring multiple dimensions of place meaning. *Journal of Environmental Psychology, 25*, 67–86.

Mulligan, M., Humphrey, K., James, P., Scanlon, C., Smith, P. & Welch, N. (2006). *Creating community: Celebrations, arts and wellbeing within and across local communities.* Melbourne: The Globalism Institute, Royal Melbourne Institute of Technology University.

Pine, B. & Gilmore, J. (1999). *The experience economy: Work is theatre and every business is a stage.* Boston, MA: Harvard Business School Press.

Relph, E. (1976). *Place and placelessness.* London: Pion.

Vigurs, K. (2009). Reconceptualising conflict and consensus within partnerships: The role of overlapping communities and dynamic social ties. Unpublished doctoral thesis, Staffordshire University, UK.

Part I

Exploring and defining the context of community festivals and events

2 Organic festivity

A missing element of community festival

Vern Biaett

Introduction

The foremost festival and event management educational texts today (Allen, O'Toole, Harris, & McDonnell, 2008; Bladen, Kennell, Abson, & Wilde, 2012; de Lisle, 2009; Getz, 2007a; Goldblatt, 2005) focus on the business, communication, operational, and risk management strategies one must learn and embrace to achieve high levels of success as an event planner. Comments such as 'the community festival was our largest fundraiser and had a major economic impact', 'we were able to gain the attention of thousands and create millions of impressions that promoted the brands of our sponsors and the place attributes of our community', 'there were no major incidents as close attention was paid to safety and security issues', and 'volunteer involvement was at an all-time high' are typical performance measures reported from event practitioners following a successful community festival. They reflect the objective and positivist business management approach that has come to dominate community festivals since the 1950s. There is no denying that many of today's community festivals have evolved into well planned and executed commercial organisms, but to sustain this environment in the future, the behavioural experiences of attendees need to become more a part of the equation. Pine and Gilmore (1999) brought to light a paradigm shift in consumptive behaviour with consumers now seeking out and demanding special and unique experiences more than they desire traditional goods and services. While the importance of placing a greater emphasis on the concept of experience in terms of event design, customer service, and analysis (Berridge, 2007; Getz, 2007b) has surfaced, there still exists little understanding of the specific kind of on-site, real-time behavioural actions that constitute attendee experiences. Community festivals should be places of out-of-the-ordinary experience, the kind described as liminoidal by Turner (1969), keeping in mind that while these experiences represent a withdrawal from everyday social structure they are also directly correlated to contextual event social structure (Turner, 1969). This type of transcendent experience leaves attendees with a sense of equality and solidarity among fellow participants as spontaneous and undifferentiated social relations form (Andrews & Roberts, 2012) and serve as a catalyst to the latent development of human and community social capital. To produce more than just temporary places of mercantile activity and entertainment, to offer uniquely distinct experiences sought after by visitors, and to allow a communal sense of heart and soul to emerge, it is essential that today's event managers possess both the aspiration and the knowledge to meet an attendee's psychological and internal behavioural needs of being physically, mentally, emotionally, socially, or spiritually engaged (O'Sullivan & Spangler, 1998): they must be aware of the social and action elements of organic festivity.

Emerging social aspects of festivity

Research informs us that bonding and bridging social capital is cultivated and grows within the ranks of those directly involved with organizing a community festival (Arcodia & Whitford, 2006), but until recently there existed a paucity of similar research and a lack of interest regarding a similar development of social capital for event attendees. The social impacts on attendees at events have gone unmeasured and are not generally familiar to event organizers due in part to this empirical and theoretical disparity. A riposte to this paradox suggests that while the physical, emotional, and collaborative creative energy that goes into planning and producing the financial, marketing, and operational aspects leads to observable increases in social capital for organizers, the typical, mostly unimaginative, passive, spectator aspects of community festival activity programming fail to provide a comparable benefit for event visitors. Fortunately, investigation into the social impacts of festivals and events has become recognized as an important research agenda (Chalip, 2006; Getz, 2010; Hede, Jago, & Deery, 2003; Weed, 2012).

Research studies that explore the experiential social aspects of festivals have begun to be published in limited, but increasing, numbers, from diverse academic fields, and exhibit a multiplicity of findings. An annotated review of literature highlights includes:

- Satterfield and Godfrey (2011) suggest that a strong sense of community exists at sporting events, with fans often expressing desire to relive the spirit of community they find present. Studies on blues festival tourism in Mississippi (King, 2010), a six-year ethnographic study of Bluegrass festival life (Gardner, 2004), and the relationships of visitors attending food festivals in South Korea (Kim, Suh, & Eves, 2010) have produced similar findings. Contrarily, Jankowiak and Todd White (1999) reported a lack of communitas as friends and family socialized only within their own group at Mardi Gras and did not engage strangers in acts of fellowship.
- Schechner (2006) and Ellis (2011) found that audiences at theatre festivals attempt to conquer individual and social fragmentation through a sharing of the arts, while conversely a study of the nouveau art Burning Man festival (Gilmore, 2010) suggests literally the complete opposite as a case of extreme luminal behaviour where event attendees have travelled so far from the norm of everyday life that they have lost an awareness of other living beings or physical objects in their immediate presence.

- Pettersson and Getz (2009) examined the event experiences of visitors at the World Alpine Ski Championships in Sweden. Results from their study suggest that visitors were social and wanted to be with other visitors.
- Community development research (Procter, 2004) informs us about civic communions, communicative performance community events, which function to draw people into a shared identity, shared visions of community and codes of conduct while bonding citizenry around the social and political structures of a specific locale.
- From the perspective of event studies, Wilks (2011) applied critical discourse analysis to post-festival in-depth interviews and concluded that bonding social capital was highly present and recognizable within friend and family groups, but was not recognized between these same type groups with similar backgrounds as had been heuristically theorized by Putnam (2000).
- Brisbane's Annual Sports and Cultural Festival, used as a case study by Whitford and Ruhanen (2013), revealed positive socio-cultural benefits for festival participants, attendees, and the wider indigenous community including the development of social capital.
- Examining how festival involvement contributes to sense of community based on community psychology theory, Van Winkle, Woosnan, and Mohammed (2013) found that the relation between festival attendance and the emotional connection factor on their brief sense of community scale suggested that festivals do contribute to sense of community. Another psychology study (Molitor, Rossi, & Brantan, 2011) analysed questionnaires from people who had attended a community festival within the past 6 months and by comparison concluded that those who had attended an event featuring activity specifically designed to increase community interaction showed increased measures of social capital as a result of these directed programming elements.

These sorts of studies are now adding social context to characterize community festival. They are defining community festival, as Neulinger (1974) and later Mannell and Kleiber (1997) defined the concept of leisure, not only objectively as a type and/or time of activity, but also subjectively as a social psychological experience.

Emergence of PX (participant experience) Theory

The classic rhetoric of festivals and events emanating from dictionaries as well as festival and event management texts define the term *event* simply as an occurrence; the term *special event* expands this meaning to include temporary and infrequent unique experiences; the definition of the term *festival* further adds ideas of community and celebration. The question must be asked, however, why are these terms defined merely as nouns, omitting the possibility they might possess significant meanings as verbs, words of creative action? Along this line of thought Van Belle (2009) coined the verb 'festivalising' and contends that we need to stop thinking of festivals only as a collection of assorted goings-on, imagining them also as action-oriented systems with transformative powers. Approaching festivity with this new perception, festive activities are not just activity for activity's sake, but rather activities that can shape, change, and have consequences. Using the viewpoint of festival as both a noun and an action verb the definition of community festival can be modified and more contextually denoted as a temporary experiential community happening of celebration with potential to affect individuals and society.

During a phenomenological study (Biaett, 2013) that explored the on-site behaviour of attendees in real time and space at community festivals, using participant observation and socially constructed grounded theory method (Biaett, 2012), substantive theory emerged from grounded data. As this continues to unfold, what has tentatively been titled PX (participant experience) Theory asserts: 'Levels of social capital bonding and bridging increase when attendees engage in more organically festive forms of activity.' With this 'immediate conscious experience approach' (Mannell & Kleiber, 1997, p. 83) social capital bonding has been observed to be strongly evident and easily recognizable within friend/family groups at all community festivals, but minimal between unacquainted peers sharing demographic similarities when attendees were primarily spectators. As community festival attendees participated in experiences that were more physical and emotional, social capital bonding increased in both the friend/family groups as well as between unacquainted peers with demographic similarities. Social capital bonding maximized for all groups when attendees participated in experiences that were creatively collaborative with roots in organic festivity. Similarly, social capital bridging was observed to exist minimally at community festivals, both heuristically in the form of direct social interaction between strangers with dissimilar demographics as well as hermeneutically by attendees possessing only a sense of primal subconscious generic communitas when attendees were only spectators. As attendees participated in more physical and emotional experiences social capital bridging increased and maximized when attendees participated in experiences that were creatively collaborative with roots in organic festivity.

While event managers have become experts at managing the economic, promotional, and operational aspects, or, in other words, the objective product and service aspects of community festivals, the future challenges will be to acquire a deeper subjective understanding of what attendee actions lead to a genuine transformational experience and how to use this knowledge to let significant human social impacts to develop out of their events. A reasonable starting point and way to proceed to gain this knowledge is with a cursory historical analysis of festivity.

Festivity: annotated antecedents

Festivity is a word used to describe festive activity; things done to celebrate. Festivity has been an integral part of the human experience since the beginning of humankind, evolving slowly through the ages from the purely organic, to the purposefully organic, to the organized, to the commercial organism. Commencing 150,000 years ago with the earliest *Homo sapiens*, into the ages of the Palaeolithic hunter-gatherers (20000 to 8000 BCE), the Neolithic farmers (8000 to 4000 BCE), and civilization's first city dwellers (4000 to 800 BCE), festivity was unrefined, natural, organic.

For the first *Homo sapiens* festivity was 'of the whole of the world and of life' (Pieper, 1965), an ever-present, everyday ingredient of living, as primitive humans did not distinguish between work and leisure (Kraus, 1971; Nash, 1953). The most primitive festivity consisted of activities unto themselves, much like we envision play (Huizinga, 1950), activities without rhyme or reason or purpose. It was spontaneous and purely organic. For our distant ancestors work, play, and festivity were all part of the same experience – the uncomplicated living of life. This basic level of festivity still exists today as those moments of special delight, bliss, ecstasy, thrill, or pleasure that one experiences and celebrates with unplanned, unprompted, impulsive shouts, crazy facial expressions, high-five hand slaps, little dances, or group hugs. Purely organic festivity is not something that can be programmed, but it is an observable behavioural indication of liminoid experience.

As the human brain developed humankind evolved into the hunter-gatherers of the Palaeolithic Age and people began to have questions of cosmogony. Logically they learned how to make weapons, develop hunting skills, and control fire, but with mythology they also learned how to deal with the pain, sorrow, and other emotions they would feel when killing animals or when one of their own would die. Logic and mythology were complementary forces of life for the hunter-gatherers and purposeful festivity was logically amalgamated with mythology. Ancient graves from this period inform us that myth was grounded in the experience of death, inseparable from liminal celebration, connected with thoughts of unknown experience, a story told to impart life lessons, and was associated with a perennial philosophy that conveys ideas of a richer, stronger, and more enduring counterpart realm of existence to be emulated and sought after (Armstrong, 2005). As mythological beings hunter-gatherers participated in festive experiences of transcendence and feelings of ecstasy. Unlike today, however, these ancient people did not separate festive activity into divisions of the sacred and the profane, continually maintaining their awareness and feelings of ever-present spirituality. While heaven was believed to possess sacred powers it was not worshipped in a religious sense as much as it was celebrated with festive activity. As the brightness and clarity of daytime gave way to the darkness and unknown terrors of night, clans consisting of approximately 150 members, linked together for purposes of protection (Dunbar, 1996), would gather around fires and bond as a group, united in a deep emotional feeling of communitas. It was here the clan, as a single communal entity, celebrated the fragility of life, birth, and death with the rhythmic beats of drumming, the wearing of masks, headdresses, and costume like attire, extemporary face and body painting (Lewis, 1980), the chanting of mantras, and dancing in lines and circles (Ehrenreich, 2006). With a lack of restraint and inhibition, a sense of abandonment, they rejoiced and moved as one entity effortlessly into a parallel mythological world through purposeful organic festivity. Renderings of these activities can be found on rock art around the world, in caverns such as Altamira and Lascaux in France (Burkert, 2001) and the Devil's Lair in Western Australia (Adams, Brooks, Farndon, Fowler, & Ward, 2005), and other places of ancient inhabitation where paintings have been discovered with depictions of armed hunters dancing among their prey, lines of female dancers, and shamans dressed as bird-like creatures flying among them having transcended into another realm. These places were certainly also sites of the first rituals, celebratory initiations where young men left their childhoods behind and were reborn as hunters and warriors with the body and mind of an adult with new understandings of life and death as a natural process not to be feared.

Archaeologists unearthing Goebekli Tepe, which sits on the northern edge of the Fertile Crescent in what is today south-eastern Turkey, have dated its construction at about 9000 BCE, near the end of the Palaeolithic Age (Curry, 2008a). This megalithic structure pre-dates Stonehenge by 6,000 years and is thought to possibly be the first human-built spiritual place. Unlike later megaliths that were adorned with symbols of farming and fertility, the carvings on the pillars at Goebekli Tepe display the hunter-gatherer fascination with death, depicting lions, snakes, crocodiles, and vultures. An area of approximately one acre has been uncovered to date, but geomagnetic surveys have charted an area of more than 20 acres, a hill that rises 50 feet from the surrounding pastoral plain. No signs of houses, trash pits, or other indications of village life have been unearthed near the site, instead thousands of gazelle bones with signs that the animals were butchered and cooked. Human bones have also been found among the ruins and Schmidt (2000) postulates it may have been a place where the dead were laid out to be among the spirits of the afterlife. These types of ritualistic celebration are considered to be the foundations of modern humanity (Rappaport, 1999). Goebekli Tepe was not a place where animals were domesticated or the land was farmed; it was a place where nomadic clans of hunter-gatherers congregated most likely for purposes of ritualistic organic festivity. In the words of archaeologist Ian Hodder, 'This shows socio-cultural changes come first, agriculture comes later' (Curry, 2008b, p. 2). It can be hypothesized that the tremendous cooperative effort required of the hunter-gatherer clans to fashion the first human-built place of purposeful organic festivity created such a socio-cultural change that this appears to have been a catalyst in their becoming farmers. Today community festival organizers can learn from history that those engaged in cooperative effort, those engaged in purposeful organic festivity, are capable of creating extraordinary social and cultural changes.

With the coming of the Neolithic Age in 8000 BCE the roving clans congregated into agrarian cultural hearths and at first the mythical narratives continued as the farmers, like the hunter-gatherers preceding them, remained on a sacred journey of life. The routine of agriculture, however, was profoundly manifested in logic, and as new ideas emerged about the meanings of this journey, celebrations grew to be ever more intervallic and purposeful in efforts to ensure bountiful harvests, revered as the fruits of a sacred marriage between soil and seed with the rain being the sexual congress of heaven and earth (Armstrong, 2005). As farming matured, festivity became ever more seasonally temporal with logical consequences and outcomes. The Egyptian festival of Opet grew out of celebrations that coincided with the annual flooding of the Nile. In northern Europe the winter solstice was observed by groups with festive activity around bonfires or large burning trees as an annual celebration to rekindle the smouldering sun during the shortest days of the year.

About 4000 BCE, as food was grown in excess and available for trade, human self-consciousness widened with the development of writing and the artistic adornment of their possessions, and the first cities materialized. These cities continued to be supported by at least nine-tenths of the total population that remained directly engaged in tillage (White, 1969), with farmers progressing at a slower pace and retaining their mythological connections to their Neolithic past longer than their city-dweller counterparts, but the collective social role of festivity remained strong for both groups. Civilized environments were diminishing places of mythology as cities considered themselves spiritual places with the ancestral divine realm relocated from the sky and mountain tops into temples and ziggurats, increasingly places of logic as man began to envision himself as the master of his own destiny. Festivity correspondingly was less spontaneous, more temporal, and spatially located at public places of human-built spirituality. It was also in this period of earliest civilizations when the ritualistic celebrations of marriage and coronation first appear, the beginnings of a modern dichotomy that often finds festivity separated into those who directly participate in an activity and others who only observe.

By 800 BCE, as civilizations prospered, the sacred ideas of mythology declined into a spiritual malaise. A transformative period erupted that would continue until 1500 CE saturating this spiritual void with organized religion and philosophy from China, India, the Middle East, and Europe offering a variety of solutions to the age-old questions of cosmogony. In this period the spontaneous roots of organic festive activity eventually came to be replaced by organized festivity and moved from group celebration to community festival. In China, as trade markets expanded during the Han and Tang dynasties, wealthy merchants kept jugglers, acrobats, magicians, and other servants (Russell, 2009) to provide festive activity. Hebrews distinguished between sacred and secular celebrations, a concept embraced by Christians who rejected Roman circus, but adopted pagan festivity into their organized religious celebration throughout the Dark and Middle Ages. Ritualistic celebrations became meticulous planned and executed acts of obedience and social harmony. Spontaneous celebrations of the mysteriously divine were supplanted with organized sports festivals and organized religious celebrations. The originally organic festive games of Olympia, first celebrated in 776 BCE, had been combined with other sports into highly organized and controlled spectacles two centuries later (Miller, 2004). In 186 CE Bacchanalia was allowed only with Roman Senate approval and during the 6th century Advent was established with dancing and other festive activities banned

(Parker, 2009). Spontaneous Dionysus traditions, which had long existed, were organized in time and space during the 12th and 13th centuries as Catholic ecclesiastic authorities restricted this behaviour to holidays in non-church public areas, inadvertently inventing carnival (Ehrenreich, 2006). In hierarchical civilized societies preceding the Enlightenment, nobility and religious leaders organized the places and times of festivity for their populace, although festive activity itself was much less controlled.

By 1600 CE organized festivity in the form of community festival had become an intricate part of life's social fabric that wove individuals and groups together, strengthened their sense of oneness from neighbourhoods to nations, and enabled them to closely bond with friends and family as they also bridged new relationships. And then, all that had become organized festivity would fall victim to a new philosophy of civilization. It was at this time Europeans, and later Americans, began to base their civilizations on the logic of capitalism, a way of life driven by the replication of resources that finds meaning in consumption, ideas that, spread through imperialism, would become recognized worldwide as the most powerful force of modernity by the 20th century. As this period of increasing industrialization progressed into the 19th century an ever more powerful and political merchant class forced the division of labour and leisure, with each reordered into defined time and space (Coalter, 1990). A decline in festivity followed a reduction in the number of holidays, an effort to establish and maintain new discipline levels required to control workers relocated from their rural roots and casual lifestyles into manufacturing metropolises (Malcolmson, 1973). Although Protestant reform against idleness encouraged a strong work ethic and saw festivity as a sin, some community festivals were still allowed to provide an outlet for the stress and anxiety of mundane urban routines (Cohen & Taylor, 1976). The time-honoured physical, emotional, and creative elements of festivity were replaced with passive activities as leisure thought flip-flopped from looking upon recreation as a time to burn up extra energy to viewing it as a recuperative period necessary to restore one's energy for work (Kraus, 1971). Community bands, college and professional sports, travelling circuses, horse racing, and spectacular fireworks shows were only some of the many public entertainment options organized during this period that shifted the behaviour of attendees at community festivals towards the passivity of amusement and spectatorship.

Festivity was also subverted for political reasons. Oktoberfest was established in Germany in 1810 CE to honour a marriage that unified Bavaria (Parker, 2009), displacing traditional autumn community festivals. During the French Revolution numerous festivals were created for purposes of political coercion (Pieper, 1965). Official May Day celebrations, originally created to appease labour movements in the late 1800s, were converted into nationalistic days of forced participation by Nazi and communist propagandists. Locally, authorities and upper-class members of society, fearing that the mix of carnival behaviour and new passion for carrying guns fostered revolutionary ideas of class upheaval, cancelled many community festivals. In conservative communities the festive activities of dancing, spontaneous wild behaviour, as well as the consumption of alcohol were banned as a form of political social engineering.

Following the Second World War civilization placed a newfound emphasis on public relations, commercialism, and technology. With regard to festivity, these changes did not transpire without controversy, as immediately a debate arose that continues today over the authenticity of what were labelled as pseudo-events that were no longer deemed celebratory but instead were literally manufactured for purposes of generating publicity and media coverage (Boorstin, 1961). In America sacred Christmas festivity became overshadowed by secular shopping and harvest festivals were replaced by commercialized Halloween. Community festivals were used as a strategy for redevelopment in rural America (Green, Flora, Flora, & Schmidt, 1990; McGuire, Rubin, Agronoff, & Richards, 1994; Wilson, Fesenmaier, Fesenmaier, & Van Es, 2001) and as a force of urban regeneration (Foley, McGillivray, & McPherson, 2012). Festivals emerged as giants of the tourism industry (Getz & Frisby, 1988) and at the turn of the 21st century community festivals were recognized as one of tourism's fastest-growing attractions (Crompton & McKay, 1997; McDonnell, Allen, & O'Toole, 1999). In general, today's public events, including community festivals, fuelled by sponsorship, revenue generation, the Internet, and social media, are valued most for their economic impacts (Jackson, Houghton, Russell, & Triandos, 2005; Long & Perdue, 1990; O'Sullivan & Jackson, 2002) and their capabilities to create branded product and place identity (De Bres & Davis, 2001; Derrett, 2003; Jamieson, 2004). Now maybe best characterized as a secular commercial organism, with attendee behaviour consisting of primarily passive spectator experiences, the modern community festival finds itself far removed from its ancestral sacred roots of organic festivity.

Conclusion: more organic festivity, less spectatorship

With the widespread proliferation of community festivals today, can the simple act of attendance in itself still be considered a liminoidal experience for those who participate? In a fast-paced world of unlimited cyber entertainment options and mega-events, extreme shopping alternatives, and an insatiable demand for hedonist experiences, can the behaviour of attendees at community festivals engaged in activities of watching performances, shopping for arts and crafts, and what seems like incessant waiting in line for food, drinks, amusements, and restrooms, be regarded as out of the ordinary and transcendent? These latter types of passive activity have been observed to be accompanied with body languages of boredom, excessive mobile phone usage, and minimal social interaction outside of friend/family groups (Biaett, 2013). It cannot be assumed that just holding a community festival produces a significant liminoidal experience or any social impact for its attendees or their communities. Event organizers need to do more; they need to incorporate the action ingredients of organic festivity.

Spontaneity is being organized out of events today with such directives as that the event experience 'must be choreographed and blocked out … a structured progression of various sights' (Silvers, 2004, p. 271). To allow for and encourage more extemporized liminoidal type experience, event planners could make use of a more *élan vital*-like approach to design elements. For example, the layout of an event does not have to be rigid, discrete, repeatable units, but can instead offer a continual flow of experience – the difference between rows of stalks in a cornfield and wildflowers in a meadow. Not knowing what is around the corner or what will occur next creates a more organic sense of adventure and surprise. Similarly, all entertainment does not have to be known about in advance or spatially and temporally confined. A community Valentine's festival of chocolate and romance in Glendale, Arizona hired, but did not advertise, a troupe of Shakespearian actors to roam freely throughout the event dressed in full costume and stop randomly for unscheduled performance. Post-event surveys revealed it to be attendees' favourite experience. The unknown happening offers the chance for spontaneous attendee reaction with out-of-the-ordinary special experience springing forth from this turbulence just as it does when lightning fills the sky or a scented candle fills a room with smoke.

From the review of our ancestral roots we have seen that organic festivity involved physical movement; spectator amusements and entertainment were unknown concepts. To create opportunities for liminoidal experiences at community festivals event planners must get attendees moving. There is no better way to do this than with the strong rhythmic beats, deeply thumping bass, and the pounding drums of loud music that provided the original elements of festive activity. During fieldwork as a participant observer, Biaett (2013) detected that when these forms of organic festive activity are present at community festivals attendees in common areas move or walk more briskly with swaying arms and hips while those near or in performance areas often break out in improvised dance both individually and in circles, conga lines, or other communal groupings. Demographic differences break down as participants of all ages, races, economic and social class, gender, and lifestyle lose themselves, bonding and bridging with others when loud music and dance get them moving.

Event organizers must not forget the importance of visual arts as an ingredient of organic festivity. Viewing unusual or rarely seen static art, such as art cars, gets people enthused, and watching performance art, such as frenetic speed painting, gets people excited. Creating art and being a collaborative part of the process and performance, however, is what leads to a liminoidal experience. Attendees engaged in making and then wearing paper party hats, painting large murals, and wearing costume-like attire to add to the décor of a community festival – all related to forms of organically festive behaviour in past generations – are having special experiences. As with music and dance, these activity ingredients have been discerned to break down social barriers leading to increased bonding and bridging between participants (Biaett, 2013).

Real festivity is so much more than passive spectatorship, having originated in the spiritualism of our distant ancestors, expressed with the performing and dramatic arts of rhythmic chanting and dancing to loud bass beats as well as visual art forms of costumes, masks, and decoration, all combined to create a sense of wild abandonment. It is these types of activities that get people out of their chairs and physically, emotionally, and collaboratively engaged in social interaction; these types of activities that can develop and increase bonding and bridging social capital; these types of activities that event producers must acquire a deeper understanding and sensitivity about en route to providing the liminoidal, authentic experience that today's community festival attendee seeks and demands. The sustainability of community festival lies in its organically festive past.

References

Adams, S., Brooks, P., Farndon, J., Fowler, W., & Ward, B. (2005). *Exploring history*. New York: Anness.

Allen, J., O'Toole, W., Harris, R., & McDonnell, I. (2008). *Festival and special event management* (4th edn). Milton, Qld: John Wiley & Sons.

Andrews, H., & Roberts, L. (eds). (2012). *Liminal landscapes: Travel, experience and spaces in-between*. London: Routledge.

Arcodia, C.V., & Whitford, M. (2006). Festival attendance and the development of social capital. *Journal of Convention and Event Tourism, 8*(2), 1–18.

Armstrong, K. (2005). *A short history of myth*. Edinburgh: Canongate Books.

Berridge, G. (2007). *Events design and experience*. Burlington, MA: Elsevier.

Biaett, V. (2012). A confessional tale: Auto-ethnography reflections on the investigation of attendee behavior at community festivals. *Tourism Today – Special Issue Event Tourism: Theory and Practice, 12,* 65–75.

Biaett, V. (2013). *Exploring the on-site behavior of attendees at community festivals: A social constructivist grounded theory approach*. Doctoral dissertation, Arizona State University, USA. Retrieved from: http://hdl.handle.net/2286/R.I.17788.

Bladen, C., Kennell, J., Abson, E., & Wilde, N. (2012). *Events management: An introduction*. New York: Routledge.

Boorstin, D. (1961). *The image: A guide to pseudo-events in America*. New York: Harper & Row.

Burkert, W. (2001). Shamans, caves, and the master of animals. In J. Narby & F. Huxley (eds), *Shamans through time: 500 years on the path to knowledge*. London: Thames & Hudson.

Chalip, L. (2006). Towards social leverage on sports events. *Journal of Sport and Tourism, 11*(2), 109–127.

Coalter, F. (1990). Analyzing leisure policy. In I.P. Henry (ed.), *Management and planning in the leisure industries*. Basingstoke: Macmillan.

Cohen, S., & Taylor, L. (1976). *Escape attempts: The theory and practice of resistance to everyday life*. London: Routledge.

Crompton, J., & McKay, S. (1997). Motives of visitors attending festival events. *Annals of Tourism Research, 24*(2), 242–439.

Curry, A. (2008a). Seeking the roots of ritual. *Science, 319,* 278–280.

Curry, A. (2008b, November). Goebekli Tepe: The world's first temple? *Smithsonian*. Retrieved from www.smithsonianmag.com/history-archaeology/gobekli-tepe.html.

De Bres, K., & Davis, J. (2001). Celebrating group and place identity: A case study of a new regional festival. *Tourism Geographies, 3*(3), 326–337.

deLisle, L.J. (2009). Creating special events. Champaign, IL: Sagamore Publishing.

Derrett, R. (2003). Making sense of how festivals demonstrate a community's sense of place. *Event Management, 8*(1), 49–58.

Dunbar, R. (1996). *Grooming, gossip and the evolution of language*. Cambridge, MA: Harvard University Press.

Ehrenreich, B. (2006). *Dancing in the streets: A history of collective joy*. New York: Henry Holt.

Ellis, R. (2011). Serving publics: International theater festivals and their global audiences. *International Journal of Humanities and Social Science, 1*(14), 110–117.

Foley, M., McGillivray, D., & McPherson, G. (2012). *Event policy: From theory to strategy*. New York: Routledge.

Gardner, R. (2004). The portable community: Mobility and modernization in Bluegrass festival life. *Symbolic Interaction, 27*(2), 155–178.

Getz, D. (2007a). *Event management & event tourism* (2nd edn). Elmsford, NY: Cognizant Communication.

Getz, D. (2007b). *Event studies: Theory, research, and policy for planned events*. Oxford: Elsevier.

Getz, D. (2010). The nature and scope of festival studies. *International Journal of Events Management Research, 5*(1), 1–47.

Getz, D., & Frisby, W. (1988). Evaluating management effectiveness in community-run festivals. *Journal of Travel Research, 27*(1), 22–27.

Gilmore, L. (2010). *Theater in a crowded fire: Ritual and spirituality at Burning Man*. Berkeley: University of California Press.

Goldblatt, J. (2005). *Special events: Event leadership for a new world*. Hoboken, NJ: John Wiley & Sons.

Green, G.P., Flora, J.L., Flora, E., & Schmidt, F.E. (1990). Local self-development strategies: National survey results. *Journal of the Community Development Society, 21*(2), 55–72.

Hede, A.M., Jago, A.L., & Deery, M. (2003). An agenda for special events research: Lessons from the past and present for the future. *Journal of Hospitality and Tourism Management, 10*(supplement), 1–14.

Huizinga, J. (1950). *Homo ludens: A study of the play element in culture*. Boston, MA: Beacon Press.

Jackson, J., Houghton, M., Russell, R., & Triandos, P. (2005). Innovations in measuring economic impacts of regional festivals: A do-it-yourself kit. *Journal of Travel Research, 43*(4), 360–367.

Jamieson, K. (2004). The festival gaze and its boundaries. *Space and Culture, 7*(1), 64–75.

Janiskee, R. (1994. Some macroscale growth trends in America's community festival industry. *Festival Management & Event Tourism, 2*(1), 10–14.

Jankowiak, W., & Todd White, C. (1999). Carnival on the clipboard: An ethnological study of New Orleans Mardi Gras. *Ethnology, 38*(4), 335–349.

Kim, Y.G., Suh, B.W., & Eves, A. (2010). The relationships between food-related personality traits, satisfaction, and loyalty among visitors attending food events and festivals. *International Journal of Hospitality Management, 29*(2), 216–226.

King, S.A. (2010). Blues tourism in the Mississippi Delta: The functions of blues festivals. *Popular Music and Society, 26*(4), 455–475.

Kraus, R. (1971). *Recreation and leisure in modern society*. New York: Appleton-Century-Crofts.

Lewis, G. (1980). *Day of shining red: An essay on understanding ritual*. Cambridge: Cambridge University Press.

Long, P.T., & Perdue, R.R. (1990). The economic impact of rural festivals and special events: Assessing the spatial distribution of expenditures. *Journal of Travel Research, 28*(4), 10–14.

Malcolmson, R. (1973). *Popular recreations in English society, 1700–1850*. London: Hutchinson.

Mannell, R., & Kleiber, D. (1997). *A social psychology of leisure*. State College, PA: Venture Publishing Inc.

McDonnell, I., Allen, J., & O'Toole, W. (1999). *Festival and special event management*. Brisbane: John Wiley & Sons.

McGillivray, D., & McPherson, G. (2012). 'Surfing a wave of change': A critical appraisal of the London 2012 cultural programme. *Journal of Policy Research in Tourism, Leisure and Events, 4*(2), 123–137.

McGuire, M., Rubin, B., Agronoff, C., & Richards, C. (1994). Building development capacity in non-metropolitan communities. *Public Administration Review, 54*(5), 426–433.

Miller, S. (2004). *Ancient Greek athletics*. New Haven, CT: Yale University Press.

Molitor, F., Rossi, M., & Brantan, L. (2011). Increasing social capital and personal efficacy through small-scale community events. *Journal of Community Psychology, 39*(6), 749–754.

Nash, J. (1953). *Philosophy of recreation and leisure*. Dubuque, IA: Wm. C. Brown Company.

Neulinger, J. (1974). *Psychology of leisure: Research approaches to the study of leisure*. Springer, IL: Charles C. Thomas.

O'Sullivan, D., & Jackson, M.J. (2002). Festival tourism: A contributor to sustainable local economic development? *Journal of Sustainable Tourism, 10*(4), 325–342.

O'Sullivan, E.L., & Spangler, K.J. (1998). *Experience marketing: Strategies for the new millennium*. State College, PA: Venture Publishing.

Parker, P. (2009). *Festivities: Webster's timeline history 186–2007*. San Diego, CA: ICON Group Publishing.

Pieper, J. (1965). *In tune with the world: A theory of festivity*. New York: Harcourt, Brace & World.

Pine, B., & Gilmore, J. (1999). *The experience economy: Work is theatre and every business is a stage*. Boston, MA: Harvard Business School Press.

Pettersson, R., & Getz, D. (2009). Event experiences in time and space: A study of visitors to the 2007 World Alpine Ski Championships in Are, Sweden. *Scandinavian Journal of Hospitality and Tourism, 9*(2–3), 308–326.

Procter, D. (2004). Building community through communication: The case for civic communion. *Journal of the Community Development Society, 35*(2), 53–72.

Putnam, R. (2000). *Bowling alone: The collapse and revival of American community*. New York: Simon & Schuster.

Rappaport, R. (1999). *Ritual and religion in the making of humanity*. Cambridge: Cambridge University Press.

Russell, R. (2009). *Pastimes: The context of contemporary leisure* (4th edn). Champaign, IL: Sagamore.

Satterfield, J., & Godfrey, M. (2011). The University of Nebraska-Lincoln football: A metaphorical, symbolic and ritualistic community event. *Forum: Qualitative social research, 12*(1), 1–17.

Schechner, R. (2006). *Performance studies, an introduction* (2nd edn). New York: Routledge.

Schmidt, K. (2000). Göbekli Tepe, Southeastern Turkey: A preliminary report on the 1995–1999 excavations. *Paléorient, 26*(1), 45–54.

Silvers, J. (2004). *Professional event coordination*. New York: John Wiley & Sons.

Turner, V. (1969). *The ritual process: Structure and anti-structure.* New York: Aldine de Gruyler.

Van Belle, D. (2009). Festivalizing performance: Community and aesthetics through the lens of three festival experiences. *Canadian Theatre Review, 138*, 7–12.

Van Winkle, C., Woosnan, K., & Mohammed, A. (2013). Sense of community and festival attendance. *Event Management, 17*, 155–163.

Weed, M. (2012). Towards an interdisciplinary events research across sport tourism, leisure, and health. In S. Page & J. Connell (eds), *The Routledge handbook of events* (pp. 57–72). Abingdon: Routledge.

Whitford, M., & Ruhanen, L. (2013). Indigenous festivals and community development: A sociocultural analysis of an Australian indigenous festival. *Event Management, 17*, 49–61.

Wilks, L. (2011). Bridging and bonding: Social capital at music festivals. *Journal of Policy Rsearch in Tourism, Leisure & Events, 3*(3), 281–297.

Wilson, S., Fesenmaier, D.R., Fesenmaier, J., & Van Es, J.C. (2001). Factors for success in rural tourism development. *Journal of Travel Research, 40*(2), 132.

3 Experiencing community festivals and events

Insights from Finnish summer festivals

Maarit Kinnunen and Antti Haahti

Introduction

This chapter concentrates on participants' perspectives at community festivals and events. The first objective is to examine what kinds of aspects are important for locals with regard to the practical arrangements of the event. Throughout this chapter, a 'local' is considered to be a person who either lives permanently in the locality or has a second home there. This is studied by comparing the opinions of locals and non-locals with the event attributes. The second objective is to find out if a community festival can differentiate itself by taking advantage of local characteristics. This research question can be approached by studying how the event visitors perceive and experience the locality and how the meaning of the place impacts upon the event experience.

The first Finnish cultural festival was a song festival in Jyväskylä, a small town in Central Finland, in the summer of 1881. The cultural focus was on the awakening ideas of the independent Finland and the event became a political manifesto against the regime of the Russian tsar. Contemporary festivals were born after the idea of arranging summer festivals in Finland was first presented by the art critic Seppo Nummi in the 1950s. The objective was to offer cultural recreation all around the country for those having a break from work. By the end of the 1970s, more than 1,000 summer events were arranged (Valkonen & Valkonen, 1994). Finland Festivals (2013), a non-profit association working for the interests of cultural event organizers, estimates that in 2012, nearly 1.9 million visits were made to various cultural festivals. The number is quite remarkable, considering that the whole population of Finland is 5.4 million.

One of the success stories of Finnish festivals is the *Kuhmo Chamber Music Festival*. It was founded in 1970 on the initiative of a young music student, Seppo Kimanen. The first festival was arranged in 3 months after the suggestion was made, and it comprised only eight concerts and 800 visitors. Gradually, it developed into its current status, the internationally esteemed classical music festival. In 2013, the festival had 71 concerts, sold over 36,000 tickets, and the number of visitors was estimated to be 6,000–8,000 (Kinnunen, 2013; kuhmofestival.fi, 2013; Subrenat, 2006). The first study of the economic impacts of the festival was made in 1987, giving an estimate of 4.5 million FIM – €1.3 million in 2011 terms – of tourism income (Karjalainen, 1991). By 1992, the tourism income boosted by the festival was already 8.9 million FIM (€2 million at the 2011 level) (Subrenat, 2006, p. 49). Iso-Aho (2011, p. 98) gives the latest estimate from 2011, stating that annually the festival produces €2.5 million for the region. In 24 years, the economic impact of the festival has nearly doubled.

So a question that should be addressed here would be: what are the benefits that are rendered to the local residents and their community? Besides the money that boosts the local economy and generates employment, there are other impacts as well. The tiny town of Kuhmo, having fewer than 10,000 inhabitants, has its own concert venue, Kuhmo Art Centre, also known as Kuhmo House. The building would not have been erected in 1993 without the influence of the festival. Kuhmo Music Institute (founded in 1993) and Kuhmo Chamber Music Centre of Excellence Virtuosi (founded in 1998) have extended the classical music competence in Kuhmo even further. Classical music has found its way into the heart of the small town, and the main actor in this process has been the chamber music festival. Additionally, the event has increased the recognition and reputation of Kuhmo beyond anything money could buy – Kuhmo's image is largely based on that of a high-quality international festival.

A more varied story is the history of *Provinssirock* (Province Rock), arranged in Seinäjoki, which has nearly 60,000 inhabitants. The festival was organized for the first time in 1979 by the live music association of the region. In the early days, it was not easy to arrange funding for the event. The enthusiastic music lovers signed personal guarantees with the bank, and one young man even convinced his father to give their home as a guarantee for the rock festival loan. Fortunately, the home was not lost, and by the end of the 1980s, Provinssirock was already an established and big player, ending up taking foreign currency loans. In 1991, the prices of the tickets were raised considerably, causing a collapse in visitor numbers and producing losses for the festival of one million FIM (€241,000 in 2012 terms). At the same time, one of the most serious recessions in Finnish history was taking place and the currency loans became a strategic trap due to heavy devaluations of the Finnish Markka. Consequently, the organizing association went bankrupt in 1992. At a moment's notice, a new music association was founded, and the festival continued the very next year (Tuulari & Latva-Äijö, 2000). In 2008, Provinssirock generated a total income of €6.7 million for Seinäjoki. In 2012, the figure was €5.3 million but the future of the festival is encouraging, despite the descending figures (Tuuri, Rumpunen, Kortesluoma & Katajavirta, 2012, p. 64).

There is a saying that is almost proverbial in Finland: 'the summer begins from the Province'. Provinssirock has been organized at the beginning of June, in the early summer, which makes it very vulnerable in terms of the weather. In 1983, for example, it snowed and there were not even leaves on the trees when the festival took place in 1985. It has rained during several festivals, causing the 1988 festival particularly to be described as a muddy hell (Tuulari & Latva-Äijö, 2000). The timing of the festival is also problematic because in the summer of 2013, there were several big European festivals arranged at the same time. This caused heavy competition that was favourable for the international stars but a nightmare for a festival that was arranged in the outskirts of Scandinavia, in the provinces. Both the lineup and the weather were problems in 2012 and 2013, causing financial losses. The summer of 2011 was a huge success with 81,000 tickets sold, but the next summer only 56,000 tickets were sold, and in 2013 this had further reduced to 42,000 tickets. Having two negative years in a row, many wondered if the governance ought to change, since an international takeover had just happened to the famous Hultsfred rock festival in Sweden. To adjust to changes in demand and timing, the festival had to make strategic decisions about its future: in 2014, Provinssirock will last two instead of three days, and it will take place two weeks later. Changing the timing reduces the weather risk considerably. More importantly, it enables the festival to operate under much improved competitive conditions in terms of the core programme. It also means a significantly better cooperative positioning as the simultaneously arranged leading Swedish rock festival Bråvalla attracts a large number of successful international acts to Scandinavia. On the other hand, the new timing means competition with other domestic rock festivals that take place during the same weekend.

Even though Provinssirock has sometimes suffered heavy financial problems, it has boosted the live music scene in Seinäjoki throughout its existence. The organizer, Seinäjoki Live Music Association (Selmu), is one of the owners of *Rytmikorjaamo*, a centre of creative work established in an old postal van depot. '*Rytmikorjaamo* is a place for work and recreation among professionals, students and researchers in the fields of music, culture, arts, communications and various business services', as the webpages of the facility state (Rytmikorjaamo, 2013). Selmu has a year-round rock club on the premises. The association also cooperates with Seinäjoki University of Applied Sciences in its degree programme in cultural management. Seinäjoki is known for its events and Provinssirock constitutes an essential part of the town's image. Since the festival generates over €5 million of tourism income annually, its influence on the town economy is remarkable.

Typically, the local community benefits from festivals and events in two ways. The economic impacts of events have been an important research area since the late 1980s and John Myerscough's (1988) classic work. The direct and indirect proceeds of events have been a major justification for politicians when granting public funding for events (Skot-Hansen, 2005). However, some researchers (e.g. Florida, 2002/2004; Kainulainen, 2005) have come to the conclusion that the image benefits for the organizing community have the strongest positive impact. Interesting events may increase the attractiveness of the locality as a domicile, and active cultural life – including events – may serve as one of the reasons why locals stay in the region. Nevertheless, both economic and image effects are fundamentally instrumental. They focus mainly on the policy view. In this study, we will concentrate on event visitors' views: what locals' hopes and desires are with regard to events, and what the influence of local characteristics is on the visitor experience of community festivals.

Events studied

The study focused on 17 festivals and events all around Finland during the years 2012–2013 (see Table 3.1). They represent the following genres: large and small rock festivals, classical music festivals, visual arts events and other cultural festivals consisting of a dance and a film festival. The studied festivals and events are established, regularly organized in the same location and most of them have become hallmark events (Getz, 2007, p. 24). They are planned, implemented and managed mainly locally. In most of the cases, a considerable number of the festival's volunteer workers are locals.

In Table 3.1, the number of inhabitants in the community is given to compare with the event size. The events are classified as small (S), medium (M) and large (L) according to the estimate of the number of daily visitors. The total number of guests is not given since it is a problematic concept and causes constant public debate. Organizers tend to stress the number of sold tickets. When we consider the impacts of the event on the local community, the number of tickets does not give the right impression of the size of the event. For example, the *Retretti Art Exhibition* lasted for several months in 2012 and sold over 40,000 tickets. It had much less of a direct impact on the environment and the local residents' life than any one-day festival with 10,000 visitors. In Finland, cultural events are typically rather small, and it is rare to have more than 10,000 daily visitors. Events of such a size are usually rock festivals or stadium concerts that cannot remain unnoticed by anyone in the neighbourhood. Despite the high number of sold tickets, Retretti went bankrupt in the early autumn of 2012 due to earlier debts and the smaller than expected amount of visitors.

The events of this study were selected not only because they represent a certain genre and take place in different localities around Finland, but also because they are arranged in different surroundings. Rock festivals are mainly arranged outdoors. Provinssirock and *Pienet Festarit Preerialla* (PFP) take place on islands: PFP is arranged on a tiny Hietasaari island of the coast of Vaasa in the Gulf of Bothnia, and Provinssirock festival area is partly on an island on River Seinäjoki. *Ilosaarirock, Ruisrock, Ilmiö* and *Ämyrock* are arranged in parks. *Kuudes Aisti* festival takes place in Helsinki, in industrial blocks dating back to the 19th century. In the early evening, the acts are performed in the courtyard but the late performances take place indoors. *Naamat* is arranged on a private farm. The camping area is in the fields of the farm, and the bands play on a small stage constructed in an opening of the wall of an old drying barn.

The selected classical music festivals can boast a unique natural environment. In Naantali, some of the concerts are held in the archipelago of the Baltic Sea. The basic idea of *LuostoClassic* is to arrange concerts in open air in the Lappish fells. Even though Kuhmo Chamber Music Festival concerts are performed indoors, various visitors mention their memories of the beautiful Lake Lammasjärvi [Sheep Lake] that lies near the concert venues Kuhmo House and Kontio School.

Visual arts events are usually arranged in buildings that are of architectural or historical interest. *Honkahovi* is an old manor house. *Naïvistic Art at Iittala* is

Table 3.1 Events studied

Genre	Event	Locality	Inhabitants	Established	Event size
Large rock	Ilosaarirock	Joensuu	73,400	1971	L
	Provinssirock [Province Rock]	Seinäjoki	57,900	1979	L
	Ruisrock	Turku	177,400	1970	L
Small rock	Ilmiö [Phenomen]	Turku	177,400	2009	S
	Kuudes Aisti [Sixth Sense]	Helsinki	588,900	2012	S
	Naamat [Faces]	Muurame	9,300	2000	S
	Pienet Festarit Preerialla [Little Festivals on the Prairie]	Vaasa	59,700	2012	S
	Ämyrock	Hämeenlinna	66,900	1974	S
Classical music	Kuhmo Chamber Music Festival	Kuhmo	9,500	1970	M
	LuostoClassic	Sodankylä	8,800	2003	S
	Naantali Music Festival	Naantali	18,800	1980	S
Visual arts	Honkahovi Summer Exhibition	Mänttä-Vilppula	11,400	1992	S
	Ii Biennale of Northern Environmental and Sculpture Art	Ii	9,400	2008	S
	Naïvistic Art at Iittala	Hämeenlinna	66,900	1989	S
	Retretti	Punkaharju	3,700	1978	M
Others	Kuopio Dance Festival	Kuopio	96,800	1970	M
	Midnight Sun Film Festival	Sodankylä	8,800	1986	S

Notes
Event size is expressed as daily visitors, estimated from the sold tickets: S = less than 5,000, M = 5,000–10,000, L = over 10,000 daily visitors.

arranged in a former school. Retretti takes place in a building especially built for this art exhibition, and the most fascinating part of the construction are the inside caves that offer artists extraordinary opportunities for the creation of 'wow' experiences. *Ii Biennale of Northern Environmental and Sculpture Art* exhibits its works in a special environmental art park that is free of charge to enter. Some of the works of art are placed in the old harbour area surrounded by the beautiful wooden houses from the 19th century.

Kuopio Dance Festival has its main programme in indoor venues. Some performances are arranged in the marketplace and in the inland harbour area. *Midnight Sun Film Festival* screenings are in a cinema, in the former school of Kitisenranta and in two large tents.

Research methods

We applied a mixed methodology approach to empirical research on the Finnish festival scene. In so doing, 1,434 web survey answers, 23 interviews and 42 narrative stories were collected. The web survey was conducted in 2012–2013, interviews were conducted in 2012 and narratives were collected in 2012. We were not interested in the artistic presentations per se, but in the other aspects of an event; we call these aspects the non-core attributes. The web survey contained questions about these attributes. Additionally, the informants were asked to describe the experience as they perceived it. To shed further light on what the informants considered desirable and desired, they were asked to give suggestions for further development. The respondents' personal values were collected using Schwartz's (1992) value structure that consists of 10 basic values: power, achievement, hedonism, stimulation, self-direction, universalism, benevolence, tradition, conformity and security. The values were measured using the Short Schwartz's Value Survey (SSVS) introduced by Lindeman and Verkasalo (2005). The profiles of web respondents are presented in Table 3.2. The youngest respondent was 12 and the oldest was 82 years old.

The interviewees had voluntarily given their contact information in the web survey. The interviews were semi-structured and the questions were the same for everyone. The interviews were recorded and transcribed. The interviews were conducted by telephone since the informants live all around Finland. The purpose was to deepen our understanding of the success factors of the event in question.

The narrative stories were collected using the Method of Empathy-Based Stories (MEBS) developed by Eskola (1988). This technique is non-active role-playing where the informant is given a description of a situation, a frame story, and asked to continue the story or to tell the antecedents. In the given frame stories, a single factor is changed at a time. Our first frame story stated that in the near future, in 2015, the festival in question would be extremely successful. The writers were asked to say what has happened. In the second frame story, the successful festival was to be arranged in the far future, in 2027. In the third

Table 3.2 Profiles of web survey respondents per genre ($n=1,434$)

Variable		Large rock	Small rock	Classical music	Visual arts	Others	Total
Gender	Male	145 (29%)	298 (49%)	20 (20%)	21 (28%)	37 (26%)	521 (36%)
	Female	360 (71%)	309 (51%)	82 (80%)	55 (72%)	107 (74%)	913 (64%)
Visitor type	Local	167 (33%)	341 (56%)	26 (25%)	22 (29%)	34 (24%)	590 (41%)
	Non-local	338 (67%)	266 (44%)	76 (75%)	54 (71%)	110 (76%)	844 (59%)
Education[a]	Basic	23 (5%)	22 (4%)	1 (1%)	3 (4%)	4 (3%)	53 (4%)
	Secondary	236 (47%)	212 (35%)	26 (25%)	32 (43%)	46 (32%)	552 (39%)
	Tertiary	245 (49%)	373 (61%)	75 (74%)	40 (53%)	94 (65%)	827 (58%)
Age	Mean	28.7	30.5	53.1	48.5	37.5	33.1
	Std Dev	9.1	7.6	14.3	14.3	13.6	12.2
Times visited	Mean	6.1	3.3	9.9	4.6	5.3	5.0
	Std Dev	5.4	3.7	9.8	5.1	7.1	5.7
TOP3 values (Schwartz, 1992)		Benevolence	Benevolence	Benevolence	Benevolence	Benevolence	Benevolence
		Hedonism	Self-direction	Universalism	Security	Self-direction	Self-direction
		Self-direction	Universalism	Self-direction	Universalism	Universalism	Universalism
Total		505 (35%)	607 (42%)	102 (7%)	76 (5%)	144 (10%)	1,434 (100%)

Notes

a Basic education = elementary and comprehensive school; Secondary education = vocational school or course, general upper secondary school (senior high), vocational upper secondary school (e.g. technical college); Tertiary education = polytechnic/university of applied sciences, university.

scenario, a negative one, the event was arranged in 2015, and it was to be considered a major disappointment. The informants were people who had answered the web survey and given their contact information. They were approached by email and asked to write a short narrative about the frame story, using a maximum of 15–20 minutes on the subject. The background of the informants was not connected with the stories. This was done in order to focus only on the logics of the stories.

The data was analysed using mixed methods. First, the web survey statements concerning the non-core attributes of the event were analysed using multivariate methods. Principal components analysis was performed to compress the data. Then the respondents were divided into four groups using K-means cluster analysis. The aim in this analysis was to find out if there were any differences in the opinions of the locals and non-locals.

Next, the combined data were used for interpretation. We made use of interviews and empathy-based stories as well as experience descriptions and suggestions for improvement given in the web survey. These were used to interpret event visitors' relation to the locality and the place. How was the locality perceived: what is the meaning of the size of the locality, are the local characteristics and authenticity meaningful? What kind of memories do the participants have and what stories do they tell of the place of the community event?

Understanding the opinions of locals and non-locals

Some of the locals visit a specific visual arts exhibition several times a summer. They probably take visiting friends and relatives there because the exhibition is considered an essential part of the cultural services of the locality. Yet, locals might appreciate the event even though they think that the core programme is not for them:

> we very seldom take part in the actual concerts and then … yeah, in the concerts that are paid for, since they are kind of … Eh … they are made for others, and it is not the business of people of Kuhmo to participate in those concerts.
>
> (Female, age 44, Kuhmo Chamber Music Festival)

Even though this description excludes the core programme from the locals, the same informant considers the event quite inclusive (Jepson & Clarke, 2013) in other aspects: 'besides buying this [festival] t-shirt I also always eat at least once in that beach restaurant [a pop-up tent restaurant that serves during the event]. It has been a new thing … so, good food and good wine.'

When locals describe their experiences, they occasionally mention the meaning of the event for the local community. The event rejuvenates the locale. In rock and classical music events, locals praise the natural environment. They also remember to thank volunteers and organizers in their experience narratives. But what do locals and non-locals think of value-laden issues like sustainability, sponsoring, social media or crowding at the community festival or event?

Opinions on the non-core attributes of the event were collected using a Likert scale from 1 to 5 (1 = 'Strongly disagree', 2 = 'Disagree', 3 = 'Neither agree nor disagree', 4 = 'Agree', 5 = 'Strongly agree'). 'Cannot say' was converted from the original value 0 to the value 3, thus changing the meaning of category 3 to 'Neither agree nor disagree/Cannot say'. Principal components analysis was conducted in total of 20 statements using varimax rotation. Those statements were omitted that loaded with a weight less than 0.500 on a single component or loaded to two components evenly. The final result comprises five components originated from 14 statements (Table 3.3) and it explains 66.8% of the total variance.

The first component is called *environmental sustainability* since it included recycling, the sorting of waste, the usage of renewable energy and ecological transport. Over 70% of the participants agree or strongly agree with the ecological statements. This opinion is 5% stronger among locals than non-locals. The second component, *local purchasing*, contains the offerings of local food and other local products at the event, as well as the use of local services. Older participants consider local purchasing more important than do the younger ones. However, local purchasing is generally appreciated: nearly 70% of all participants agree or strongly agree with promoting local products and services at the event. Interestingly, there are no particular differences among locals and non-locals with regard to this factor. The third component concerns *social media*: following the event on social media, and sharing photos and feelings on social media during the event. There are no differences in the opinions of locals and non-locals with regard to this. Quite obviously, the younger participants use social media more than the older ones. The fourth component is about *crowding*: queues, the visibility of security personnel and the ease of moving around. Even though there are no statements concerning crowds as such, all the given statements make sense only with larger crowds. Locals wish for more crowds than non-locals but the component actually correlates strongest with age. The final component concerns *sponsors* in general and with the values that the respondent shares, and on this there are no particular differences between locals and non-locals. The use of sponsors is unanimously approved but over 60% of all respondents agree or strongly agree that a sponsor with values shared by the participant has a positive effect.

When we compare the opinions of locals and non-locals by cultural genres, the most interesting component is the crowding (see Figure 3.1). Crowds are not normally tolerated in classical music festivals or in visual arts events. But, as can be seen from the figure, in both of these genres, locals actually wish for more crowds. The same is true to a lesser extent with the dance and the film festival. What is the explanation for this contradiction? Partly it is due to the fact that the locals, who answered the survey concerning classical music and visual arts events, were on average 5–7 years younger than the corresponding non-locals. As the cultural event is arranged near by, people are able to attend it more easily.

Table 3.3 Structure of the opinions on non-core attributes: the results of the principal components analysis (n=1,434)

Factors	PC1: environmental sustainability	PC2: local purchasing	PC3: social media	PC4: crowd	PC5: sponsors
It is important to sort waste and promote recycling during the event	0.849				
Renewable energy sources must be used in the event	0.836				
During the event I want to move/travel ecologically	0.800				
There must be local products for sale at the event		0.841			
Additional services (transport, food, guarding, etc.) must be produced locally		0.812			
There must be local food available at the event		0.789			
During the event, I share my feelings using social media services (Facebook, Twitter, Google Plus, etc.)			0.859		
I share photos taken during the event on the web			0.858		
I follow the event also on social media (Facebook, Twitter, etc.)			0.720		
Queuing should be made part of the fun				0.724	
It must be possible to move around (wander/dance) during the event				0.687	
Security guards should be clearly visible				0.621	
The use of sponsors is acceptable at this kind of event					0.835
Event sponsorship that aligns with my own values has a positive effect on my mood					0.694
Eigenvalues	3.43	2.28	1.27	1.22	1.17
% of variance	24.47	16.26	9.07	8.73	8.32
Cronbachs alpha	0.831	0.800	0.769	0.443	0.496

Notes
Coefficients under 0.400 omitted. KMO = 0.761.

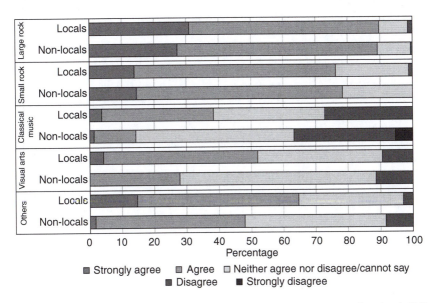

Figure 3.1 Opinions of locals and non-locals by genre in regard to crowding (*n*=1,431).

Additionally, classical music events tend to have special offers for younger participants. This seems to attract more locals than non-locals. Thus, the events featuring classical music or visual arts, which normally have a middle-aged audience, get a younger audience from the local community.

The sum variables based on the principal components analysis were used in K-means cluster analysis. The resulting four visitor groups were named as hedonists, activists, omnivores and universalists (Table 3.4). *Hedonists* are young (on average, aged 30), they want to have fun, love crowds and reflect on and about their feelings on the web. They participate in rock festivals with their friends. *Activists* are positive young people (average age 31) who value

Table 3.4 Value dimensions revealed: the result of K-means clustering with the final cluster centres and F-values (*n*=1,423; missing groupings = 11)

Principal component	Hedonists (n = 474)	Activists (n = 428)	Universalists (n = 332)	Omnivores (n = 189)	F
Social media	4.00	4.22	2.24	2.10	1,098.04
Environmental sustainability	3.52	4.58	4.39	3.28	465.14
Local purchasing	3.42	4.30	4.19	3.15	294.37
Sponsors	3.81	4.34	3.86	3.65	77.98
Crowd	3.89	4.07	3.76	3.39	47.56

universalism, benevolence, security, hedonism, self-direction and stimulation. All the value-laden event attributes are important for them and they are eager to share their feelings on social media. The proportion of females (73%) is the biggest in this group. *Omnivores* are those that visit the most versatile cultural events and are the oldest of the groups (on average, aged 40). They do not like large crowds and they do not use social media. Within the omnivores, the proportion of those who participate in the event with their family or with their partner is larger than in any other group. Of the omnivores, 53% are men while in other groups there are only 30–40% males. *Universalists* are on average 37 years old. Even though their appreciation of universalism is not necessarily as high as for young activists, they consider universalism more important than any other value, while activists have various values of similar weight. Universalists seem to shun social media. The universalists have the highest educational level within our groups: 63% of them have tertiary education.

In Table 3.4, the F-values reveal that the use of social media contributed most for the clustering, followed by environmental sustainability and local purchasing. Even though hedonists are young and omnivores are 'old', their opinions are quite similar on green issues. Neither of these two groups considers local purchasing very significant, and their opinions on environmental sustainability are weaker than for activists and universalists. Hedonists and omnivores think that waste should be sorted and recycling promoted at the event, but for them it is 'all the same' if the event uses green energy. They do not care much for ecological transport either.

How are locals and non-locals distributed into these stereotyped groups? The proportions are quite close to each other (Table 3.5). There are slightly more activists and universalists among locals (56% vs. 52%). We can conclude that locals value environmental sustainability more than non-locals, and that locals wish for more people to attend the community events.

The participants of a small, free-of-charge festival, Ämyrock, differ considerably from the average: 41% of its visitors are activists, 27% universalists, 13% omnivores and merely 19% hedonists. Generally, the proportion of hedonists in rock festivals is over 30%. Ämyrock is a genuine local festival and the tradition of participating is passed on through generations (Case Box 3.1).

Table 3.5 Distribution of clusters of locals and non-locals (n = 1,423)

	Locals (n = 585)	Non-locals (n = 838)
Hedonists	189 (32%)	285 (34%)
Omnivores	68 (12%)	121 (14%)
Activists	185 (32%)	243 (29%)
Universalists	143 (24%)	189 (23%)

Case Box 3.1: Ämyrock: 39 years of free hippie feeling

> I wish it would not rain but in most Ämys it is quite probable.
>
> (female, 53 years)

Kari Peitsamo carries a guitar and walks into the festival area. It is only a minute before he is scheduled to play. He has been on stage in Ämyrock 30 times and as he starts his set, the crowd sings along: 'Peace and love is the spirit of *Ämy* people...'. Peitsamo wrote the song for the 25-year-old Ämyrock and now he does not have to sing at all since the adult males in the front row take care of that.

Ämyrock is the oldest free-of-charge rock festival in Finland. It was founded in 1974 and will be celebrating its 40th anniversary in 2014. The event is organized in Hämeenlinna, which has 67,000 inhabitants. Over 60% of the participants are locals, and taking part in Ämyrock runs in the family. 'With mommy and my granny', says a 13-year-old girl about her companions at the festival. The mean age of the web survey respondents of Ämyrock was 35; the youngest one was 13 and the oldest 63 years old. 'I have been there as a teenager, messing around as a single and [now I participate in the event] as a mother', writes a 31-year-old female. The average number of visits in Ämyrock was eight, and the most important motive for participation was that taking part in the event is already a tradition.

In Finland, rock festivals are not considered family events. Ämyrock is an exception. Even though there is a licensed bar in the area, the festival is suitable for children and the 'beer drinking adults stayed quite well in the designated boozing areas, at least until the early night'. The presence of young children calms people down. Ämyrock has been a non-commercial festival since its inception (Järvelä, 1997). 'The organizers are on the visitors' side and the visitors want to support the background organization by behaving properly and using money in the

Figure 3.2 In Ämyrock, the soap bubble tools are provided by the organizers (photo: Sami Lindfors).

area', says a 36-year-old male. Over 75% of the respondents are willing to pay a little bit more if the proceeds go towards a good cause. Such a strongly benevolent attitude is quite exceptional among the studied events. In 2013, the theme of the festival was 'Stop poaching!', speaking out against the on-going poaching of wolves in Finland. Ämyrock is a hippie-ish event acknowledging sustainable values, just like its audience.

Visitors' TOP3 values were benevolence, self-direction and universalism. This is reflected in the opinions on the green values of the festival. Nearly 100% of the respondents agreed or strongly agreed on sorting waste and the promotion of recycling at the event. Over 80% thought that the event should use renewable energy, and nearly 80% wanted to move around ecologically during the event. There are not many cars around the festival area – instead, lots of bicycles are parked nearby. Ämyrock participants consider local purchasing very important: over 70% agree or strongly agree on local purchasing issues.

Since the festival is free of charge and it is organized by a local non-profit music association, people do not expect any big stars to perform there. Local bands are appreciated as well as – naturally – Kari Peitsamo. There is a saying that it always rains in Ämyrock. However, people do not let it disturb them. The overall feeling is very laid-back, free and easy. In 2013, the area was decorated beautifully with flowers, the children loved the possibility to blow soap bubbles, and teenagers did graffiti painting. A local improvisation theatre, a cheerleading team and a drumming group were given the opportunity to perform. Ämyrock is a small-scale and cosy festival to which people love to return. It attracts around 2,000 visitors each year. For more information: www.amyrock.org.

Local characteristics as a competitive advantage

In this section, we will investigate how the locality and the place are seen in community festivals. How is the locality perceived: what is the meaning of its size, are the local characteristics and authenticity meaningful? What kind of stories or memories do participants tell of the event place? When we are talking about established events, the locality is known for its events. Joensuu is famous for Ilosaarirock and Sodankylä would hardly be internationally known without the Midnight Sun Film Festival. In the Finnish summer, cultural events are spread around the country and even quite distant locations might receive thousands of visitors.

When cultural events are arranged outside the bigger cities, the importance of nature is obvious. All the studied classical music events are arranged in very small localities and the surrounding nature fascinates the visitors. In some of the events, a distinctive spirit of the place, *genius loci*, was observed. 'There was a silent moment in the performance. At the same time, the wind got more intense. The nature and the music came into one. I still get goose bumps when I think about it' (male, 65 years, LuostoClassic). LuostoClassic is arranged in a stunning natural environment (Case Box 3.2). It is an extraordinary classical music event also in the sense that it attracts visitors who have never before attended a classical music concert – the combination of the exceptional natural environment and open-air classical music makes people curious and willing to explore.

Case Box 3.2: LuostoClassic: classical music in a stunning natural environment

I had never before visited Aittakuru and it was somehow … in a sense … I was enthusiastic there.

(female, 47 years, LuostoClassic)

Figure 3.3 LuostoClassic concert at Aittakuru [Granary Ravine] (photo: Ilpo Okkonen).

The very basic idea behind LuostoClassic is to have musical performances in the open air, surrounded by Lappish fells. The three outdoor venues are Aittakuru [Granary Ravine], Ukko-Luosto and Ahvenlampi [Perch Pond]. In Finnish mythology, the Overgod *Ukko* is the god of the weather just like Roman Jupiter, Greek Zeus or ancient Scandinavian Thor (Haavio, 1967, pp. 148–178). Aittakuru is a ravine amphitheatre by Pyhä Fell. The ravine was formed by the melting waters of the Ice Age. After the Ice Age, rock fragments gradually disintegrated from the walls of the cliff and there is a large amount of scree on the bottom and slopes of the gorge. The stage of the amphitheater is at the bottom of the ravine and there is a tiny pond in front of it. The audience sits tens of metres above, by the slopes of the ravine. The place is just breathtaking.

Ukko-Luosto is the place for big orchestras, 'The heavens alone provide the roof and great old pine trees form the walls of Ukko-Luosto concert hall', as the event web pages describe. There are several stages around the audience at the bottom of Luosto Fell. Kalevi Aho composed his Luosto Symphony specifically for this place, and the orchestra and the choirs are supposed to be scattered into different stages and the audience is in the middle of the space.

The third venue is a large pond, Ahvenlampi. There is a small roofed stage on a tiny spit of land, and the audience sits on the opposite bank. Since the stage is so close to the water, there is no need for sound reproduction equipment. The water transfers the sound.

LuostoClassic has been organized since 2003 and it has a couple of thousand visitors each year. For more information: www.luostoclassic.fi.

A typical visitor to the Kuhmo Chamber Music Festival comes from the Helsinki metropolitan area, i.e. the south of Finland. The distance between Kuhmo and Helsinki is 600 km, and the mental distance is even larger. This seems to develop topophilia (Tuan, 1974/1990), the emotional attitude towards the place. A visitor perceives the place differently from the local inhabitant. Local residents might never notice or pay no more attention to the things the visitor might see. Kuhmo is a small town in a sparsely populated area; one can breathe fresh air, enjoy the silence and have a walk in the woods in total solitude. Furthermore, the local residents seem very natural and genuine in the eyes of a city dweller. When the nature experiences are combined with the memories of the people encountered during the event, the effect of the place becomes more personal and lasts longer.

The small size of the locality can influence the overall festival atmosphere. As a 50-year-old male interviewee from the Kuopio Dance Festival puts it:

> And then actually, as it is in Kuopio which is not a particularly big city ... that kind of significant event in a smallish town makes it comprehensive. At least you get the kind of a feeling that there the whole town is dancing and playing for that week. And it is not lost like it would be if it was an event among other events in some kind of a metropolis or in a big city.

A similar kind of ambience is offered by the Midnight Sun Film Festival (Case Box 3.3). A tiny locality in Finnish Lapland, in the middle of nowhere, combines with the white nights of the northern summer to set the stage for an extraordinary festival experience.

Case Box 3.3: Midnight Sun Film Festival: a world-class film festival in the middle of nowhere

> Woodstock is fucking nothing if you have been to the Midnight Sun Film Festival.
>
> (D.A. Pennebaker, in von Bagh, 2010, p. 305)

The Midnight Sun Film Festival has taken place since the late 1980s in Sodankylä in Finnish Lapland. The festival was founded by Finnish filmmakers and it is known for the presence of Peter von Bagh and Aki and Mika Kaurismäki. The initial idea was quite eccentric: to watch movies throughout the night at the time when the sun does not set at all, in a distant location that has practically no other activities at the same time. Sodankylä is 900 km from Helsinki, on the northern side of the Arctic Circle, and it has less than 9,000 residents. The small size of the event locality is very important. 'Sodankylä kind of transforms into this film place, kind of a different place for the time of the festival', says a 36-year-old male interviewee.

The festival can boast guests like Michael Powell, Jacques Demy, Francis Ford Coppola and Miloš Forman, and still 'you can come across a world-class celebrity in a local pizzeria'. The cheerful organization attitude is described by Jim Jarmusch (von Bagh, p. 290):

I was asked to participate in other festivals as well but they always send so formal invitations: *We cordially invite your presence.* Then I got a fax from Aki and Mika [Kaurismäki] and it read: *Come to Lapland. You can drink as much beer as you want.*

Figure 3.4 Peter von Bagh discussing with Miloš Forman at Midnight Sun Film Festival in 2008 (photo: Santeri Happonen).

The festival claims to be an anti-Cannes event for genuine film lovers, without red carpets, adulation or heavy film marketing efforts. The extraordinary atmosphere comes from the combination of a constant flow of films, informal attitude, the distant and small location and the white nights. As the festival web pages (MSFF, 2013) put it: 'Films are shown in four venues for 24 hours a day, and the actual time is easily forgotten as the sun shines as brightly at 4 a.m. as it does at 4 p.m.' In 2013, the festival sold 27,000 tickets and had around 100 screenings. The number of actual visitors can be estimated to be around 3,000 since an average participant watches nine movies (Salokangas, 1996, p. 24). For more information: www.msfilmfestival.fi.

Events are important occasions to spend time with family and close friends. However, the event also serves as a place for reunion for those who once lived there. 'You meet childhood friends and listen to good music', as a 39-year-old female describes her experience in *Ilosaarirock*. Locals mention that at the event, they meet former schoolmates and other old friends who moved away a long time ago. On the other hand, those who had left their hometown recount that at the event, they meet both those who stayed in the area and those who left at some point but return, year after year, for the community festival.

When the interviewees were asked what would ruin the event, change of place is mentioned. 'Well, if it was transferred e.g. to Nurmes [neighbouring municipal] ... Transferring would ruin the event. It kind of cannot be transferred,

Kuhmo Chamber Music was born in Kuhmo and it will be buried there if it was closed down', says a 44-year-old female interviewee about the importance of the place. In her remarks, place refers to a wide context, the whole town. When a 49-year-old male visitor of Naïvistic Art at Iittala was asked the same question, he used a narrower concept of place, the venue: 'Mmm ... maybe if it would be transferred to some kind of DDR style concrete bunker...' Even though visitors want the event to be renewed every year, changing the locality or the venue would not be tolerated.

The place may be meaningful also for a rock festival visitor.

> The Törnävä area is a kind of, well, actually you do not necessarily spend much time there otherwise, so when you are there, instantly you have Provinssi[rock] memories in your mind even if it was in the middle of the winter,

a 27-year-old male interviewee suggests. At rock festivals, the campsites have a special meaning and create memorable experiences (Case Box 3.4).

Case Box 3.4: Camping places in rock festivals

> Ilosaarirock and spending the night in the camping area in a military tent is part of the summer
>
> (female, 41 years, Ilosaarirock)

Rock festivals attract thousands of people to localities that do not necessarily have enough accommodation capacity for their non-local participants. Thus, most of the rock festivals arrange temporary, pop-up campsites. They are memorable places for those who overnight there. A member of the organizing team of Provinssirock says that earlier there were lots of people at the campsite who had not bought a ticket for the festival at all. The atmosphere of the camping place was enough for them. However, the open area attracted thieves, and nowadays festival campsites are guarded and access is usually granted only for those who have a ticket for the event. A worker at the Ilosaarirock campsites confirms that there are still people who come merely for the festival camping experience – they might not leave the campsite at all even though they have a ticket for the festival.

The camping area is an important place for pre- and after-partying. There the carnival goes on after the core programme at the festival site has ended. It is part of the festival experience to deliberately stay awake, in many cases, with the help of alcohol. Campers tend to be more and more tired towards the end of the event. An empathy-based story picturing a successful Ilosaarirock 2015 describes camping life in the festival:

> And we twanged the guitar and rattled whatever gear we could find, sang well out of tune, now and then delicately in tune as well, also those who never otherwise sing. Folks in the neighbouring tent were similar-minded, a real guitarist was found there, one who really could also play, more songs, hooray!

For obvious reasons, camping places are mainly used by non-locals. Among the studied events, a small festival, Naamat, is arranged on a private farm quite far from the centre of the locality. The festival has loyal visitors who want to return year after year. Its 800 tickets have been sold out for several years in a row even before the programme was published. In 2013, the event was sold out in four minutes. Here also the locals tend to spend the night on the field, camping. Overnight staying is a bodily experience: people go to sauna, swim naked in a pond, queue for breakfast, some wander around barefoot, football is played in the field. Many participants describe their experience like spending the weekend in a summer cottage with friends. 'Collective, open, caring, warm, different, being in the field with a big bunch of buddies', describes a 28-year-old male, casually defining the characteristics of a hypercommunity (Kozinets, 2002). The field camping is an essential part of the festival experience, in both the good and the bad aspects: 'I haven't participated any more since I want to sleep at night and that is not possible at Naamat' (female, 41 years). For more information. naamat.info.

Figure 3.5 A swim after sauna at Naamat rock festival (photo: Anssi Toivakka).

In empathy-based stories describing an imaginary failure of the community festival, the local people and the local characteristics of the community were absent.

Food services do not work, there is no atmospheric pancake or salmon place, no cafes with cheese cakes and, above all, the local is absent, even in the food arrangements, instead everything comes from somewhere else (from Helsinki?) and tastes industrial.

Another visitor describes a fictitious, unsuccessful Midnight Sun Film Festival: 'Sodankylä is polished, alcoholics and poor people are taken away and bars are closed from the locals.' The writer shudders at the thought of hiding the unfortunate part of the population. Additionally, the idea of closing off the services from the locals and favouring the visitors contradicts the feelings of togetherness and egalitarianism that are an essential part of the sense of community in events and festivals. It is the local people and the tastes and smells of local food that give the event its authenticity and the special touch worth remembering.

Altogether, the locality, the place and the local people build an authentic experience that cannot be replicated anywhere else. Some of the events might have constructed the differentiated local image with decades of hard work; some might have concentrated on choosing a memorable venue. Nevertheless, since Finns are nature lovers and the surroundings are of importance, summer events that offer authentic local characteristics and the opportunity to have bodily, open-air experiences seem to have steady foundations.

Conclusion and discussion

This chapter has focused on two separate questions: How do the participants view the festival when it takes place in their home community? And how do local characteristics differentiate an event? We studied these questions among the participants of various summer festivals in Finland during the summers of 2012 and 2013. The festivals represented the following genres: large rock festivals, small rock festivals, classical music festivals, visual arts events and other cultural festivals consisting of a dance festival and a film festival. The study included altogether 17 festivals and events all around Finland.

A multivariate analysis of 1,434 web survey responses resulted in classifying the visitors into four clusters that were hedonists, activists, omnivores and universalists. We may characterize these clusters as follows: hedonists are young crowd lovers that want to have fun at rock festivals with their friends, reflecting their feelings on social media. Activists are young people who are positively disposed towards the event and for whom the value-laden event attributes are important. Omnivores visit the most versatile cultural events, and they are the oldest of the groups. They do not particularly value traditions even though their attitude towards large crowds and social media is traditional. Universalists consider universalism more important than any other value. Within local event participants, there are more activists and universalists than among non-locals.

In analysing differences and similarities between locals and non-locals, the following observations may be made: the local audience wishes for more crowds. They also place more stress on the environmental sustainability of the event. Locals and non-locals have similar attitudes towards local purchasing, the use of social media and sponsors. It is worth noting that local participants lower the average age in classical music and visual arts events. A typical visitor at such an event does not want large crowds. However, the opposite seems true when considering young locals' views.

The importance and significance of local characteristics were also studied. In 23 interviews, 42 narrative stories and responses to open questions in the aforementioned web survey, new light was shed on aspects of locality. Feelings of authenticity and the sense of place seemed strongly connected in the responses. It can be concluded that a special natural environment creates a more attractive and memorable event. On the other hand, festivals and events produce memories that are connected to a specific place that could be an event venue or a pop-up campsite. The local scenery, an established venue, local people and local food are of utmost importance to the visitors. The event would be ruined if it were transferred to another locality or place, if the local people were excluded from the event or if there were no local food available. Indeed, the local characteristics and authenticity were shown to give a competitive advantage to community festivals and events.

The results cannot be generalized since the respondents were not randomly selected. In addition, the number of responses is heavily biased towards rock festivals. The studied events promoted the web survey in a way they considered appropriate. Most of them used Facebook, which means that the respondents are also biased towards those favouring social media.

In discussing the visitors to the community festivals in Finland, there is a reason to comment on the definition of community festival, given the context of our findings. All human societies always find reasons for celebrating. Feasts were meant to entertain, educate and to offer escape as well as aesthetic pleasure, just like contemporary experiences (cf. Pine II & Gilmore, 1999). Most often like-minded groups create their social identity in these events. To celebrate happenings, common experiences and cultural festivals are at the core of humanity, and also at the core of experience economy. The editors of this book define community festivals as follows:

> Community festivals are defined as themed and inclusive community events or series of events, which have been created as the result of an inclusive community planning process to celebrate the particular way of life of people and groups in the local community with emphasis on a particular space and time.
>
> (Jepson & Clarke, 2013, p. 7)

Community festivals are or have become an integral part of the life of their communities in most of our cases. They were often constructed by local enthusiasts as in the case of Kuhmo, where the Kuhmo Music Society was founded in 1966 to promote interest in music. An outsider to the locality, the young Seppo Kimanen, proposed to the society that an international group of top musicians come over to Kuhmo to perform chamber music there in the summer of 1970. The intention was to establish a permanent festival for chamber music. The society activities were continued all year, and enthusiastic artists, students, locals and visitors alike helped in establishing the successful international chamber music festival (kuhmofestival.fi, 2013; Subrenat, 2006).

The Kuhmo Chamber Music Festival is an example of a locally coordinated activity combined with the entrepreneurial vision of an artist acquainted with the place. Kimanen saw the opportunities in the creation, establishment and successful internationalization of this community festival.

There is an evolution of the meetings of the like-minded from festivities to community festivals. One realizes that in most cases, limiting oneself to the 'inclusive community planning process to celebrate the particular way of life of people and groups in the local community in a particular space and time' definition holds true only partially. Community festivals are also entrepreneurial platforms for cultural entrepreneurship where initiators may see an extension of their original ideas into something else with collaborators and resource providers. The stage in the community, i.e. the place and the locality, is often the motive for the establishment, but the success depends on meeting the ambitions and wishes of the actors and stakeholders.

References

Eskola, A. (1988). Non-active role-playing: Some experiences. In A. Eskola, A. Kihlström, D. Kivinen, K. Weckroth & O.-H. Ylijoki (eds), *Blind alleys in social psychology: A search for ways out* (pp. 239–311). Advances in Psychology 48. Amsterdam: North-Holland.

Finland Festivals. (2013). Festivaalien käyntimäärät 2012 [The amount of festival visits in 2012]. Retrieved from www.festivals.fi/tilastot/alatilastot/#.UlLO0xDPbO4.

Florida, R. (2004). *The rise of the creative class: And how it's transforming work, leisure, community and everyday life*. New York: Basic Books. (Original work published 2002)

Getz, D. (2007). *Event studies: Theory, research and policy for planned events*. Amsterdam: Elsevier.

Haavio, M. (1967). *Suomalainen mytologia* [Finnish mythology]. Porvoo: WSOY.

Iso-Aho, J. (2011). An introduction to festival management: Old ways, new directions. In M. Brindle & C. DeVereaux (eds), *The arts management handbook: New directions for students and practitioners* (pp. 95–119). New York: M.E. Sharpe.

Järvelä, J. (1997). *Homma kävi: Erään pikkukaupungin pophistoria* [Job well fixed: The pop history of a smalltown]. Hämeenlinna: Karisto.

Jepson, A. & Clarke, A. (2013). Events and community development. In R. Finkel, D. McGillivray, G. McPherson & P. Robinson (eds), *Research themes for events* (pp. 6–17). Wallingford: CABI.

Kainulainen, K. (2005). *Kunta ja kulttuurin talous: Tulkintoja kulttuuripääoman ja festivaalien aluetaloudellisista merkityksistä* [Municipalities and cultural economy: Interpretations of the meanings of cultural capital and festivals for regional economy]. Tampere: Tampere University Press.

Karjalainen, T. (1991). *Kuhmo Chamber Music Festival: The structure of the festival's economy and the economic impact of the festival*. Arts Council of Finland, Research and Publications Unit.

Kinnunen, H. (2013, 14 July). Kuhmon Kamarimusiikki auttaa ensikertalaisia valitsemaan sopivan ohjelman [Kuhmo Chamber Music Festival helps the first-timers to choose a suitable programme]. *Yle Kainuu*. Retrieved from http://yle.fi.

Kozinets, R.V. (2002). Can consumers escape the market? Emancipatory illuminations from Burning Man. *Journal of Consumer Research, 29*, 20–38. doi: 10.1086/339919.

kuhmofestival.fi. (2013). History of the Kuhmo Chamber Music Festival. Retrieved from www.kuhmofestival.fi/history.htm.

Lindeman, M. & Verkasalo, M. (2005). Measuring values with the Short Schwartz's Value Survey. *Journal of Personality Assessment, 85*, 170–178. doi: 10.1207/ s15327752jpa8502_09.

MSFF. (2013). Festival webpages. Retrieved from www.msfilmfestival.fi.

Myerscough, J. (1988). *The economic importance of the arts in Britain.* London: Policy Studies Institute.

Pine II, B.J. & Gilmore, J.H. (1999). *The experience economy: Work is theatre & every business a stage – Goods & services are no longer enough.* Boston, MA: Harvard Business School Press.

Rytmikorjaamo. (2013). Webpages of the facility. Retrieved from www.rytmikorjaamo. com.

Salokangas, M. (1996). 'Sodankylän henki': Yhteisyys ja yksilöllisyys elokuvajuhlilla ['The spirit of Sodankylä': Community and individualism in film festivals]. *Sosiologia, 1*, 23–33.

Schwartz, S.H. (1992). Universals in the content and structure of values: Theory and empirical tests in 20 countries. In M.P. Zanna (ed.), *Advances in experimental social psychology* (Vol. 25, pp. 1–65). New York: Academic Press.

Skot-Hansen, D. (2005). Why urban culture policies? In J. Robinson (ed.), *EUROC-ULT21 integrated report* (pp. 31–39). Helsinki: EUROCULT21.

Subrenat, J.-J. (2006). *Listen, there's music from the forest: A brief presentation of the Kuhmo Chamber Music Festival.* Kuhmo: Kuhmon kamarimusiikin kannatusyhdistys.

Tuan, Y.-F. (1990). *Topophilia: A study of environmental perception, attitudes, and values.* New York: Columbia University Press. (Original work published 1974)

Tuulari, J. & Latva-Äijö, J. (2000). *Provinssirock: Ihmisten juhla – Historiallinen kooste Provinssirockista ja sen tekijöistä 1970–2000* [Provinssirock: The party of people – The historical collage of Provinssirock and its makers 1970–2000]. Seinäjoki: Rytmi-Instituutti.

Tuuri, H., Rumpunen, S., Kortesluoma, A. & Katajavirta, M. (2012). *Etelä-Pohjanmaan kesätapahtumat 2012, kävijäprofiili, kävijätyytyväisyys ja aluetaloudellinen vaikuttavuus* [Summer events 2012 of South Ostrobothnia, visitor profile, visitor satisfaction and regional economic impact]. Seinäjoki: Seinäjoen ammattikorkeakoulu, Markkinatutkimuspalvelut. Retrieved from http://etelapohjanmaa.fi/kulttuuri/documents/kesatapahtumat2012.pdf.

Valkonen, K. & Valkonen, M. (1994). *Festival fever: Finland Festivals.* Helsinki: Otava.

Von Bagh, P. (2010). *Sodankylä ikuisesti* [Sodankylä forever]. Helsinki: WSOY.

4 Festivals and sense of community in places of transition

The Yakkerboo Festival, an Australian case study

Michelle Duffy and Judith Mair

Introduction

> I think it gives the people something to really look forward to. Yakkerboo's coming, something to work on and everything, and I think it gives them pride in the fact that our town has a great festival. Now when you talk about the town we live in to other people, I think it helps to give them pride.
>
> (Yakkerboo Festival committee member, 2013)

The underlying assumption that lies behind the festival event is that it functions as a community-building activity. The festival is, as anthropologist Robert Lavenda describes it, 'people celebrating themselves and their community in an "authentic" and traditional way, or at least emerging spontaneously from their homes for a communitywide expression of fellowship' (1992, p. 76). Hence, participation in a community festival is an interactive process that produces a sense of a social reality for a 'located' group identity, and, although a temporary event, the festival has implications for a group's identity/identities that extend beyond this time period and specific geographical location. Embedded within these sorts of ideas about the festival is an understanding of a clearly articulated relationship between place and community, with the festival a means to represent this intersection. Yet there are other processes involved, specifically the ways in which different actors understand and activate ideas about place, and how place and its various constituents (human and non-human) are connected and networked. These frameworks of place point to the ways in which heterogeneous relations of people, processes and materials are important to constituting meanings about a place and community. This also means that the festival is something that activates and is activated by ideas and issues about 'community' identity and 'place' that are already in circulation. We need to acknowledge, though, that there is inequality in any constitution of community and place. As Clarke and Jepson (2011, p. 8) point out, political relations are significant to the creation of a festival because there are particular individuals who are the power brokers of that community, 'those who hold direct power over the festival and its construction'. A community festival is therefore constituted out of a complex set of power relations that nonetheless serve to define notions of belonging.

Various processes can create a sense of belonging, which in turn constructs assumptions about identification, in terms of social location (gender, race or class), with regard to narratives of identity (Fortier, 1999; Probyn, 1996), and how these various constructions are attributed ethical and political value (Yuval-Davis, 2006). However, given the various forms of identification, belonging is never fixed and coherent, but rather fragmented, partial and mobile (Appadurai, 1991; Bauman, 2001). Hence, notions of belonging require work (Crowley, 1999) as they involve the struggles around defining and determining what is actually involved in belonging. In this chapter we wish to explore the impact of shifting place boundaries on communities, and how such shifts raise questions around the sense of connectedness to a place and its community.

Our focus is on the rapid changes occurring at Melbourne's peri-urban fringe, and how the goals of one festival – the Yakkerboo Festival, a long-held event in Melbourne's south-eastern growth corridor – addresses what have become contested notions of identity, place and belonging in this space of transition.

Constructing place and community in sites of change

The Great Australian Dream of home ownership and its links to an idealised free-standing house for the modern nuclear family has been central to the making of Australian suburbia. Yet the recent push behind the development of peri-urban regions raises a number of important challenges to this dream because of the strategic, spatial, economic and environmental significance of these sites (Buxton et al., 2006).

High housing prices, rising costs of petrol, economic restructuring and changing employment opportunities, as well as growing anxieties about environmental sustainability in the face of climate change, have combined in different ways to challenge the taken-for-granted processes of urban and suburban growth. Moreover, many rural communities that experience the advancing urban frontier have expressed frustration over their loss of a sense of place, as farming land and pastures are transformed and subdivided into 'amenity' or 'lifestyle' residential blocks. Some question the inevitability of metropolitan sprawl (Green, 2010) and destruction of the rich social fabric of rural places in order to create so-called 'inauthentic' and 'placeless' suburbs dominated by a car culture and supposedly lacking any sense of community and belonging (Qviström, 2012).

One popular form of creating community has been to generate events that serve to create a sense of shared identity and belonging. Festivals have long been understood in just this way (Gibson & Connell, 2005; Kong & Yeoh, 1997; Quinn, 2003). These events tend to support ideas of place-based identities so that participants come to feel connected and united (Derrett, 2003; Duffy & Waitt, 2011; Dunphy, 2009; Mulligan et al., 2006). More importantly, what underpins the festival is the desire to promote social cohesion, and attempts to create this are made through discourses of an official 'imagined' community (Anderson, 1983). This draws on aspects of the daily lives of a group or community as a means to reinforce particular socio-political, historical and spatial affiliations

(Duffy & Waitt, 2011). Such a framework has been used by governing bodies such as local councils and businesses with the expectation that these events will produce a range of social and economic benefits. Festivals are often staged for broad social goals (Finkel, 2010; Wood, 2005) and much of the research on festivals has begun with the underlying premise that such events sustain social benefits through their economic implications. Yet, these are complex processes with potentially divisive outcomes, and raise many issues, particularly around what is meant by 'the community' and how such a formation is inclusive. Further, some research suggests that rather than encouraging community, festivals can operate as spaces of exclusion (Quinn, 2003).

Taking a case study approach, this chapter examines these ideas through a focus on the annual Yakkerboo Community Festival, held in Pakenham about one hour south-east of Melbourne, a once rural community that is now undergoing processes of rapid urbanisation.

The Yakkerboo Festival has run for almost 40 years, with little significant change to its format, and continues to include traditional community festival components of street parade, art show and craft market. This chapter explores how such a long-held festival may or may not continue to hold relevance for a community undergoing significant social, demographic and cultural change. Through a close examination of the aspirations of festival organisers involved in Yakkerboo, we explore the role community festivals may have in creating stronger communities in the new growth corridor of the City of Cardinia, located on Melbourne's south-eastern boundary. Through this, we consider the impact rapid urbanisation has on notions of *community* for those living at the peri-urban edge, given the differing needs, perceptions and histories of established and emerging communities.

Festivals and community literature

Much festival research focuses on the positive outcomes of holding festivals, from early work by Falassi (1987) and Turner (1984) on communitas, to more recent work that considers festivals as places of social inclusion (Johnson, Currie & Stanley, 2011) and as places where strong communities may be built (Derrett, 2003). Even so, while festivals may aim to be inclusive, there remains a set of exclusive practices through boundary marking that delineates certain individuals as belonging or not: for example, in marking out a community through notions of cultural or subcultural affiliations, pre-requisite knowledge that facilitates appreciation of festival practices and meaningful participation, as well as any costs incurred that may deter an individual's involvement in attending a festival (Gibson & Connell, 2012). A critical role performed by festivals, as Johnson et al. (2011, p. 69) suggest, is that they may 'engage sections of the community not normally participating in community and political activities'. In this way, festivals act, as Gibson and Connell (2012, p. 9) point out, as 'hybrid economic affairs ... a central meeting place for different parts of local economies'. Moreover, the formal and informal economic activities associated with festivals are also valuable in creating notions of place and community (Fincher & Iveson, 2008), activities that provide positive feedback into place investment in terms of the economy, but just as importantly in the processes that constitute and support notions of local community identity (Derrett, 2003).

There are often ways to facilitate access to festivals for the local community too, such as no or only a nominal entry fee or donation, thus giving greater access for lower socio-economic groups to cultural activities (Arcodia & Whitford, 2006; Carlsen, Ali-Knight & Robertson, 2007). The lack of formality associated with an outdoor setting compared to a theatre or opera house also helps to broaden access to many activities, particularly arts and culture (Carlsen et al., 2007).

Other often-cited benefits of holding festivals include the opportunity for local people to become involved, either through volunteering or taking on temporary or casual paid work. Volunteering allows people to mix with others across a wide spectrum of backgrounds and interests (Finkel, 2010). In either case, this gives local community members the opportunity to develop skills and experience that will assist them in seeking further employment, a measurable outcome, and will also increase community capacity more broadly (Johnson et al., 2011). Arcodia and Whitford (2006) argue that while there are clear economic benefits for communities that host them, festivals are predominantly a social phenomenon with the potential to provide a variety of positive social outcomes. They suggest that festivals may facilitate the development of social capital in three main ways – by building community resources, by encouraging social cohesiveness and by giving the public opportunities for public celebration.

Other potential benefits for communities in holding festivals include the use of the festival space as a place to increase tolerance and understanding of community diversity. Festivals often encompass a range of different programming, which might highlight cultural and ethnic diversity or involve minority groups (Carlsen et al., 2007; Finkel, 2006). Indeed, it is sometimes the case that a festival can provide a focus for an otherwise marginalised group within a community (Gorman-Murray, 2009). Finkel (2010) suggests that such goals or benefits act as a source of pride for organisers, and can act as a catalyst for community members to become involved.

However, alongside the benefits it is important to consider the negative impacts that festivals may have on a community. These can be particularly apparent when the event is seen to be a space of exclusion for certain groups or individuals within a community. In research carried out in the context of the 'Up Helly Aa' festival held in Lerwick, Shetland, Finkel (2010) illustrates how gender differences play out in the traditional festival roles taken on by men and women. Men are allowed to take part in the procession, which is the main event of the festival, while women are restricted to cooking for the festival. Some women state that they are happy with this gender division, seeing it as representative of the traditions of the festival; however, Finkel (2010) argues that such a structure ignores equity and diversity and that this is not a good role model for a modern community. Quinn (2003) also notes that some festivals and events are exclusive to elite audience groups (often cultural or arts events), and that the high prices for such events act as barriers to inclusivity (Waterman, 1998). Carlsen et al. (2007) also note that festivals may need to change over time in order to widen their support base in the local community, as the local community itself may change over time. The implicit suggestion here is that some festivals fail to change in step with the community that they were developed for, and over time may begin to lose their relevance to local people. This is an important point in relation to the case study of this chapter, and one to which we will return.

The Yakkerboo Festival

The Yakkerboo Festival takes place annually in Pakenham, in the outer south-east of Melbourne, Victoria. Part of Australia's rapidly growing peri-urban areas, this once rural environment is quickly being levelled and coated in asphalt and housing slabs. Rapid population growth is already evident: in 2006 the population numbered 19,644; it currently numbers around 33,999 residents (Australian Bureau of Statistics, 2011) and is estimated to expand to slightly over 57,500 in the next two decades (Grant, 2009). The Casey–Cardinia growth corridor, where Yakkerboo takes place, is beginning to be framed as a place that will not only face rapid social, cultural, economic and environmental transformation (with all the attendant challenges), but also where new and exciting urban–rural assemblages can be enabled. Even so, a key concern that is constantly raised is how to ensure that a sense of community is valued and facilitated given the demographic and land use changes occurring.

The Yakkerboo Festival, whose name derives from an Aboriginal word meaning place of green pasture, started in the mid-1970s and has not altered substantially since then. It has a range of components including the street parade, which is probably the best-known part of the festival. However, there is also a street market, a funfair, fireworks, an art show and a twilight carnival. Each part of the festival has its own feel, with the street parade and funfair aimed primarily at families with young children, and the twilight carnival attracting teenagers and young people. The art show is aimed at both local and national artists, with prizes of up to AU$4,000 on offer. The festival is essentially a version of the type of event that is held in most communities around the world, and retains elements of a farm-based culture and a country agricultural fair.

Data collection, analysis and discussion

This research took a qualitative approach, and used both interviews with key stakeholders and participant observation to collect data. This allows us to acknowledge the multiple meanings that are constructed as people engage and form relationships with the world around them (Crotty, 1998). Purposive sampling was used to identify those individuals who possess detailed knowledge and familiarity with certain aspects of the community (Jennings, 2001), while snowball sampling provided access to interviewees who were referred and recommended by others (Biernacki & Waldorf, 1981). Participants were interviewed by one or both of the authors and each interview was recorded with permission and transcribed. Interviews lasted between 20 and 60 minutes. Data were subjected to a qualitative content analysis that explored relevant themes as they arose. These codes formed the basis of a theoretically informed analysis (Miles & Huberman, 1994). During the festival, which was attended by both authors, participant observation notes and photographs were taken, providing rich data, and 'incontestable evidence' of what had been observed during the case study (Stake, 1995).

Yakkerboo and its (rural) community

Originally starting in the 1970s as a community festival by the then Pakenham Shire, the Yakkerboo Festival maintains a focus on bringing members of 'the community' together. The Pakenham Shire was severed from the Berwick Shire in 1973, and then was incorporated into the new Cardinia Shire in 1994. The local council 'wanted something for the municipal recreation and something [for the community] to do', noted one Pakenham resident who had been involved in its organisation for almost 25 years when interviewed, 'when the festival started, Pakenham was just a little country town'.

The Yakkerboo Festival continues to be held, although support has waxed and waned, and while its future may be in some doubt the primary role of this festival remains clearly (and proudly) stated on the festival webpage:

> Yakkerboo prides itself in providing a free festival for the people, by the people, and it is the people volunteering their time in Yakkerboo, who are the heart and soul of the event.... *Festivals like Yakkerboo are the glue that holds communities together. The Yakkerboo Community Festival has become part of making new residents feel welcome, it is the vehicle for new residents to work and play beside established residents*, and, importantly, it brings children together; happy, laughing, celebrating and playing together ... it is about celebrating our strong, cohesive and well-functioning community and local business and industry.
>
> (Yakkerboo Festival, n.d.; emphasis added)

The location and population size of Pakenham in the 1970s meant its residents had to be relatively self-reliant, which in turn has meant that a more conservative definition of community, one with an emphasis on locality, tradition and a sense of neighbourliness (Lavenda 1992), has been a key defining characteristic of Yakkerboo. These rural origins and, indeed, the taken-for-granted ideas about what constitutes rural festivals, are understood particularly by longer-term residents as important as a means to connect individuals and social groups to a particular location, something that was affirmed – and even mourned – by one participant, who exclaimed:

> I probably liked it better ten years ago before [Yakkerboo] got bigger ... I knew nearly every person, or most of the people in Pakenham. I don't know that now. I could walk up the street ... and we wouldn't know anyone. You miss that.

A councillor and ex-president of the festival acknowledged the inherently nostalgic flavour of the Yakkerboo Festival, and the focus is deliberately on the old township of Pakenham with very little acknowledgement of the more recent changes to Pakenham or even other places within the shire. Even so, the dimensions of the Pakenham community are not easily delineated. As stated on the festival's webpage and echoed by others interviewed, the function of this festival is also one that seeks to reconnect and recreate community, that 'Yakkerboo means that for one moment people are brought together', and this is understood as a significant thing given people are seen to be less community oriented than in the past. In many ways this festival differs little from festivals we may see anywhere else – the opening event, the street parade, consists of various floats showcasing the local community groups, volunteer organisations, kindergartens and primary schools – and these groups are a means to anchor the event within this location and community. Indeed, people watching the street parade were heard to comment on the differences between this parade and those of previous years, and one family noted that this particular spot in the street was where they always stood to watch the parade. Another long-term festival organiser also noted that Yakkerboo functioned as a form of community reunion, explaining, 'the festival is a little bit like a mini 'back-to' because people come back to the festival and they haven't been around for a few years'. Such comments reflect traditions and familiarity, both important concepts in local community festivals.

One of the key parts of the festival is the appearance of Mr Yakkerboo. Mr Yakkerboo is the name given to a bunyip-like creature originally created by schoolchildren in Pakenham. The origin of the word *bunyip* has been traced to the Wemba-Wemba or Wergaia language of Aboriginal people of South-Eastern Australia, but these local children had made individual papier mâché tiles that were then stuck onto a wire frame to form the outline of the creature, described imaginatively by one local as having a 'crazed buck-toothed grin' and that you would feel 'the earth shudder as the bilious bunyip moved his morbidly obese body' (*Berwick Star*, April 2011). As the then festival committee's president explained, 'He is his own personality, he's not like anything' (*Berwick Star*, March 2011). Why this particular creature is less clear. The bunyip is a mythical creature originating in Aboriginal mythology that lives in swamps, riverbeds and waterholes. Perhaps it connects to the region's terrain and local stories. The region around Pakenham, and in particular the areas in which the Casey–Cardinia growth corridor is located, lies between streams and drainage lines that channel water from the upland area just to the north of the town (Sinclair Knight Mertz, 2005). Much of what was designated swamp land was reclaimed about 20 years ago, although in winter this low-lying area is prone to flooding and is often covered in mist, particularly at night. Nonetheless Mr Yakkerboo appears to be a favourite especially among younger children, as we found when attending the 2013 festival parade. One small girl eagerly asked us if we were also going to have some of Mr Yakkerboo's birthday cake and ice cream, while a young boy excitedly waiting for the start of the parade told those around him, 'I love Mr Yakkerboo! He's my favourite!'

Much of the community involvement and investment in the festival centres on the street parade, where schools, community organisations and volunteers design floats that process along the streets during the parade. Our observations at the 2013 event were that those involved in the street parade strongly reflected the existing, older identity of Pakenham, one that maintains strong connections to its rural past and communities. For example, the parade featured the schools and kindergartens from the original part of town; as well as organisations such as the Country Fire Authority, State Emergency Service and St John's Ambulance, all of which have been active in Pakenham for many years; and a range of volunteer groups reflecting the heritage of the area, such as the Country Woman's Association. In short, the parade reflected the identity of the traditional rural townscape. However, this is a place under transition, and in spite of the strong presence of local community groups, it was difficult to see any major contribution from the new growth areas during the parade.

Yakkerboo and Cardinia's (changing) communities

Stakeholders of the event recognise the need to change and better engage with the community (or more precisely, new communities) that are now living in Pakenham. One idea proposed by the organising committee is to take Mr Yakkerboo round the schools, presumably including those built in new housing estates on the outskirts of the town, in order to build up the enthusiasm levels of the children (*Berwick Gazette*, May 2011). Yet, at the recent festival parade, there appeared to be less participation from the schools and kindergartens built recently in the growth areas. While it may simply be a matter of time before these children become part of the festival, it may alternatively be the case that for those moving to the outer suburbs involvement in such long-established community traditions is a low priority compared with settling into new homes and adjusting to new workplaces, or long commutes, and may not even be desired (Lynn & Monani, 2010). Then again, for some of the stakeholders we spoke to, while there is an expectation that change is occurring, and with it a change in what the community of Pakenham is, there is a sense that such change needs to be minimised, that this is 'our festival' and something should be done to defend it. This type of response is reminiscent of the study by Carlsen et al. (2007) that highlights a common failing among festivals to adapt to changing circumstances. A third response has also opened up, one that recognises that change is inevitable and that the festival lends itself to such change. As one participant pointed out, the festival can target the sort of growth happening within the region, and a multicultural type festival is possible; however, such a radical change is 'just a little too early at this point'.

It is interesting to consider whether it is likely that those new entrants to the Pakenham region will eventually share the notions of community and belonging that currently exist in the region, perhaps by some form of social osmosis, or whether active steps may need to be taken in order to encourage this process. At the same time, the local council must address the question of whether new residents want to be connected with an existing community. It may also beg the question as to whether the new entrants to the community would feel any sense of connectedness to the existing notion of community, given that it reflects another time and arguably another place. If community is an ever-evolving construct, then surely the newcomers will contribute as much to any new notions of community as the existing residents. However, the current format of the event does not appear to encourage active participation by newcomers. This point is acknowledged by the event organisers, who note that the festival is in need of a revamp (*Berwick Gazette*, May 2011), yet what form any future revamp will take is currently uncertain.

A strand of festival research has sought to understand the role and function of festivals in terms of processes of identity, belonging, social inclusion and exclusion (Barraket, 2005; Duffy, Waitt & Gibson, 2007; Gorman-Murray, 2009; Mulligan et al., 2006; Waitt & Duffy, 2010). This research suggests that when listening closely to the stories that unfold at festivals, what is often expressed is a considerable emotional investment and a strong desire for place-based attachment. Our data suggests that there are long-held issues around territoriality embedded within such events that suggest this peri-urban region is distinct from the assumed urban–rural dichotomy. In addition, people living here value this difference through expressions of boundedness to specific localities and regions.

Our research also underlines the points made by Carlsen et al. (2007) about festivals failing to change to keep pace with changes in the composition of the local community. It seems that in the case of Yakkerboo, the festival has not accepted, or indeed paid any heed at all to the changing demographics of the community in Pakenham, and it can be argued that in doing this, the festival is now acting almost (but not intentionally) as a space of exclusion for new community members.

Conclusion

Lyndon Terracini, founder of the Northern Rivers Performing Arts (NSW, Australia), argues that the ways in which place, arts and cultural practices intersect are more than simply programming cultural activities in a particular place or region. The event of a festival, he declares, 'should be about fundamentally understanding what resonates within the people who live there, left there, or died there; and about translating those deep local associations for the benefits of a much wider audience' (Terracini, 2007, p. 11). There is, then, a deep emotional significance in the relationships created and built up between people, place and festivals, and this has implications for any festival that seeks to create, support and celebrate ideas about community and identity. Yet, we need to be mindful in the conceptualisation that *community* and *place* are not interchangeable entities (Massey, 1994), and that different understandings and activations of these terms are an inherent part of place-making processes (Cresswell, 2004). Drawing on aspects of the daily lives of a community is a means to reinforce particular socio-political, historical and spatial affiliations. A festival programme tends to support notions of boundedness to particular places and people, and this can ensure that certain people *feel* (re)connected and (re)united to that of the group or community. However, if the festival fails to keep pace with changes in the community, can new entrants to the community ever feel connected or united in the first place? It is precisely this problematic notion of feeling that needs closer consideration.

The challenge for a community festival like Yakkerboo is to closely examine how local place and a sense of community are constituted and given meaning over time through the transitory situatedness of social relations at crucial moments, which occur in work connections, sites of retail and commerce, education and health facilities, faith, the local social and community structures (such as sport and personal interests, as well as the connection between interest groups), and through informal social relations that 'just happen' in the everyday. However, the changes wrought by development in peri-urban regions often lead to anxieties and concerns about the social impacts of change, and the community-building events of the past become a vehicle for reinforcing a sense of who a community is. This, of course, is not to say that a festival like Yakkerboo will not change or adapt – and indeed, many of those involved in its organisation recognise the need for the festival to both celebrate the township's past and find ways to involve recent arrivals to the area. However, it is important not to underestimate the difficulty of this task.

References

Anderson, B. (1983). *Imagined communities*. London: Verso.

Appadurai, A. (1991). Global ethnoscapes. In R.G. Fox (ed.), *Recapturing anthropology* (pp. 191–210). Santa Fe, NM: School of American Research Press.

Arcodia, C. & Whitford, M. (2006). Festival attendance and the development of social capital. *Journal of Convention and Event Tourism, 8*(2), 1–18.

Australian Bureau of Statistics. (2011). *National regional profile: Cardinia*. Retrieved from www.abs.gov.au/ausstats/abs@nrp.nsf/lookup/LGA21450Main+Features120072011.

Barraket, J. (2005). *Putting people in the picture? The role of the arts in social inclusion* (Social Policy Working Paper No. 4). Melbourne.

Bauman, Z. (2001). *Community: Seeking safety in an insecure world*. Cambridge: Polity.

Berwick Gazette. (2011, 30 March). Tracing birthday origins. Retrieved 3 June 2013 from http://berwick.starcommunity.com.au/gazette/2011-03-30/tracing-birthday-origins.

Berwick Gazette. (2011, 11 May). Fresh blood for Yakkerboo. Retrieved 3 June 2013 from http://berwick.starcommunity.com.au/gazette/2011-05-11/fresh-blood-for-yakkerboo.

Berwick Star. (2011, 6 April). The luck less monster. Retrieved 3 June 2013 from http://berwick.starcommunity.com.au/gazette/2011-04-06/the-luck-less-monster.

Biernacki, P. & Waldorf, D. (1981). Snowball sampling: Problems and techniques of chain referral sampling. *Sociological Methods & Research, 10*(2), 141–163.

Buxton, M., Tienan, G., Bekessy, S., Budge, T., Mercer, D., Coote, M. & Morecombe, J. (2006). *Change and continuity in periurban Australia: Monograph 1 A review of the literature*. Melbourne: RMIT.

Carlsen, J., Ali-Knight, J. & Robertson, M. (2007). Access: A research agenda for Edinburgh festivals. *Event Management, 11*, 3–11.

Clarke, A. & Jepson, A. (2011). Power and hegemony within a community festival. *International Journal of Event and Festival Management, 2*(1), 7–19.

Cresswell, T. (2004). *Place: A short introduction*. Malden, MA: Blackwell Publishing.

Crotty, M. (1998). *The foundations of social research: Meaning and perspective in the research process*. Sydney: Allen & Unwin.

Crowley, J. (1999). The politics of belonging: some theoretical considerations. In A. Geddes & A. Favell (eds), *The politics of belonging: Migrants & minorities in contemporary Europe* (pp. 15–41). Aldershot: Ashgate.

Derrett, R. (2003). Festivals & regional destinations: How festivals demonstrate a sense of community & place. *Rural Society, 13*(1), 35–53.

Duffy, M. & Waitt, G. (2011). Rural festivals and processes of belonging. In C. Gibson & J. Connell (eds), *Festival places: Revitalising rural Australia* (pp. 44–59). Clevedon: Channel View Press.

Duffy, M., Waitt, G. & Gibson, C. (2007). Get into the groove: The role of sound in generating a sense of belonging through street parades. *Altitude*. Retrieved from www.altitude21c.com.

Dunphy, K. (2009). Developing and revitalizing rural communities through arts and creativity: Australia. In N. Duxbury, H. Campbell, K. Dunphy, P. Overton & L. Varbanova (eds), *Developing and revitalizing rural communities through arts and creativity: An international literature review and inventory of resources*. Vancouver: Creative City Network of Canada, Centre for Policy Studies on Culture and Communities, Simon Fraser University.

Falassi, A. (1987). Festival: Definition and morphology. In A. Falassi (ed.), *Time out of time: Essays on the festival* (pp. 1–10). Albuquerque: University of New Mexico Press.

Fincher, R. & Iveson, K. (2008). *Planning and diversity in the city: Redistribution, recognition and encounter*. Houndmills: Palgrave Macmillan.

Finkel, R. (2006). Tensions between ambition and reality in UK combined arts festival programming: Case study of the Lichfield Festival. *International Journal of Event Management Research, 2*(1), 25–36.

Finkel, R. (2010). 'Dancing around the ring of fire': Social capital, tourism resistance and gender dichotomies at Up Helly Aa in Lerwick, Shetland. *Event Management, 14*(4), 275–285.

Fortier, M. (1999). Re-membering places and the performance of belonging(s). *Theory, Culture and Society: Performativity and belonging, 16*(2), 41–64.

Gibson, C. & Connell, J. (2005). *Music and tourism*. Clevedon: Channel View Press.

Gibson, C. & Connell, J. (2012). *Music festivals and regional development*. Aldershot: Ashgate.

Gorman-Murray, A. (2009). What's the meaning of ChillOut? Rural/urban difference and the cultural significance of Australia's largest rural GLBTQ festival. *Rural Society, 19*(1), 71–86.

Grant, M. (2009, 2 April). Population to explode. *The Gazette (Star New Group)*.

Green, S. (2010, 12 February). Pushing the boundary. *The Saturday Age: Insight*, pp. 15, 21.

Harvey, D. (2008). The right to the city. *New Left Review, 53*, 23–40.

Jennings, G. (2001). *Tourism research*. Milton, Qld: John Wiley and Sons.

Johnson, V., Currie, G. & Stanley, J. (2011). Exploring transport to arts and cultural activities as a facilitator of social inclusion. *Transport Policy, 18*, 68–75.

Kong, L. & Yeoh, B. (1997). The construction of national identity through the production of ritual and spectacle. *Political Geography, 16*(3), 213–239.

Lavenda, R. (1992). Festivals and the creation of public culture: Whose voice(s)? In I. Karp, C. Mullen Kreamer & S. Lavine (eds), *Museums and communities: The politics of public space* (pp. 76–104). Washington, DC: Smithsonian Institute Press.

Lynn, M. & Monani, D. (2010). *Final report: Building family and community resilience in Cardinia Growth Corridor – A case study of Officer*. Windermere: Narre Warren.

Massey, D. (1994). *Space, place and gender*. Minneapolis: University of Minnesota Press.

Miles, M.B. & Huberman, A.M. (1994). *Qualitative data analysis: An expanded source-book*. Beverly Hills, CA: Sage.

Mulligan, M., Humphrey, K., James, P., Scanlon, C., Smith, P. & Welch, N. (2006). *Creating community: Celebrations, arts and wellbeing within and across local communities*. Melbourne: Globalism Institute, RMIT Print Services.

Probyn, E. (1996). *Outside belongings*. New York and London: Routledge.

Quinn, B. (2003). Symbols, practices and mythmaking: Cultural perspectives on the Wexford Festival Opera. *Tourism Geographies, 5*(3), 329–349.

Qviström, M. (2012). Contested landscapes of urban sprawl. *Landscape Research, 37*(4), 399–415.

Sinclair Knight Mertz (SKM). (2005). *Melbourne 2030 Casey–Cardinia Growth Corridor, shallow watertable constraints on urban development*. Melbourne: Department of Sustainability and Environment, Victoria.

Stake, R.E. (1995). *The art of case study research*. Thousand Oaks, CA: Sage.

Terracini, L. (2007). *A regional state of mind: Making art outside metropolitan Australia* (Platform Papers 11). Sydney: Currency House.

Turner, V. (1984). Liminality and the performative genres. In J. MacAloon (ed.), *Rite, drama, festival, spectacle: Rehearsals toward a theory of cultural performance* (pp. 19–41). Philadelphia: Institute for the Study of Human Issues.

Waitt, G. & Duffy, M. (2010). Listening and tourism studies. *Annals of Tourism Research, 37*(2), 457–477.

Waterman, S. (1998). Carnivals for elites? The cultural politics of arts festivals. *Progress in Human Geography, 22*(1), 54–74.

Wood, E.H. (2005). Measuring the economic and social impacts of local authority events. *International Journal of Public Sector Management, 18*(1), 37–53.

Yakkerboo Festival. (n.d.) Retrieved from http://yakkerboo.org.au/about.

Yuval-Davis, N. (2006). Belonging and the politics of belonging. *Patterns of Prejudice, 40*(3), 197–214.

5 New and old tourism traditions

The case of Skieda in Livigno, Italian Alps

Margherita Pedrana

Introduction

Taking as their starting point the concept of social capital, Rodríguez-Pose and Storper (2006) separate it in their research into community and society. The two different concepts start from how we understand the different kinds of social capital. Society is considered to be all the features and institutions linked to a specific area. Community represents the informal institutions linked to the social relationships and connections in that society.

Community events are often based on traditions and on the social need to be interconnected to each other, creating and maintaining the sense of ownership to a community or a place. However, community events may also have other functions. Especially in tourist destinations, they are linked to the destination's image and may present the social tissue of the place to the outside. Sometimes they are not a part of the community tradition, but rather have the purpose of communication and promotion.

This chapter will focus on the Skieda event in Livigno, Italy, which started in the late 1990s. The chapter will be organised as follows: first, the differences between community and society in the literature on social capital are analysed. Second, what we understand of community and its features are presented, focusing in particular on community events and their functions. Finally, the case of Skieda in Livigno is presented, leading to overall chapter conclusions.

Livigno is a small village in the Italian Alps, which is also a tourist destination in both winter and summer. The local community is strongly reliant on the tourism industry, which constitutes the main economic resource together with retail (Livigno is also a duty-free area). However, until the 1960s, the local population lived on agriculture and animal husbandry. Many local community traditions and events are still alive; however, new events come and change the social fabric. The Skieda is a full week of festivals based around a special skiing discipline. Telemark is based on a traditional style of skiing, with a 'free heel', which was also how the original Livigno inhabitants used to ski. The success of the discipline and of the Skieda event depends largely on the local community, which has started to understand how the old traditions may be important in the future and may help Livigno to gain a competitive advantage in order to attract new tourists.

Events can be considered as very important in both tourism and destination management. Despite this importance, however, there is a lack of literature, especially in the field of community events. Events play a key role in tourism development, mainly in developing and restructuring destinations. The role and the impacts of such events have been analysed and discussed in the literature (Getz, 2008). The relationship between events and tourism is quite obvious. Events create induced effects on tourism and on all the services linked to the events themselves as well as the correlated aspects such as ancillary services, amenities, etc. The impacts of events occur on both the demand side and the supply side. From a demand point of view, the implications are pertinent to people who move for events and the impacts pertain not only to the event and the destination for that specific time, but also to the destination image, destination marketing and tourist area as a whole. On the supply side there is the attraction of visitors: fostering a positive image of the destination may also help to renovate the urban and tourist infrastructure and define and attract other target markets in specific periods of time. In this sense the Destination Management Organisation (DMO) is involved as an actor on the supply side. However, the purpose of the DMO must be not only for the duration of the event, but should become a long-term strategic partner.

For the purposes of this chapter events are defined as a 'spatial–temporal phenomenon, and each is unique because of interactions among the setting, people, and management systems – including design elements and the program' (Getz, 2008, p. 404). This includes a variety of implications. Above all, events are temporally and spatially defined, in a specific time and space, and they have implications that may be long-term, especially if destination image and economic impacts are considered. In order to be successful, not only for the event itself but also for the image of the destination, the organisation of such events has to consider many factors. First, the inclusion of the destination in the organisation, especially from a touristic and a managerial point of view, has to be negotiated in order to have effects not only during the event, but also in the future. Second, the design element and the programme have to be well known not only by the organisers, but also by the destination and in particular by the DMO, in order to help promote a positive destination image during the event.

The complexities of the literature on events can be divided into two points of view, underlining event management and the tourism aspects. Formica (1998) followed the specific route of what concerns the literature on event and tourism. Early attempts to underline the impact of tourism events on a destination include Gunn and Wicks (1982) and Ritchie (1984). Moreover, in the following decades, there have been many studies on specific events and on the economic impacts of festivals and events on the local area and community (see, for example, Crompton, 1999; Crompton & McKay, 1994; Getz, 1989, 1991; Hawkins & Goldblatt, 1995).

Especially in Dwyer, Mellor, Mistillis and Mules (2000a, 2000b), many important features of event impact assessment and models are highlighted. In order to understand the impact of events and above all forecast the implications and effects of events on the territory from an economic point of view, academics have analysed the economic aspects of events through a model of analysis. Moreover, they try to understand both the tangible and intangible impacts of events on the destination, especially in event management literature.

The literature on events identifies different kinds of events. The first class of events is the business one, which includes fairs, conventions and meetings – the so-called MICE industry (Meetings, Incentives, Conventions and Exhibitions). For example, Spiller (2002) comments on the history of convention events; Davidson (2003) discusses the connection between business and pleasure as regards travel and tourism. The second definition of events is represented by sports events. There is a huge literature on sports tourism, which can also be linked to specific events and festivals (Gibson, 1998; Weed, 2005, 2006). The third class of events is cultural events and festivals, which include both cultural and religious festivals. This field of study is strongly linked with cultural tourism and literature (Carlsen & Getz, 2006; Quinn, 2006; Richards, 2007). The literature has particularly focused on the economic impacts and legacies of mega events such as the Olympic Games and the World's Fair. There are also some examples of mega-event impacts on civil community(ies) (Glynn, 2008). However, there are other implications both from a cultural and a social point of view. Following the literature on social capital, especially on community and society differences, the chapter will seek to define the significance of community events.

Social capital: community vs society

The debate on social capital and what really defines it has long been followed by researchers and is fuelled by a large literature (Sabatini, 2005). In fact, discussions of social capital are made more difficult by the lack of an accepted definition.

Putnam, Leonardi and Nanetti (1993) can be thought of as being at the centre of this debate with their book *Making Democracy Work: Civic Traditions in Modern Italy*. After this publication many different authors and academics have tried to define social capital in various research environments in order to understand if there are connections between social capital and economic development and growth (Durlauf & Fafschamps, 2005). Granovetter (1985) and Coleman (1990) have started to argue the embeddness of social capital and its possible positive effects on the economic development of a group of people. On the other hand, other research has criticised the 'power' of social capital (Durlauf, 1999). Moreover, it has been argued that a lack of social capital will lead to a lack of social relationships and a lack of trust (Fukuyama, 1995, 1999; Putnam, 2000).

This chapter will concentrate on the subtle differences in social capital between communities and societies. In Rodríguez-Pose and Storper (2006), the difference between community and society has been strongly underlined. With community the features of group life include elements such as social conventions and rules, traditions, interpersonal relationships and informal networks. They allow for sustained collective action and they require a lot of local and complex personalised information. These informal networks are based on trust and membership giving many advantages to the individual such as the power of coordination. There are also enforcement mechanisms and informal or moral sanctions. Community is usually considered in the literature as a second-best solution, whereas societies are the best solution to market failures (North, 1990). On the other hand, society is compared to an institution, with its formal rules and formal organisation. The sanctions provided are not only of a moral and informal nature, but can also be imposed through a more formal and costly enforcement mechanism. The legal system, together with property rights and bureaucracy, is the main feature of society, and is transparent and visible. Community, on the other hand, has less formalised rule-enforcement mechanisms and has been empirically studied through density association and participation in economic, civic, social and professional associations, in order to capture group life. Both community and society are linked to specific territories and have different ways of binding people together. Rodríguez-Pose and Storper (2006) argue that both community and society are 'mutually necessary and complementary' and that the relationship and influence between the two may facilitate or contrast economic development, especially at a local level. There has to be an interaction between community and society in order to be effective on local economic development, where the two authors see the relationship between responsibility (society) and autonomy (community). Moreover, speed of change also has to be investigated in order to understand the real possible future implications for economic development.

For the purposes of this chapter, the focus will be on community and on the specificities of social capital at the local community level. Communities are connected by means of informal rules and informal traditions that are particular to a local area. In the case of tourism, community may be in direct contrast with tourists who come from outside the area and change the local social cultural context. However, the local community may also be one of the very factors that attract tourism into the area. The DMO may be seen as a formal society and it has to emerge from the local community. The success of a tourism destination, not only from a social and cultural point of view but also from the perspective of sustainability, is linked to the interconnections between community and society, between formal and informal rules.

Community events

As shown in the first paragraphs, events may be understood as a potential pull factor for a tourism destination. They are often an expression of community, as we have defined in the previous paragraph. Event purposes may be different according to the functionality. However, whatever goal the event has (economic, tourist or political), the event strategy should be based on fostering 'community development, culture, sport, leisure, health or other aims' (Getz, 2008, p. 408). Community involvement is stronger for traditional and cultural events. However, it may become institutionalised by the revival of old traditions in a new manner, such as in our example of the Skieda in Livigno. The development of community events may also increase social capital, especially with regard to small-scale community events (Molitor, Rossi & Branton, 2011). Moreover, community events may also build community and togetherness with linkages to other members of the community, especially if these events are shared (Albinsson & Perera, 2012).

Research concerning community events has mainly focused on economic impacts. However, there are some examples of anthropological, social and cultural studies (Cunneen & Lynch, 1988; Delamere, 2001; Greenwood, 1972). These studies have often focused on resident perceptions of event impacts and on the social impacts of events (see, in particular, Fredline, 2006; Xiao & Smith, 2004).

As shown in Fredline and Faulkner (2000), there are some variables that influence the community's reactions to events. These include the geographical proximity to activity concentration and the involvement in tourism. The case study demonstrates that many inhabitants of Livigno are involved in tourism activities. Therefore, they receive benefits from both the tourism and events industries. This is especially the case as regards sporting events, such as in this case study whereby the creation of a fan community together with a loyalty programme has helped to make the event successful (Yoshida, James & Cronin, 2013).

With community events, it is widely understood that events are driven by the community. They are in direct contrast with corporate events, which are more concentrated on industry or a specific corporate purpose (Stokes, 2008). Obviously, in the tourism perspective there may be both approaches, because there are many corporate interests (tourism) and community interests, and the aims of each group have to be shared and interconnected. In the community-driven approach, no particular stakeholder is dominant, but there are one or several stakeholder group strategies and collaborative decision-making. With regard to tourism and sports events, the community contribution is often made by the DMO and the public support for initiatives. Community events are therefore not only events driven by the community or based on traditional and cultural purposes, but they may also be sports events that benefits the community and help attract new tourists, especially in the low season, and they are sustainable events for the community.

The following case study demonstrates the initiative of a group of people that is keen to stage a revival of Telemark skiing. Moreover, this kind of sporting event and festival has become strongly rooted within the local community because many people were interested in the old modernised Telemark technique. The year 2014 marks the 20th anniversary of Skieda, which is a sustainable initiative both for inhabitants and for tourists, because there are many people who come from abroad to participate in the event, which is held in the low season. In this case the sustainability has been achieved through community participation in the organisation of the event, which attempts to empower the community and share the benefits for the host population (Schulenkorf, 2012).

The case of Skieda in Livigno

Livigno is a small village in the heart of Italian Alps, very close to the border with Switzerland, within the Italian province of Sondrio. The inhabitants (almost 6,000 according to the Italian National Census of 2011 – ISTAT) of this small mountain village offer hospitality and retail services. Livigno is a touristic area both in winter and in summer. In both seasons, Livigno is a tourism destination with many different characteristics.

Many of its inhabitants are involved directly or indirectly with tourism activities. Figures 5.1 to 5.3 show the analysis of arrivals in Livigno. Figure 5.1 shows the number of arrivals from 2009 to 2012.

Figures 5.2 and 5.3 represent, respectively, the winter season and the summer season. The percentage of foreign tourists is higher during wintertime (more than 60% of the total tourist arrivals), whereas in the summertime almost three out of four tourists are Italian or domestic tourists.

Among the winter arrivals, the top 10 countries of origin of foreign tourists are Poland, Germany, Czech Republic, Belgium, Denmark, Russia, Switzerland, United Kingdom, Sweden and South Africa.

Livigno offers a variety of events, especially concentrated in the sports sector. It has also been the location for the 2005 World Mountain Bike Championships. There are numerous different big competitions during both winter and summer. The winter season starts with La Sgambeda, an international FIS (Fédération International de Ski – International Ski Federation) approved popular cross-country ski race during December. There is a portfolio of events (Ziakas & Costa, 2011) aimed to foster economic and community development and to attract more international tourists, especially during low season periods (see www.livigno.eu).

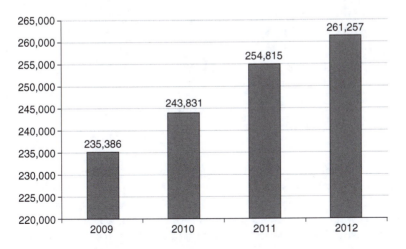

Figure 5.1 Arrivals in Livigno (2009–2012) (source: Azienda di Promozione e Sviluppo Turistico di Livigno, 2013).

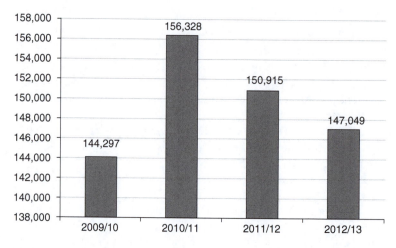

Figure 5.2 Arrivals in winter seasons in Livigno (2009/2010–2012/2013) (source: Azienda di Promozione e Sviluppo Turistico di Livigno, 2013).

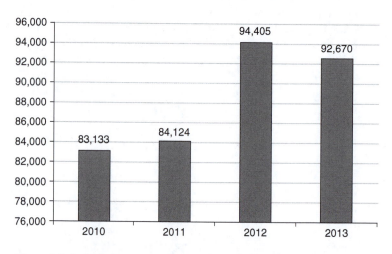

Figure 5.3 Arrivals in summer season (2010–2013) (source: Azienda di Promozione e Sviluppo Turistico di Livigno, 2013).

The revival of traditional/authentic skiing (known as Telemark) has been adopted by Livigno within a specific festival that has taken place annually since 1994. It fulfils a desire to rediscover the pleasure of skiing with a specific style and turn technique that provides a contrast with Alpine skiing which is more and more dominated by speed. Telemark brings to these modern kinds of skiing the good points from an old tradition, giving them something new. In this sense we may define Skieda as a community event because it started from past traditions, renewed with different features and meanings as well as, from a social and cultural point of view, being updated with new materials and techniques.

The Skieda telemark skiing festival was established in 1994. Telemark skiing, also called free-heel skiing, is a type of downhill skiing and can be considered a minority sport. The specific feature of this kind of skiing is that the boot is attached only at the toe, leaving the heel to rise from the skis, in a similar manner to cross-country skiing. Due to the free heel, the skier goes into a lunge position when he turns (the so-called telemark turn technique). Telemark turns are quite peculiar, as the heel of the outside ski is flat, with the knee at a 90° angle, whereas the inside ski slides back under the skier's body with a flexed knee and raised heel. Telemark turns first appeared before 1866 and were used especially during the Open Christiania in 1868, when the Norwegian Sondre Norheim used the technique in a ski competition (Blikom & Molde, n.d.; Lert, 2002). The name originates from the Telemark region of Norway, where the cambered ski was invented. After having invented the Telemark turn, Norheim and other skiers used and refined parallel skiing techniques, spreading the Telemark turn all over the world (Lund, 2007). Since the first decade of 20th century, the Telemark style has been replaced by newer techniques, especially in the Alpine countries, resulting in a decline in its popularity starting from the mid-1940s. These newer techniques allowed shorter turns, especially in downhill skiing (Droste & Strotmann, 2002).

For the purposes of this chapter, what is crucial is the revival of the Telemark technique in the 1970s in the United States. This revival was inspired by the Norwegian Alpine ski racer Stein Eriksen (Kleppen, 1986). Modern Telemark skiing has been primarily a reaction against the development of high-tech equipment in Alpine skiing and the dominance of shorter and faster ways of skiing (Parker & McDonald, 1988). This reaction was inspired by not just the use of old skis, but also the emphasis on traditional clothing.

The Telemark revival started in Crested Butte, Colorado and in the northern part of the Green Mountains, in Vermont (www.catskillsfreeheel.com/p/history. html).[1] The two main leaders of the Telemark revival were Dickie Hall and Filippo Pagano (as known as Telemarkfil) in the north and south of Vermont, respectively. Pagano also opened the first Telemark Ski School in the eastern United States at Bromley Mountain. Combining the experience of cross-country and Alpine skiing, and aided by high-tech technologies, Telemark skiers started to grow in number. A desire to rediscover the traditional style as well as the backcountry helped spread the Telemark culture (McGee, 2012). In Sexten, Italy in 1983 a demonstration by Professional Ski Instructors of America at Interski brought the Telemark technique to the attention of the public. The demonstration revived the old Telemark style in the Alps, where, despite being an old technique, it was seen as something of a novelty. The resurgence of the Telemark style of skiing that had been adopted by American skiers gave it a sort of modernisation (McGee, 2012).

The growing attention paid to the new/old Telemark discipline is also thought to be due to the spread of festivals and competitions organized by the North

American Telemark Organization (NATO) and New England Telemark (NET). Many of these festivals started in the United States and Canada (e.g. Téléfestival at Mont Comi from 1983; Bromley Mountain in Vermont from 1985). In Europe there are many telemark festivals, including the Skieda, now one of the world's largest. It usually takes place in the low season at the end of March or the first week of April. From its beginnings in 1994 and during the last 20 years it has used the name 'Free Heel Fest', in order to be more international, while at the same time also using its local name. The low season was chosen to stage the festival because it helps the community attract new visitors by extending the winter tourist season. Moreover, the chosen period also allows the Skieda participants to be the sole focus of attention from the local community and industry.

Figure 5.4 shows the number of Skieda participants, who come from all over the world, over the last 10 years.

The Skieda organising team hope to make it one of the most important Telemark festivals in the world. In the 2014 festival, there will be many initiatives based on it being the 20th anniversary year. The festival will last 1 week and include many initiatives together with courses to meet all participants' needs. The festival programme is composed of a variety of events: there are races in different disciplines (Downhill, Bergans Derby freeride race, Telekilometro lanciato), excursions, courses (some for children also) and cultural evenings.

Figure 5.4 also shows that from 2003 to 2013 the number of participants has more than doubled, with a generally increasing trend, with the exception of some years such as 2005, 2011 and 2012, in which the number of participants decreased. In Figure 5.5, the nationalities of participants in 2013 are analysed. The number of Italians (1,061 in 2013) has been excluded from the graph in order to better show the number of participants from other nations.

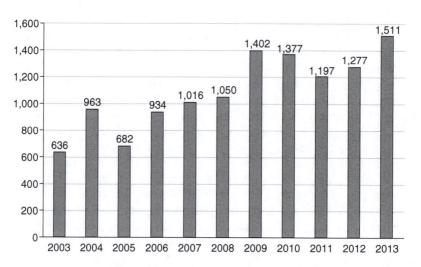

Figure 5.4 Skieda participants (2003–2013) (source: Azienda di Promozione e Sviluppo Turistico di Livigno, 2013).

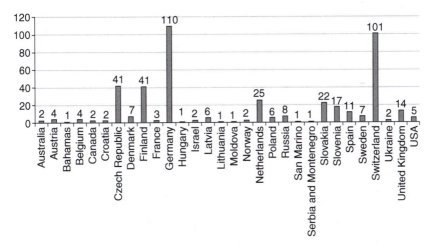

Figure 5.5 Nationalities of foreign Skieda participants (2013) (source: Azienda di Promozione e Sviluppo Turistico di Livigno, 2013).

Skieda is a big Telemark festival and may be considered as a community event, because there is great attention from both the international and the local community. The success of the event is underlined by its 20-year history and legacy, and the increasing number of participants year after year. The chosen period (low season) helps in finding competitively priced accommodation and the right environment and atmosphere for the event and its participants.

Conclusions

Social capital has been addressed as the solution of many development and growth problems. However, there have been many different suggestions in defining what we really mean by social capital. We have assumed a separation into two main kinds of social capital: community and society. In showing the role of the community, this chapter has focused specifically on the community events in destination and tourism development. They have to involve the community, also giving the community some benefits, and overall be sustainable for the local population.

The case of Skieda shows the revival of old traditions in skiing that were widespread in the Alpine areas, together with the participation of many international tourists and the host community. The success of the initiative in the past 20 stagings of the festival has been quite assured by the spread of the Telemark revival, the choice of the period (low seasonality) and the revival of local traditions linked to the Telemark world. This event has helped the local community attract new tourists who are Telemark enthusiasts, and has infused in the local community a kind of skiing that was traditionally rooted in the territory and in the local area.

Acknowledgement

The author thanks Matteo Dessì and Fabiana Salvadori from Azienda di Promozione e Sviluppo Turistico of Livigno for data on tourism in Livigno and on the Skieda festival.

Note

1 For more information, see www.catskillsfreeheel.com/p/history.html.

References

Albinsson, P.A. & Perera, Y. (2012). Alternative marketplaces in the 21st century: Building community through sharing events. *Journal of Consumer Behaviour, 11*, 303–315.

Blikom, A. & Molde, E. (n.d.). *Sondre in the history of skiing: Sondre Norheim – The skiing pioneer of Telemark.* Retrieved 30 December 2013, from www.sondrenorheim.com/history.htm and www.sondrenorheim.com/skisbindingsstyle.htm.

Carlsen, J. & Getz, D. (2006). Strategic planning for a regional wine festival: The Margaret river wine region *festival.* In J. Carlsen & S. Charters (eds), *Global wine tourism: Research, management and marketing* (pp. 209–224). Wallingford: CABI.

Coleman, J.S. (1990). *Foundations of social theory.* Cambridge, MA: Harvard University Press.

Crompton, J. (1999). *Measuring the economic impact of visitors to sports tournaments and special events.* Ashburn, VA: Division of Professional Services, National Recreation and Park Association.

Crompton, J. & McKay, S. (1994). Measuring the economic impact of festivals and events: Some myths, misapplications and ethical dilemmas. *Festival Management and Event Tourism, 2*(1), 33–43.

Cunneen, C. & Lynch, R. (1988). The social meanings of conflict in riots at the Australian Grand Prix Motorcycle Races. *Leisure Studies, 7*(1), 1–19.

Davidson, R. (2003). Adding pleasure to business: Conventions and tourism. *Journal of Convention and Exhibition Management, 5*(1), 29–39.

Delamere, T. (2001). Development of a scale to measure resident attitudes toward the social impacts of community festivals, Part 2: Verification of the scale. *Event Management, 7*(1), 25–38.

Droste, P. & Strotmann, R. (2002). *Telemark skiing.* Oxford: Meyer & Meyer Sport.

Durlauf, S. (1999). The case 'against' social capital. *Focus, 20*, 1–4.

Durlauf, S. & Fafchamps, M. (2005). Social capital. In P. Aghion & S.N. Durlauf (eds), *Handbook of economic growth* (vol. 1B). North-Holland: Elselvier.

Dwyer, L., Mellor, R., Mistillis, N. & Mules, T. (2000a). Forecasting the economic impacts of events and conventions. *Event Management, 6*(3), 191–204.

Dwyer, L., Mellor, R., Mistillis, N. & Mules, T. (2000b). A framework for assessing 'tangible' and 'intangible' impacts of events and conventions. *Event Management, 6*(3), 175–189.

Formica, S. (1998). The development of festivals and special events studies. *Festival Management and Event Tourism*, 5(3), 131–137.

Fredline, E. (2006). Host and guest relations and sport tourism. In H. Gibson (ed.), *Sport tourism: Concepts and theories* (pp. 131–147). London: Routledge.

Fredline, E. & Faulkner, B. (2000). Host community reactions. A cluster analysis. *Annals of Tourism Research*, 27 (3), 763–784.

Fukuyama, F. (1995). *Trust: The social virtues and the creation of prosperity*. New York: The Free Press.

Fukuyama, F. (1999). *Social capital and civil society*. Paper presented at the International Monetary Fund conference on Second Generation Reforms, Washington, DC.

Getz, D. (1989). Special events: Defining the product. *Tourism Management, 10*(2), 135–137.

Getz, D. (1991). *Festivals, special events, and tourism*. New York: Van Nostrand Rheinhold.

Getz, D. (2008). Event tourism: Definition, evolution, and research. *Tourism Management, 29*, 403–428.

Gibson, H. (1998). Sport tourism: A critical analysis of research. *Sport Management Review, 1*, 45–76.

Glynn, M.A. (2008). Configuring the field of play: How hosting the Olympic Games impacts civic community. *Journal of Management Studies, 45*(6), 1117–1146.

Granovetter, M. (1985). Economic action and social structure: The problem of embeddedness. *American Journal of Sociology, 91*, 481–510.

Greenwood, D. (1972). Tourism as an agent of change: A Spanish Basque case study. *Ethnology, 11*, 80–91.

Gunn, C.A. & Wicks, B.E. (1982). *A study of visitors to Dickens on the Strand*. Galveston, TX: Galveston Historical Foundation.

Hawkins, D. & Goldblatt, J. (1995). Event management implications for tourism education. *Tourism Recreation Research, 20*(2), 42–45.

Kleppen, H. (1986). *Telemark skiing: Norway's gift to the world*. Oslo: Det Norske Samlaget.

Lert, W. (2002). A binding revolution. *Skiing Heritage Journal, 14*(1), 25–26.

Lund, M. (2007). Norway: How it all started. *Skiing Heritage Journal, 19*(3), 8–13.

McGee, J.S. (2012). *Cross-country skiing*. USA. Morris Book Publishing.

Molitor, F., Rossi, M. & Branton, L. (2011). Increasing social capital and personal efficacy through small-scale community events. *Journal of Community Psychology, 39*(6), 749–754.

North, D. (1990). *Institutions, institutional change, and economic performance*. Cambridge: Cambridge University Press.

Parker, P. & McDonald, S. (1988). *Free-heel skiing: The secrets of telemark and parallel tech*. London: Diadem Books.

Putnam, R. (2000). *Bowling alone: The collapse and revival of American community*. New York: Simon & Schuster.

Putnam, R., with Leonardi, R. and Nanetti, R.Y. (1993). *Making democracy work: Civic traditions in modern Italy*. Princeton, NJ: Princeton University Press.

Quinn, B. (2006). Problematising 'festival tourism': Arts festivals and sustainable development in Ireland. *Journal of Sustainable Tourism, 14*(3), 288–306.

Richards, G. (ed.). (2007). *Cultural tourism: Global and local perspectives*. New York: Haworth.

Ritchie, J.R.B. (1984). Assessing the impacts of hallmark events: Conceptual and research issues. *Journal of Travel Research, 23*(1), 2–11.

Rodríguez-Pose, A. & Storper, M. (2006). Better rules or stronger communities? On the social foundations of the institutional change and its economic effects. *Economic Geography, 82*(1), 1–25.

Sabatini, F. (2005). *Social capital as social networks: A new framework for measurement* (Working Paper no. 83). Università La Sapienza, Roma Dipartimento di Economia Pubblica.

Schulenkorf, N. (2012). Sustainable community development through sport and events: A conceptual framework for Sport-for-Development projects. *Sport Management Review, 15*, 1–12.

Spiller, J. (2002). History of convention tourism. In K. Weber & K. Chon (eds), *Convention tourism: International research and industry perspectives* (pp. 3–20). New York: Haworth.

Stokes, R. (2008). Tourism strategy making: Insights to the events tourism domain. *Tourism Management, 29*, 252–262.

Weed, M. (2005). Sports tourism theory and method: Concepts, issues and epistemologies. *European Sport Management Quarterly, 5*(3), 229–242.

Weed, M. (2006). Sports tourism research 2000–2004: A systematic review of knowledge and a meta-evaluation of methods. *Journal of Sport and Tourism, 11*(1), 5–30.

Xiao, P. & Smith, S. (2004). Improving forecasts for world's fair attendance: Incorporating income effects. *Event Management, 6*(1), 15–23.

Yoshida, M., James, J.D. & Cronin Jr., J.J. (2013). Sport event innovativeness: Conceptualization, measurement, and its impact on consumer behaviour. *Sport Management Review, 16*, 68–84.

Ziakas, V. & Costa, C.A. (2011). Event portfolio and multi-purpose development: Establishing the conceptual grounds. *Sport Management Review, 14*, 409–423.

Websites

www.catskillsfreeheel.com/p/history.html
www.istat.it
www.livigno.eu
www.skieda.com
www.socialcapitalgateway.org
www.telemarknato.com

6 'Whose festival?'

Examining questions of participation, access and ownership in rural festivals

Jodie George, Rosie Roberts and Jessica Pacella

Introduction

Within Australia, as elsewhere, much of the tourism and event studies literature highlights the important contribution of regional festivals to rural communities in terms of social cohesion, regional identity and fiscal viability (e.g. Brennan-Horley, Connell & Gibson, 2007; Getz & Andersson, 2008; Gibson & Stewart, 2009). However, definitions of what may constitute a 'rural community' remain problematic. There exists a detailed scholarship that challenges the long utilised oversimplification of the rural which we will not rehearse here (see, for example, Cloke, 2006); in summary, the construction of the rural as a singularly agrarian space that is definite only in binary relation to the urban has been extensively problematised. Instead, more recent attempts to define the rural community have focused on concepts of the multiscalar, recognising that however conceptualised, these spaces are inevitably influenced by the global, the national and, more locally, the specificity of their own contexts and the bodily experiences of their residents (Gorman-Murray, Darian-Smith & Gibson, 2008). In this way, it is possible to acknowledge the presence of both long histories of diversity and contemporary narrations of community identity (Woods, 2007), particularly within the Australian context, the focus of the case study for this chapter.

One of the important ways that this narration of community identity may occur is through festival events, which provide a concentrated time- and place-specific lens through which to examine how rural communities define themselves, both internally and to those outside the community, and how these might vary. In particular, festivals are understood to have a powerful effect on how 'places' and 'social relations' are made and remade (Getz, 2010), representing an important opportunity for beneficial economic and social outcomes, particularly within the rural landscape. This is the case even for those festivals aimed primarily at local community members, as they often also attract tourists and, in those rural areas affected by differential infrastructure needs and government expenditure, provide an opportunity for economic gain and cultural innovation that, ideally, is driven by the community itself (Gibson, Waitt, Walmsley & Connell, 2010).

Most commonly, festivals are held to celebrate a particular aspect of the rural place and are often categorised according to the focus of the celebration, such as food, music, sport, art and agriculture. According to a large-scale study conducted by Gibson and Stewart (2009), approximately 2,800 festivals are held annually within New South Wales, Victoria and Tasmania alone. The majority of these festivals are small (often fewer than 10,000 attendees), not for profit and visited predominantly by locals, yet generate a significant income of more than AU$550 million across the three states.

In part, these economic benefits result from the diversified employment opportunities, increased community infrastructure and networking relationships that develop through collaboration between local stakeholders during festival events (Alves, Cerro & Martins, 2010; Cameron & Gerrard, 2008). Beyond the financial narratives that form the predominant focus of much of the scholarship in the area, literature drawn from cultural, event and tourism studies suggests that festivals may also contribute significantly to the social and cultural capital of the community in numerous ways. Specifically, these may include providing opportunities for increased leadership and management (Gibson et al., 2010); identifying rallying points of celebration for the community (Smith, 2009); binding communities through their interconnections of individuals, cultures and place (Getz, 2010); increasing social inclusion and preserving local culture through celebrations of diversity and identity (Alves et al., 2010); and increasing the number of tourists to an area and, by extension, economic stability and the likelihood of local development (Çela, Knowles-Lankford & Lankford, 2008). Such outcomes are particularly important within the rural context, as the changing modes of primary production, the impacts of climate change and the instability of continuing outmigration challenge the viability of some rural areas.

As Brennan-Horley et al. (2007, p. 72) suggest:

> Against this backdrop of uneven fortunes, numerous places in inland Australia have sought to reinvent themselves through staging festivals.... Small, struggling towns in rural Australia have prompted festivals of all sorts, both as a community-building exercise and because they can attract wealthy, usually urban, visitors. In Australia, as in many other parts of the world, the tourism spin offs deriving from the promotion of festivals are seen as one means of redressing rural decline.

However, festivals within the rural context may also be problematic, subject to criticisms of inauthenticity, the gentrification of sites, the overcommodification of culture, conflicting agendas of various stakeholders and the influence of neoliberalisation on tourism policy which may increase the danger that only that which qualifies as economically rational will be recognised (Gibson et al., 2010). Further literature (e.g. Reid, 2011; Robertson, Rogers & Leask, 2009; Smith, 2009) suggests that issues may also include increased infrastructure requirements, selective and differential distribution of benefits across the community, environmental degradation, the fractured nature of Liminal zones within the event space that work to obscure the delineation of spaces of work and play, and selective representation of culture and identity. Issues of identity may be particularly pronounced as multiple stakeholders associated with the festival event, including organisers, community groups, residents (those who attend and those who do not), tourists, local business owners, government employees and media, to name a few (Hede, 2007), identify what they believe the 'rural space' *should* involve (Reid, 2011). Significant tensions may arise particularly between policy makers who are concerned with the economic and marketing aspects of the event and community members, whose concerns may be more locally based (Robertson et al., 2009). As Smith (2009, p. 136) suggests, 'It is often difficult to reconcile differing priorities, especially in the case of festivals that were initially developed as community events, but which have since become reorientated towards tourism.'

Stakeholders may also have a vested interest in which images of the rural are circulated more widely. According to Bell (2006), there exists a 'transnational rural' that defines how the rural is imagined globally and how this may be normalised, such as the pastoral ideals of Europe, which are circulated to represent the rural even in arid landscapes such as Australia and Asia, and thereby further shape what may be celebrated as 'rural' and what it means to be a person of that 'place', most often singular in nature. Examples of this can be seen in the gendered depiction of the Australian frontier, as a mythical space in which the male conqueror subdues the untameable landscape (see, for example, Dixon, 1995). However, within these and other images of the 'rural', certain actors may be absent, or at the very least underrepresented, as rural bodies are most often presented as predominantly white and heterosexual (Gorman-Murray, Pini & Bryant, 2013). According to Neal and Agyeman (2006), this absence of the other, whether gendered, racialised or class based, may be evoked in order to avoid disrupting spaces of non-modernity, here specifically the rural. Thus, issues of representation are clearly an important consideration when planning festivals. As Gibson et al. (2010, p. 281) argue:

> as an officially endorsed event, festivals always have the capacity to selectively seek and represent some elements of local cultures and identities, while evicting others, intensifying social exclusion – inadvertently or otherwise…. In various ways, local social tensions may be refracted through festivals.

Despite the extensive body of research discussed within this chapter, literature within the event tourism field is still in the early stages of development, requiring a continued development of both knowledge and theory. In particular, much of the existing research's primary concerns have been with the urban experience, generalised understandings of festival contributions to the community, quantitative data and economic considerations (Alves et al., 2010), research foci that often result in festivals viewed primarily as a 'product' rather than an embedded celebration of community identity (Picard & Robinson, 2006). In contrast, using a qualitative approach, this research seeks to provide a detailed understanding of issues arising from differential access and participatory practices of particular groups' engagements with festivals, focusing on the South Australian context, itself termed the 'Festival State' and yet significantly underresearched when compared to other Australian states.

Method

As part of a larger project that examined multiple rural festivals across South Australia, this qualitative study seeks to develop a better understanding of community members' experience of festivals and how festivals might contribute to community identity and place making within the rural context. This chapter focuses specifically on the findings from the Kangaroo Island Art Feast, a 10-day celebration of local art, food and wine across 34 venues involving approximately 150 artists and associated professionals within the culinary and viticultural fields. Located 120 km south-west of Adelaide, this choice of the Art Feast festival as a case study serves as a useful space through which to understand the discursive complexities of local community and tourism events due to its historical development as an isolated community, its cultural and economic diversity (or otherwise at times) and the differing levels of community support and engagement with the event. The festival was celebrating its 10th anniversary as a community-based event run only by volunteers, while also seeking to enlarge its audience, in particular to mainland tourists. In this way, the festival presented an opportunity to examine possible tensions related to intersections between concepts of growth, community, identity and event ownership. The promotional materials themselves reflect this juxtaposition of a focus on the local with a desire to expand, stating:

> The new Kangaroo Island Art feast brand projects a sophisticated modern image that retains a regional, community feel.... The Kangaroo Island Art Feast committee is developing Art Feast from a community festival for locals and visitors already coming to Kangaroo Island into a community-at-heart festival that markets itself professionally to attract people to visit Kangaroo Island specifically for Art Feast.
>
> (Kangaroo Island Art Feast, 2012, p. 4)

This attempt to attract visitors is particularly important given the isolated location of the festival that requires individuals to drive an hour-and-a-half from the state capital city, Adelaide, and then take a further 45-minute ferry ride to reach the festival destination. To address this, the event attempts to create a singular community of the entire island by threading across the landscape a thematic unity of art, wine and produce, based in multiple venues.

Using a mixed method approach of in-depth interviews with community members, festival tourists and event organisers as well as participant observation and analysis of promotional materials, this research examined the emergence of competing discourses of 'place' in regional and rural areas, disentangling the ways concepts of the 'local', 'community' and 'rurality' are constructed and circulated in relation to the festival event. During interviews, attendees and organisers were asked about their past experience with the festival, the aspects they engaged with most and why, how they thought the festival presented and impacted upon the community itself, who they thought might attend the festival or not, and their own motivations for involvement. Some 15 participants drawn from a range of ages, genders and relationships with the larger community were chosen to reflect the diverse audience taking part in order to ensure a cross-section of the community that reflected the complexity of perspectives on this festival, including the grass-roots response of local community members and the perceptions of tourists and local council members.

Discussion

According to an increasing body of research literature (e.g. Alves et al., 2010; Getz, 2010; Gibson & Stewart, 2009) and ongoing developments within government policy, festivals represent a significant social and economic opportunity for celebration and regeneration within rural communities, particularly in the context of a rapidly modifying primary production industry, climate change and outmigration. In particular, festival events are understood to provide a diversified economic base for the community (Gibson & Stewart, 2009), decreased uncertainty in relation to seasonal fluctuations in tourism and, most significantly for this research, a 'rallying' point of celebration around which to build, strengthen and extend notions of local community and shared civic identity (Alves et al., 2010; Çela et al., 2008; Getz, 2010; Smith, 2009). However, these outcomes may be made particularly complex by the need to address the diverse and often competing expectations of multiple stakeholders associated with the festival event.

We examine the lived experience of these complexities in relation to the Kangaroo Island Art Feast and its contributions to notions of rurality and community. Two significant themes are explored, including how discourses of the 'local' are constructed, circulated and celebrated (or otherwise) through the event and its participants and how particular elements of culture may be highlighted or obscured by the festival event, and together, the effect these outcomes may have for notions of community.

Celebrating the 'local'

Although highlighted as an important mechanism of tourism, and by extension economic sustainability, within Australia, the majority of rural festivals appear to cater primarily to a local audience rather than a large tourist body, as suggested by Gibson et al.'s (2010) study of events held across the eastern states of Australia that found that on average, almost two thirds of attendees were drawn from the local area. The promotional material of the Kangaroo Island Art Feast reflects this focus on the local. In emails circulated to previous festival attendees (made up of both locals and tourists), participants are invited to enjoy the opening night celebrations as an inclusive space in which individuals are known to one another, evoked through an informal languaging of the familiar: 'Opening night promises colour, excitement, *community* artworks, digital projections, *locally* composed music and, *once the official bits are done*, party music by a *local* DJ and musicians' (email communication, 17 September 2012; emphasis added). Similarly, this focus on the local is emphasised in the booklet circulated to prospective sponsors of the event, who are themselves termed 'Friends of Art Feast':

> In 2012, the tenth Art Fest bursts into life with a street fiesta in King-scote.... This colourful, exciting, *community* celebrations promotes Art Fest venue attractions, *local* food and wine, and has roaming street performers, Island school children leading a multi-cultural parade with large scale art-works to herald the festivities; surrounding buildings lit up with digitally projected images to a *locally* created musical score.
>
> (Kangaroo Island Art Feast, 2012, p. 2; emphasis added)

Moreover, when the event's venue was required to change in order to accommodate inclement weather, the informality of the communication (often associated with a more 'laidback' environment such as the rural) was evident: 'A weather forecast of wind and rain for tomorrow evening has seen the opening night team implement Plan B (bless you Fleur, Andrea, Cath and Lara)' (email communication, 27 September 2012). In this way, prospective festival sponsors and participants are made aware of the local nature of the event and perhaps more significantly, within the final email passage, implicitly identified as a local themselves, familiar with other members of community who are referred to only by their first names, despite the wide circulation of the email to individuals outside the community.

Similarly, in the festival programme, constant references are made to local produce and individuals including 'local craftsmen', 'local award-winning photographer' and 'the selection is seasonal and fresh, handmade and local'. Through a very public farewell to a former organiser within a mass-produced programme given out to every attendee, the festival participant is further inter-pellated as a 'local' through the invitation to honour an important community member for his dedication to the event: 'Without him, we would have no Kanga-roo Island Art Feast. Rest in Peace dear friend' (Kangaroo Island Art Feast, 2012, p. 18).

From these passages, it appears that the promotional discourses of the festival work to (re)inscribe the community in certain ways to those participating, creating a narrative of place that assumes a close-knit community where individual members are known by everyone. This occurs even as the event itself seeks to widen their audience to a larger numbers of tourists, with the committee describing the current position of the event as one that is shifting from a 'community festival for locals and visitors already coming to Kangaroo Island into a community-at-heart festival that markets itself professionally to attract people to visit Kangaroo Island specifically for Art Feast' (Kangaroo Island Art Feast, 2012, p. 4).

However, the tension of this focus on multiple audiences and the growing nature of the festival were evident in the discrepant responses by festival attendees.

Many participants were pleased by the historical internal focus of the event, concerned with how it might change under the pressures of tourism and commercialisation:

> That's what's nice about living in the country. If you did it in the city it would have to be bigger and better and more sophisticated. I think it would be a shame to lose that because that's what's special about Kangaroo Island. It's like stepping back 40 years. It's a nice place to live and I think that fact that it is hard to get here, it's expensive to get here, is what saves it; otherwise it will be loved to death like the rest of Australian coastlines.
>
> (Kangaroo Island Art Feast local artist)

In contrast, others suggested that a shift to a greater outward focus was necessary to ensure the sustainability of the event:

> One thing that worries me about this festival is that islanders love it but it's got to be for mainlanders too and it's an expensive little exercise for them to come over here. I don't think people think 'I'll go over to Kangaroo Island Art Feast' because it's really expensive. And so it's dependent on how much the locals can spend, and you just hope you can sell something.
>
> (Kangaroo Island Art Feast local artist)

Perhaps most surprising, however, was the lack of awareness about the event *at all* by some community members, belying the discursive centrality of the local portrayed in the promotional materials. In particular, upon arrival at the hotel situated only 100 metres from the opening night street festival, when asked why we were visiting, our response that we were there for the 'big event' was surprisingly greeted with 'Oh, are you here for the wedding?' Subsequent discussion revealed that the receptionist of one of the largest hotels on the island was not familiar with the festival that would be happening for the next 10 days, located only metres from her establishment. While anecdotal, this unexpected exchange suggests that the representation of the rural community as singularly engaged with the festival may not be accurate.

However, this disengagement may also reflect the unique nature of the festival, as it is spread over the entirety of the island, and thus, in many ways, echoes the perpetual challenge of awareness that usually exists instead between the rural and the urban environments (Cloke, 2006). Interestingly, participants highlighted the strength of this disparate approach, suggesting that the Art Feast showed 'a different kind of pace' to other rural festivals, in which the aim was to 'slowly absorb it' across multiple venues and days, rather than experience all aspects of the festival within a single concentrated space and time. Visitors are invited to experience the event by 'talking to the locals' rather than simply following the event programme, creating a feeling of 'authentic engagement' with the rural.

Underlying these different perspectives on how the festival may be experienced and by whom is a question of primary aims. Is it a celebration of local produce and artistic endeavours only for those living within the community? Alternatively, is it intended as a situated moment of cultural consumption for prospective tourists, or, most likely, a combination? The shifting answers to this question as the festival grows have, in turn, influenced how the key concepts examined in this chapter, including the 'rural', 'local' and 'community', are constructed and promoted within Kangaroo Island's discourses of identity. Primarily, there is a promotion of a 'small town feel ... small enough that you feel it's really community based', even as the event is widely promoted by large state-based tourism bodies in an attempt to increase its attendance. This tension is reflected in the literature (e.g. Gibson et al., 2010; Reid, 2011; Robertson et al., 2009; Smith, 2009), which suggests that as festival events shift to focus more specifically on the tourist market, concerns may arise within the community regarding issues of gentrification, commodification and conflicting stakeholder interests, as identified in the literature review.

Querying the 'local'

Engagement with the Art Feast and the larger community of Kangaroo Island showed that some issues of commodification and ownership were already being raised by several artists who actively chose not to participate because of practices they see as exclusionary. This included what one artist termed the 'enormous commissions' artists must pay to the committee in order to show their works as part of the Art Feast, which they do, he suggested, because 'most artists are so desperate to have their work sold they will sign any contract'. Other artists indicated that they could not afford the commission charged and thus were not included in the programme for the festival, despite their presence as ongoing members of the artistic community.

Some individuals have decided to openly declare their independence from the festival event, flying a flag at their particular venue to signify their opposition not to the event itself, but to the administrative aspects of the festival that they found objectionable:

> anybody who endeavours to take over a whole arts community, hyperbolise it, sell the thing, put money in their pockets is not okay with me. The smaller the community the less you can kick out ... and that keeps people from complaining.
>
> (Kangaroo Island local artist)

Similarly, as another community member stated in relation to the more bureaucratic aspects of the festival:

> I don't want to be involved. Somebody wants to tell you too much and as an artist myself I need to be independent. There are a few around here that want to be independent [but] they are afraid because there's nowhere to hang their [work].

While problematic, such issues of power in relation to 'social and cultural relations' within tourism appear ubiquitous (Clarke & Jepson, 2011). According to Church and Coles (2007, p. 5), 'The allocation and distribution of benefits (often money and knowledge) inevitably result in winners, losers and rivalries among the individuals and/or groups involved.' This suggests that while the aims and intentions of certain individuals may be enabled by festival events within the rural context, in contrast others may be disenfranchised, whether it is as a result of financial circumstances, relational networks with those organising the event or concerns regarding the rural identity being celebrated. For some participants in the Art Feast, this frustration is significant:

> You know this island has enough artists on it now and even enough profes-sional artists on it now that on October long weekend there are going to be a whole bunch of places to go and see art without having to have a festival. So I think that's what I would prefer.
>
> (Kangaroo Island local artist)

Thus, the traditional discourses of a singular, unified rural community con-structed and circulated for the purposes of event promotion are here challenged by those individuals who object to the commissions charged in association with the festival. Interestingly, through this objection, artists in turn create their own community of individuals whose tactics (in de Certeauian terms) both express frustration and actively circumvent the intended use of space (an institution's 'strategies') to recreate their own understandings of the place and identity of Kangaroo Island during the festival.

Issues of diversity were also raised as a matter of concern by some community members. Research within the rural context has highlighted the complexity of race in the construction of competing ruralities (Neal & Agyeman, 2006), and, in par-ticular, in relation to festivals (Robertson et al., 2009). There is not sufficient scope within this chapter to explore this in depth, but within the context of the Kangaroo Island Art Feast, one local business owner explained that her attempts to introduce points of difference within the community were problematic: 'Not to be negative, it's really hard for the locals to embrace this culture and this type of food.' Local Aboriginal perspectives also appeared absent within the festival, the traditional histories of 'Karta' or 'Land of the Dead' (the term given to Kangaroo Island due to its mysterious abandonment several thousand years ago) and more contemporary Aboriginal practices seem obscured from the narrative of place presented by the event. In this way, the reality of contemporary rural landscapes that are informed by complex demographic movements appears absent within the festival space, highlighting the problematic question of who may be considered a 'local' within the rural context.

Nevertheless, other participants were enthusiastic about the opportunities they saw created by the festival to encourage diversity and development, suggesting that it gives artists 'something to work towards rather than putting all the paint-ings under the bed ... it's become bigger and bigger and bigger ... and a lot more people are participating. I think It's great' (Art Feast participant). Similarly, another participant highlighted the significant encouragement of local community members made possible by the festival:

> The artists and food and wine producers, chefs and restaurants need more outlets for their creativity and this festival does that.
> It also has a 'feel good' effect on the island community … a celebration of what we can achieve if we put our mind to it.

The economic benefits of the festival for the rural community were also highlighted by several: 'Art Feast brings a lot to the island … I wouldn't be surprised how much it adds to our economy. I think it would be quite substantial' (Art Feast local artist).

Building community

These complex considerations of the multiple perspectives of the local may be particularly important at this juncture for the Art Feast, which has now celebrated its 11th anniversary. According to a UK-wide study of festival leaders and the evaluations of festival stakeholders (Robertson et al., 2009), the length of a festival was inversely correlated with its post-event engagement with the community's level of event satisfaction. This reflects an interesting shift in the measure of success for events held within the rural context in terms of whom the event is for and whose interpretations are given the most weight. As a festival ages, and in many cases becomes increasingly professionalised for the purposes of tourist consumption, it may be that the perceptions of tourists are prioritised over those of local community members.

However, these shifting measures of communities of significance may be problematic not only in terms of the perceptions and engagement of individual residents, but also more broadly, in the sustainability of the event itself. Over the past two decades, much has been written on the issue of sustainability within tourism (e.g. Alves et al., 2010; Getz & Andersson, 2008; Reid, 2011), with a significant body of research suggesting that tourism practices should be conceptualised not through top-down processes that impose outside institutional strategies for success, but through an active engagement with residents themselves (Alves et al., 2010; Hall, 1991; Mattessich & Monsey, 1997; Reid, 2011). Specifically in relation to 'festival sustainability', Getz and Andersson (2008) suggest that ongoing success must be understood as multifaceted, involving environmental, cultural and organisational considerations that take into account the complex needs of various stakeholders, in particular those of the local community.

This may be particularly pertinent to the Kangaroo Island context, where the recently staged Surf Music Festival was shut down after only its first year due to high levels of expense that made future events untenable, including a final government-sanctioned payout of AU$400,000 to reimburse businesses left out of pocket. The primary blame for the festival's demise was framed as a lack of engagement with local knowledges, which suggested that the event timing and location did not respect the local environment or the purpose of the festival itself. In a letter published in *The Islander* on 16 February 2012, the writer states:

> Without prior knowledge of its native and human inhabitants, its economy or of its surfing potential [various organising bodies] once again tarnish the Island's reputation and damage priceless heritage by implementing plans without the consultation of residents, the conservation based Council Development Plan (2011) and without considering the Island's unique rare and threatened ecology.

In contrast, the Kangaroo Island Art Feast highlights its considered community-based development over the past 10 years, emphasising the consultation process with a wide range of community members. As it attempts to transition to a larger event that focuses more significantly on the tourism market, however, it seems imperative that organisers take into account the views of those local community members who are at odds with the discursive representations and administration of the festival event. According to Larson and Wikström (2001), such moments are not uncommon, with consensus and conflict rarely mutually exclusive, but instead one or the other governing relationships at particular times, as some individuals challenge aspects of the event and others attempt to address these. For the Kangaroo Island Art Feast, this may suggest that the projected period of growth may also coincide with increasing conflict, as the central notions of 'rural', 'local' and 'community' presented by the event organisers are questioned and challenged by the community members who act as subjects within this discursive construction. However, conflicts may in turn create opportunities to implement more formal and strategic consultation processes with the wider community, and thus ensure these discursive constructions are representative of that community, as suggested by the promotional materials of the event.

Conclusion

Concepts of the 'local' may be discursively enacted to strengthen feelings of community within the rural landscape, particularly during festival events that seek to celebrate specific notions of identity. This may be especially significant at an event like the annual Kangaroo Island Art Feast, where the disparate locations and extended period of the festival can create feelings of disconnect, even within the festival. The festival itself presents a unique opportunity to promote the place, its produce and its artists to both the wider community and to the tourist population, whose presence provides increased economic and development opportunities. Such opportunities may be particularly significant as the rural landscape continues to shift away from traditional notions of primary production. However, the discourse of 'local community' may also be challenged by residents who do not feel able to participate in the event, due to issues of cost, desire for independence, or even a lack of awareness of the event itself. These issues present important challenges that must be acknowledged to ensure the sustainability of the event, particularly in light of other island festivals that have failed. Thus, as highlighted by Brennan-Horley et al. (2007) and Clarke and Jepson (2011), the complexities of the rural space and, specifically, the rural festival suggest there always exists the capacity for conflict in terms of discursive construction and circulation of identity, but for the most part, communities appear to be engaged in a project of beneficial promotion based on the passions of particular community members. The Kangaroo Island Art Feast appears to be no exception, attempting to celebrate the artistic and primary products of a community they frame as simultaneously sophisticated and modern within a traditional regional setting.

We argue that these findings, though specific to the South Australian context, provide a useful understanding for wider festival and event scholarship that seeks to examine how celebrations of place may act to both include and exclude. This chapter also sought to highlight the impact of cultural festivals for those involved in regional development, as critical considerations regarding the meaning of 'local' within the context of tourism may have important policy outcomes for the rural landscape.

Through participants' diverse stories of 'place', this research reveals the complex ways in which festivals construct local cultures for both residents and visitors and how these individuals in turn contribute to shaping festivals through their own participatory practices.

References

Alves, H., Cerro, A. & Martins, A. (2010). Impacts of small tourism events on rural places. *Journal of Place Management and Development, 3*(1), 22–37.

Bell, D. (2006). Variations on the rural idyll. In P. Cloke, T. Marsden & P. Mooney (eds), *The handbook of rural studies* (pp. 149–160). London: Sage.

Brennan-Horley, C., Connell, J. & Gibson, C. (2007). The Parkes Elvis Revival Festival: Economic development and contested place identities in rural Australia. *Geographical Research, 45*(1), 71–84.

Cameron, J. & Gerrard, J. (2008). *Thinking and practising values: Community enterprises in the food sector – Report on the Community Enterprises in the Food Sector Workshop.* Newcastle: Centre for Urban and Regional Studies.

Çela, A., Knowles-Lankford, J. & Lankford, S. (2008). Local food festivals in Northeast Iowa communities: A visitor and economic impact study. In M. Robertson & E. Frew (eds), *Events and festivals: Current trends and issues* (pp. 70–85). Abingdon: Routledge.

Church, A. & Coles, T. (2007). Tourism, politics and the forgotten entanglements of power. In A. Church, & T. Coles (eds), *Tourism, power and space* (pp. 1–42). Abingdon: Routledge.

Clarke, A. & Jepson, A. (2011). Power and hegemony within a community festival. *International Journal of Event and Festival Management, 2*(1), 7–19.

Cloke, P. (2006). Conceptualising rurality. In P. Cloke, T. Marsden & P. Mooney (eds), *The handbook of rural studies* (pp. 18–28). London: Sage.

de Certeau, M. (1984). *The practice of everyday life*. Berkeley: University of California Press.

Dixon, R. (1995). *Writing the colonial adventure: Race, gender and nation in Anglo-Australian popular fiction, 1875–1914*. Cambridge: Cambridge University Press.

Getz, D. (2010). The nature and scope of festival studies. *International Journal of Event Management Research, 5*(1), 1–47.

Getz, D. & Andersson, T.D. (2008). Sustainable festivals: On becoming an institution. *Event Management, 12*, 1–17.

Gibson, C. & Stewart, A. (2009). *Reinventing rural places: The extent and impact of festivals in rural and regional Australia*. Wollongong: University of Wollongong.

Gibson, C., Waitt, G., Walmsley, J. & Connell, J. (2010). Cultural festivals and economic development in nonmetropolitan Australia. *Journal of Planning Education and Research, 29*, 280–293.

Gorman-Murray, A., Darian-Smith, K. & Gibson, C. (2008). Scaling the rural: Reflections on rural cultural studies. *Australian Humanities Review, 45*, 37–52.

Gorman-Murray, A., Pini, B. & Bryant, L. (2013). Introduction: Geographies of ruralities and sexualities. In A. Gorman-Murray, B. Pini & L. Bryant (eds), *Sexuality, rurality, and geography* (pp. 1–20). Lanham, MD: Lexington Books.

Hall, C. (1991). *Introduction to tourism in Australia: Impacts, planning and development*. South Melbourne: Longman Cheshire.

Hede, A. (2007). Managing special events in the new era of the Triple Bottom Line. *Event Management, 11*(1/2), 13–22.

Kangaroo Island Art Feast. (2012). *Sponsorship proposal*. South Australia: Kangaroo Island Art Feast.

Larson, M. & Wikström, E. (2001). Organising events: Managing conflict and consensus in a political market square. *Event Management, 7*(1), 51–65.

Mattessich, P. & Monsey, B. (1997). *Community building: What makes it work – A review of factors influencing successful community building*. Saint Paul, MN: Wilder Publishing Center.

Neal, S. & Agyeman, J. (eds). (2006). *The new countryside? Ethnicity, nation and exclusion in contemporary rural Britain*. Bristol: Policy Press.

Picard, D. & Robinson, M. (2006). Remaking worlds: Festivals, tourism and change. In D. Picard & M. Robinson (eds), *Festivals, tourism and social change: Remaking worlds* (pp. 1–31). Clevedon: Channel View Publications.

Reid, S. (2011). Event stakeholder management: Developing sustainable rural event practices. *International Journal of Event and Festival Management, 2*(1), 20–36.

Robertson, M., Rogers, P. & Leask, A. (2009). Progressing socio-cultural impact evaluation of festivals. *Journal of Policy Research in Tourism, Leisure and Events, 1*(2), 156–169.

Smith, M. (2009). *Issues in cultural tourism* (2nd edn). Abingdon: Routledge.

Woods, M. (2007). Engaging the global countryside: Globalization, hybridity and the reconstitution of rural place. *Progress in Human Geography, 31*(4), 485–507.

Part II
Exploring and defining community festival and event communities

7 'Wha's like us?'

Scottish Highland Games in America and the identity of the Scots' diaspora

Jenny Flinn and Daniel Turner

Heres's tae us; wha's like us?
Damn few, and they're a deid.
Mair's the pity.
    (Traditional Scottish toast)

This chapter is concerned with the relationship between events and community identity. Events and festivals offer opportunities for communities to come together to construct and communicate a shared cultural identity and meaning to the world (see Andrews & Leopold, 2013; Jepson & Clarke, 2013). Events can also provide a focal point for these communities to reaffirm and strengthen their shared bonds and to articulate their position within wider society. As such, the study of such community events offers the opportunity to develop a deeper understanding of the lives and values of the groups that create them, a chance to understand not just the cultural form itself, but also the cultural meaning symbolised by participation in the event. In an increasingly multicultural world, in which the power of events to foster social capital and community cohesion is increasingly recognised, and sought-after by a range of policy makers, funding bodies and 'legacy' planners (Foley, McGillivray & McPherson, 2011; Getz, 2013), understanding this relationship between events and their communities is of increasing interest from both an academic and practical perspective.

To deepen this understanding this chapter focuses, in particular, upon the articulation of Scottish cultural identity by the North American Scots' diaspora and their use of traditional Scottish Highland Games as part of this process. Through developing an understanding of the history, first of the diaspora, and then, second, of the Highland Games movement, the chapter will suggest that the relationship between events and identity is both complex and multifaceted. It is argued here that the Games serve a twofold purpose. First, and most obviously, the Games serve as a rallying point for the diaspora to celebrate their Scottish history and to find an 'ontological anchor' rooting them collectively to their past. Second, and more interestingly, we will suggest that such Games also enable the diaspora to position themselves in their new North American community, by enabling them to portray themselves as central to the modern North

American cultural identity. In doing so, this chapter will highlight that cultural events are a complex phenomenon, enabling simultaneous production and consumption of a multitude of ideas by communities in possession of similarly multifaceted identities.

Diasporic identity

The term diaspora refers to a scattering, with Sim (2012) establishing that the concept was first used to refer to the Jews when they were exiled from their homeland in Israel. Over time this term has been adapted to refer to any group of people who have been exiled from a country or migrated elsewhere. As such, the term diaspora can be seen to describe the dispersal of human migratory populations from their homelands (Braziel, 2008). On further exploration it can be seen that there is some contention regarding the defining characteristics of diaspora but as Butler (2001) points out, it is generally agreed that in order to be defined as a diasporic community there must be a minimum of two destinations; there should be a relationship to the real or imagined homeland; and there should be a self-awareness of the group's identity. Furthermore, Butler (2001) suggests that the diaspora must exist over at least two generations.

However, regardless of the intricacies of the definitions, diaspora as a concept can be seen to centre upon the global migration of a population from a 'homeland' to a new host community. This resettling then raises interesting questions regarding the cultural identity of the diasporic community. In his discussion of globalisation, Miles (2001) distinguishes between 'traditional' and 'global' identities. For him, traditional identities are firmly fixed to a place and space with the individual ascribed an identity at birth in relation to the community into which they were born and the values, attitudes and beliefs of that group. A lack of migration and movement means that identity, in the traditional world, is 'unproblematic' (Miles, 2001, p. 144), given to the individual, fixed to a place and carried through life. Indeed Billig (in Stewart-Leith & Sim, 2012) refers to such simple identity as 'banal nationalism', suggesting that, for those who remain within a fixed locale for the majority of life, their national identity is almost subconscious, unchallenged and, crucially, reinforced by the surrounding reference points of everyday life.

However, as Miles (2001) goes on to argue, in an age of globalisation, with migration such as that undertaken by diasporic groups, identity becomes less fixed, less localised and inherently problematised as a result. This is particularly the case for diasporic groups that have a relationship to the real or imagined homeland (see Butler, 2001) but live and exist within a new host community and, unsurprisingly, there is a considerable literature afforded to the identities formed in such circumstances across the diasporic communities of the world (see Brah, 1996; Butler, 2001; Hall, 1997; Safran, 1991). These scattered populations may officially be citizens of one state, but feel alienated from the cultural life of their host community, essentially an outsider on the inside. For these groups, identity is far more complex and subjective, less prescribed and increasingly a work in progress, open to redraft, reproduction and alternative representation (Hall, 1997) as they seek to navigate their position between the void of home and host. Often this navigation is a fraught process, with the twin threats of rebuff and charges of disloyalty if they attempt to integrate into the host community matched with the consequences of permanent outsider status as a result of failing to assimilate (Stewart-Leith & Sim, 2012). Navigating this process can create, to borrow from Fanon's work on colonialism (cited in Hall, 1997, p. 226), 'individuals without an anchor, without horizon, colourless, stateless, rootless – a race of angels'. As such, the cultural identities and practices of diasporic groups are a complex but compelling phenomenon.

The Scots diaspora

As mentioned previously, Scotland is a country with a strong diasporic community with it being estimated that 20% of the Scottish-born population live outside Scotland, and there are between 28–40 million Scots diaspora living worldwide (Scottish Government, 2010). This is of particular interest given that the population of Scotland itself is only 5.2 million. The Scots diaspora are spread around the world with the largest diasporic communities living in the United States (5.5 million), Canada (4.2 million), England (0.8 million) and Australia (0.5 million) (Sim, 2012). This chapter focuses on the Scots diaspora in the United States as the largest of the diasporic communities.

While emigration from Scotland can be traced back to the aftermath of the first Jacobite uprising, waves of mass emigration occurred during the 18th and 19th centuries (Mitchison, 1981); a period that is commonly referred to as the Highland Clearances. This was a time of significant agricultural reform with traditional farmers being removed from the land in order to make way for more profitable sheep farming. This reform was largely seen to be supported by the government, but as Richards (2010) argues, the recognition of the substantial efforts to kick-start the highland economy is lost beneath revulsion at the forced evictions carried out by hereditary aristocratic landowners. This displacement saw the highland population being forced to coastal areas where the farmland could not sustain the rapidly growing communities (Mitchison, 1981). Thus, much of the highland population were forced to emigrate to colonies in Canada and the United States. A further wave of mass emigration took place in the early 19th century when, as in Ireland, the potato crop failed causing further migration and forcible eviction.

Richards (2010) suggests that the revulsion felt at the surge of clearances that took place during the famine years is bitterly sustained to this day, by the oral traditions of the Highlands both at home and overseas. The notion of continued attachment is central to diasporic communities with diaspora being identified to have 'historical roots and destinies outside the time/space of the home nation' (Clifford, 1997, p. 255) and to be a part of an enduring transnational system than includes the homeland as a place of attachment and not as something left behind. Therefore, for diaspora, links between metaphorical, imagined and physical homes are established between individual and collective pasts through memories and nostalgia (Agnew, 2005). As will be witnessed, despite the often unpleasant circumstances of their migration many Scots migrants looked back fondly on their previous life. Stories of the 'old country' would be passed down through generations causing diasporic views of the homeland to change over time. The notion of nostalgia is inextricably linked to identity; this can be of either a lived or learned nature and may be described as a 'yearning to return to or relive a past period' (Fairley & Gammon, 2005, p. 183). Therefore, as Butler (2001) suggests, diasporic representations of the home country often diverge markedly from reality and are part of the project of constructing diasporic identity rather than homeland actuality. In the case of the Scots diaspora it often seen that their identity is rooted in an overly romantic view of the homeland leading to expatriate Scots 'often viewed from the homeland as being more "Scottish than the Scots", wearing tartan in quantities in inverse proportion to the strength of their Scottish ancestry' (Sim, 2012, p. 99). As will be witnessed through the case of Highland Games, diasporic behaviour displayed during celebrations outwith Scotland often reinforces this romanticised view of the homeland.

History of the Highland Games

The Scottish Highland Games are an important cultural event for communities not only in Scotland, but also around the world. The history of the Games is much contested due to the fact that very few documentary records exist (Jarvie, 1991), with much information relating to highland culture and traditions being passed down through the generations by word of mouth. While some would argue that the origins of the Games can be traced back to the Irish Scotti (Brewster, Connell & Page, 2009; Burnett, 2000; Ray, 2001), it is widely believed that there are two key periods that can be associated with the Highland Games as we now know them. The first official records of prearranged and designated sporting events taking place in the Highlands stem from the 11th century when it was the custom of clan chiefs to summon their clansmen to periodical gatherings for hunting, the practice of military exercises and the transaction of clan business generally. Of particular note is the Braemar Gathering, organised during the reign of King Malcolm III, where clansmen would compete in races and strength events to identify post runners to deliver messages on behalf of the king and the strongest warriors to become his bodyguards (Brewster et al., 2009).

Such gatherings continued to grow and gather momentum until the Jacobite Rising of the mid 18th century. Following the Scots defeat at the Battle of Culloden the Act of Proscription came into effect on 1 August 1746 outlawing many highland traditions such as the wearing of kilts, playing of bagpipes and gatherings, all of which were viewed as acts of warfare (Donaldson, 1986). The introduction of this law along with others such as the Heritable Jurisdictions Act, which removed feudal authority from Clan Chiefs, were an attempt to assimilate the Scottish Highlands, crushing the clan system and ending the Highlanders' ability to revolt.

Following the repeal of these laws in 1782 Highlanders were able to re-engage with their old customs/traditions making a conscious effort to retain features of Scottish culture such as dance and music (Webster, 1973). The re-emergence of Highland Games occurred at a time when it was generally agreed that the roots of modern-day Highland Games could be linked to an event organised by the St Fillans Society at Falkirk in 1781 (Brewster et al., 2009; Donaldson, 1986; Jarvie, 1991; Webster, 1973). However, it was not until the 1820s that the Highland Games were brought back to the forefront of Scottish society, forming part of the Victorian social calendar. It was at this time that the popularity of the Highland Games spread across Scotland, taking place not only in the Highlands but also the Lowlands, emerging as an important community event, affording formal organisation and annual occurrence (Grant, 1961; Jarvie, 1989, 1991). The popularity of the Highland Games was further accelerated thanks to Queen Victoria, who was widely known for her love of the Highlands, attending her first Gathering at Braemar in 1848. The approval of Her Majesty along with the support of wealthy patrons, interest from the media and curiosity of the public allowed the Highland Games to thrive, reaching their peak in the 1940s when it is estimated that over 200 events were taking place across Scotland on an annual basis (Webster, 1973).

Although Scotland has changed significantly since this time, its Highland Games have not. According to Reynolds (2011) the Games remain community events with a relatively standard programme. Reynolds surmises that Highland Games comprise a number of 'essential' sporting and cultural activities including 'Heavy' competitions such as tossing the caber; track and field competitions that are open to competitors of all ages; rituals and ceremonies involving a Games Chieftain; competitions and displays by solo pipers and highland dancers; and the appearance of at least one pipes and drums band. In addition to these 'essential' features of the Highland Games they often also comprise a number of optional activities such as tug of war, hill and road races, back-hold wrestling and musical entertainment. These novelty activities have formed part of the Games from an early age, often being introduced to attract larger audiences and increase competitor numbers (Ray, 2001). It is worth noting that while present-day Highland Games tend to follow a specific structure and format similar to that of the 1820s it is likely that today's Games have different values and meanings to their audience than in the past (Jarvie, 2003).

Sadly, since the 1940s Highland Games in Scotland have been in decline. Such was the failure of these events in the post-war recession that the majority of Games still in existence today are actually more contemporary events, founded after 1961 (Brewster et al., 2009) when new funds became available as a result of an increased recognition of the role of local festivals in developing tourism (Felenstein & Fleischer, 2003). Despite this growth of 'new' Games, numbers continue to dwindle, with Brewster et al. (2009) identifying that 20% of Highland Games in Scotland failed between 2000 and 2007. Much of this decline can be attributed to the change in funding for the Games, which initially relied upon wealthy patrons and in more recent times the support of local authorities and other public-sector funding agencies. As Jarvie (2003) suggests, the Games occupy a third (unwanted) space between highly commercialised sport and state-sponsored sport; a space that marginalises traditional Scottish sport, ensuring that they remain unsupported and unable to reach their full potential. Furthermore, a number of Highland Games have suffered due to a lack of interest among the younger generation, a common issue faced by community events (Brewster et al., 2009). As Reynolds (2011) highlights, while Highland Games have adjusted from their early role as celebrations funded by elites, competition for public interest and funding along with the arrival of numerous other leisure alternatives has made the environment in which they operate increasingly hostile. The challenge faced by Highland Games in Scotland are further emphasised in a report commissioned by the Scottish Government (DTZ, 2007) that found that a lack of business knowledge, committed volunteers, missed opportunities and a lack of financial support were a threat to the sustainability of Highland Games. However, despite being in decline in Scotland, Highland Games are flourishing overseas with one of the key drivers in the continuity of these events being the diaspora of Scottish migrants who have a desire to keep highland traditions alive. This is particularly true in parts of America where Highland Games can attract crowds of up to 50,000 people (Jarvie, 2003).

Highland Games and the North American Scots diaspora

The Highland Games first took place in America in the 1860s following the Highland Clearances and were a means of helping Scots migrants unite. The Games enabled the Scottish American diaspora to reaffirm a sense of the homeland, allowing them to connect with others in the same migrant position, thus developing a sense of community/group identity. Donaldson (1986, p. 3) describes the celebrations of the Games and the people involved as

> celebrating their love of their country and their heritage that could not be destroyed. This love has passed on to succeeding generations, and has remained strong enough to stir those whose hearts are in the Highlands whether they have actually been there or not.

As has been mentioned previously, despite the often desperate circumstances surrounding their emigration many Scots migrants looked back on their homeland with fond memories that they passed down through generations (Ray, 2001); this can be witnessed in the Highland Games which promote a romantic history of Scotland, involving kilts, bagpipes and rough bravado, on a global scale.

A reasonable amount of academic research has been undertaken on Highland Games in America but the majority of this has been from an American viewpoint (Brewster et al., 2009). This is concerning given the important role that the Scots American diaspora play in defining and representing Scottish identity on a global scale and as such this chapter represents our attempt to make a Scottish reading of an American Games.

For this chapter, the focus is on the Long Island Highland Games, an event taking place in New York each year under the auspices of the Clan MacDuff. The event, now held at Old Westbury Gardens, has taken place annually since 1960. Like most Highland Games in the United States, participants take part in a range of traditional events, including the caber toss, putting the stone and tossing the sheaf alongside entertainment such as traditional music and dancing and activities relating to genealogy and opportunities for the several thousand guests in attendance to trace their own heritage and history. In many ways, the form of the event chimes strongly with Radhakrishnan's (2003) view of diasporic groups and their practices in general in that it is a nostalgic gaze back to an idealised image of the homeland. The event is steeped in the 'homely, rural past of the forefathers' (McCrone, 2001, p. 100) and the overly sentimental 'Kailyard' literary tradition of the early 1900s, which presented an idealised view of rural Scottish life. The event organisers' description of the Games and their wider events calendar reflects this: 'We have Burns Suppers, we teach Scottish Gaelic, have bagpipe lessons, highland dancing, we get involved in the whole culture.' This romanticised Scottishness serves an important role, it enables the diaspora to connect with one another around a common reference point, affording an opportunity to bond and find common purpose and meaning. The accuracy of the event, its real 'Scottishness', is not essential. Indeed, the hyperreality of the event, with its simulation of a time gone by, of clans and communities, is actively sought, offering as it does a feeling and image of being 'connected to connectedness' (Ray & McCain, 2012, p. 978). If the scattering of a diasporic group away from their home community with a fixed, traditional identity creates an uncertainty of being, then the Games represent an ontological anchor, a fixed point through which certainty and sense of place can be assured. This is particularly clear in the case of an American Highland Games, where the fabled homogeneous melting pot is seen to remove these cultural moorings. As one clan member at the Games suggested: 'In New York everyone's got their piece of the apple and I just wanted to see if there was anything to do with Scotland … everyone's searching for something in America.' However, the relationship between the Games and the Scots diaspora can be seen as much more complex than offering a simple bonding point. Identity formation is both subjective and multitudinous in nature (Brah, 1996). One cultural practice, such as the Games, can serve several purposes in terms of identity creation.

In addition to allowing the diaspora to bond with one another, activities such as the Long Island Games enable the Scots expatriates to position themselves *against* their host community. Being Scottish becomes a badge of pride, something to separate the migrants from other ethnic groups within their host community. In essence, being Scottish provides the individual with a badge of 'distinction' (Bourdieu, 1979), an expression of the self and a marker of difference from others (Andrews & Leopold, 2013). In this case of the Games, one senior clan member expressed this neatly:

I grew up during the depression and I remember my mother making fried oatmeal at dinner time, she used to put fried onions and things in it. I remember telling people 'we're so poor that we have to have fried oatmeal'. Then one day my wife bought me a Scottish cookbook and there was a recipe for fried oatmeal! It wasn't because we were poor. It was because we were Scottish.

In this context, Scottish heritage elevates the individual, taking them beyond the poverty surrounding them. In contrast to Craig's tale (cited in Ray & McCain, 2012) of the affluent American who traces his privileged life back to an ancestry of hardship in the 'old country' with bittersweet impact, here the impoverished American becomes the noble clansman, a cultured Scot, protecting the traditions of his heritage, ensuring their survival and in doing so, demonstrating their superiority to those surrounding them in destitution.

This highlights that, in addition to *bonding* the individual to their diasporic community, a cultural event such as the Games can also enable that diaspora to identify their collective identity via their *difference* from the host community. However, it can also be seen that participation in the Games also, simultaneously, serves a third purpose. Namely, positioning the diaspora *within* their host community and enabling them to display their connection to their new cultural identity as Americans.

Despite the hyper-Scottishness of the Long Island Games, it did depart from the Kailyard in places. In addition to the traditional activities, the Games programme regularly includes some distinctly *American* cultural practices. The event is opened with a small parade, of which a major aspect is a parade of serving military personnel, something unusual in traditional Scottish events but commonplace at American cultural occasions. In keeping with other accounts of such events (Roberts, cited in Sim, 2012), there is a distinctly American feel to aspects of the programme as classic cars are exhibited and arm-wrestling contests take place; fitting with the hegemonic masculinity typically displayed at such events (Bueltmann, 2010) but not the traditional Games programme as recognised in Scotland. The Games programme then, reflects its creators, being simultaneously Scottish and American. However, more than this, the Games speak to what type of America the diaspora represents. Speaking with organisers, participants and audience members, a recurring theme emerged regarding what it meant to be 'Scottish'. Repeatedly, when asked about why their Scottish heritage was important, evocative images of Scotland as a place of 'freedom', 'fraternity' and 'independence' were put forward by those in attendance. Individuals discussed their image of Scotland as a place when a man could make a life from mastery of the land, the sweat of his brow and his own quiet endeavour. These values, while indicative of the romanticised tartanry of the Kailyard, also speak strongly to the values of American Frontierism, an era vital to the settlement and success of the nation and a period mythologised in the American psyche as a tale of survival, persistence, self-reliance and independence (Hine & Faragher, 2000). By valorising these values within their cultural heritage as Scots, the diaspora simultaneously lay claim to a foundational brick of American cultural identity, staking a claim at the centre of American life for themselves.

Event organisers took pride in outlining the openness of their event, and the pride they took in allowing non-Scots to witness and participate in the Games: 'we don't differentiate, we have a classification "friend of Scotland" so if you just want to be a member you can … some members have no Scottish links at all, they're just interested. The secretary of the club is Jewish!' This openness is important, non-Scots are invited into the Games to bear witness this claim to American identity, to validate the diaspora not only as no longer on the outside of American identity, but as integral to its creation; gatekeepers of the frontier spirit.

Overall therefore, examining events such as Highland Games in North America allows for a nuanced understanding of cultural identity to be developed. Rather than a fixed identity as Scots or Americans, as outsider or insider, the diaspora can be seen to simultaneously create and display three different identity claims though their participation in the Highland Games. They bond with one another as exiles from the homeland finding an ontological anchor point in their shared history. They distinguish themselves from their non-Scottish peers through their display of cultural heritage and practice. And simultaneously, they locate themselves within the very heart of their new community by laying claim to the cultural values underpinning this new identity.

Conclusion

Throughout this chapter we have witnessed the ways in which events can provide a focal point whereby communities can reaffirm and strengthen their shared bonds and articulate their position to wider society. The use of traditional events, such as the Highland Games, can be particularly important in the creation of identity for diasporic communities who often find their identity to be inherently problematised due to the fact that they wish to maintain the identity of their home country but similarly wish to create an identity that will be accepted by the host nation. In the case of the North American Scots diaspora it can be suggested that the Highland Games in fact serve a threefold purpose.

First, the Games offer a rallying point for the diasporic community to celebrate their Scottish heritage and provide an 'ontological anchor' rooting them collectively to their past. The identity constructed around the Games represents a highly romanticised interpretation of Scottish culture based on stories that have been passed down through the generations of diaspora and thus offers a representation of the homeland that can diverge markedly from reality.

Second, this romanticised Scottishness serves an important role in enabling the diasporic community to bond around a common purpose and meaning. However, the relationship between the diaspora and the Games can be seen to be much more complex than offering a simple bonding point.

Third, as well as providing the opportunity to bond with one another, events such as the Games allow the diaspora to affirm and display their difference to the home identity. Their diasporic identity becomes a badge of pride, something that separates them from the home identity and, indeed, from other ethnic groups within the host community.

As Bourdieu (1979) suggests, being Scottish provides the individual with a badge of 'distinction', a maker of difference that can be openly displayed via events such as the Games. We suggest that the Games offer the Scots diaspora the opportunity to position themselves within their North American community by enabling them to portray themselves as central to modern North American cultural identity, thus developing a connection to their new cultural identity as Americans.

What is clear is that the relationship between diasporic identity and events is complex one, as can be seen in the case of the Highland Games such events can offer a multitude of opportunities to create identities of both difference and acceptance simultaneously.

References

Agnew, V. (2005). Introduction. In V. Agnew (ed.), *Diaspora, memory and identity: A search for home* (pp. 3–18). Toronto: University of Toronto Press.

Andrews, H. & Leopold, T. (2013). *Events and the social sciences*. London: Routledge.

Bourdieu, P. (1979). *Distinction: A critique of the judgement of taste*. London: Routledge.

Brah, A. (1996). *Cartographies of diaspora: Contesting identities*. London: Routledge.

Braziel, J.E. (2008). *Diaspora: An introduction.* Oxford: Blackwell.

Brewster, M., Connell, J. & Page, S.J. (2009). The Scottish Highland Games: Evolution, development and role as a community event. *Current Issues in Tourism, 12*(3), 271–293.

Bueltmann, T. (2010). Manly games, athletic sports and the commodification of Scottish identity: Caledonian gatherings in New Zealand to 1915. *The Scottish Historical Review, 89*(228), 224–247.

Burnett, J. (2000). *Riot, revelry and riot: Sport in Lowland Scotland before 1860*. East Linton, Scotland: Tuckwell Press.

Butler, K.D. (2001). Defining diaspora: Refining a discourse. *Diaspora, 10*(2), 189–219.

Clifford, J. (1997). *Routes: Travel and translation in the late twentieth century.* Cambridge, MA: Harvard University Press.

Donaldson, E.A. (1986). *The Scottish Highland Games in America.* Gretna, LA: Pelican Publishing.

DTZ. (2007). *An analysis of minority indigenous sports in Scotland*. Edinburgh: Scottish Executive.

Fairley, S. & Gammon, S. (2005). Something lived, something learned: Nostalgia's expanding role in sport tourism. *Sport in Society, 8*(2), 182–197.

Felsenstein, D. & Fleischer, A. (2003). Local festivals and tourism promotion: The role of public assistance and visitor expenditure. *Journal of Travel Research, 41*, 385–392.

Foley, M., McGillivray, D. & McPherson, G. (2011). *Event policy: From theory to strategy.* London: Routledge.

Getz, D. (2013). *Event tourism: Concepts, international case studies and research*. New York: Cognizant.

Grant, I.F. (1961). *Highland folk ways*. London: Routledge.

Hall, S. (1997). Cultural identity and diaspora. In K. Woodward (ed.), *Identity and difference* (pp. 51–58). London: Sage.

Hine, R. & Faragher, J. (2000). *The American West: A new interpretive history.* New Haven, CT: Yale University Press.

Jarvie, G. (1989). Culture, social development and the Scottish Highland Gatherings. In D. McCrone, S. Kendrick & P. Straw (eds), *The making of Scotland: Nation, culture and social change*. Edinburgh: Edinburgh University Press in conjunction with the British Sociological Association.

Jarvie, G. (1991). *Highland Games: The making of the myth*. Edinburgh: Edinburgh University Press.

Jarvie, G. (2003). Highland Games, ancient sporting traditions and social capital in modern international communities. *Studies in Physical Culture and Tourism, 10*(1), 27–37.

Jepson, A. & Clarke, A. (2013). Events and community development. In R. Finkel, D. McGillivray, G. McPherson & P. Robinson (eds), *Research themes for events* (pp. 6–17). Wallingford: CABI.

McCrone, D. (2001). *Understanding Scotland: The sociology of a nation* (2nd edn). London: Routledge.

Miles, S. (2001). *Social theory in the real world*. Oxford: Sage.

Mitchison, R. (1981). The Highland Clearances. *Scottish Economic and Social History, 1*, 4–24.

Radhakrishnan, R. (2003). Ethnicity in an age of diaspora. In J. Braziel & A. Mannur (eds), *Theorising diaspora: A reader* (pp. 119–131). Oxford: Blackwell.

Ray, C. (2001). *Highland Heritage: Scottish Americans in the American South*. Chapel Hill: University of North Carolina Press.

Ray, N. & McCain, G. (2012). Personal identity and nostalgia for the distant land of the past: Legacy tourism. *International Business and Economics Research Journal, 11*(9), 977–989.

Reynolds, G. (2011). *Scotland's Highland Games: Challenge in an ageing world*. Unpublished master's thesis. Glasgow: Glasgow Caledonian University.

Richards, E. (2010). *The Highland Clearances*. Edinburgh: Berlin Ltd.

Safran, W. (1991). Diasporas in modern societies: Myths of homeland and return. *Diaspora, 1*(1), 83–99.

Scottish Government. (2010). *Diaspora engagement plan: Reaching out to Scotland's international family*. Edinburgh: Scottish Government.

Sim, D. (2012). Scottish devolution and the Scottish diaspora. *National Identities, 14*(1), 99–114.

Stewart-Leith, M. & Sim, D. (2012). Second generation identities: The Scottish diaspora in England. *Sociological Research Online, 17*(3).

Webster, D. (1973). *Scottish Highland Games*. Edinburgh: Macdonald Printers.

8 Football on the weekend

Rural events and the Haitian imagined community in the Dominican Republic

Nicholas Wise

Much research has assessed sporting events and community identity (see Alegi, 2010; Arthur & Andrew, 1996; Burdsey, 2008; Gaffney, 2008; MacClancy, 1996; Shobe, 2008). This study both recognises and relates critically to research focusing on the role of sport and the events, or the gatherings, that transient communities establish to help create a sense of place abroad (Grainger, 2006; Werbner, 1996; Wise, 2011; Yassim, 2013). There is a need to focus on 'sense of community' in rural locales and how 'common' locally organised weekend sporting events can foster social cohesion among transnational groups. Furthermore, there is also a need to focus on the social impacts of events, in order to understand how they contribute to social capital and belonging among local populations. By acknowledging the significance and role of sport in local communities, researchers contribute social and cultural understandings to why people use sport and events for the purpose of social cohesion, especially among migrant groups.

This chapter contributes a particular understanding of the impact of local sporting events to immigrant communities by focusing on the case of the Haitians in the northern Puerto Plata province of the Dominican Republic. An initial interpretation of Haitian football matches on the weekend represents the focus of this chapter, and relates to the idea of escapism, because, as will be discussed below, the Haitian community is faced with prejudices and struggles in a country where they are often referred to as 'others' (Wise, 2011). Escapism, according to Tuan (1998, p. 5) 'has a somewhat negative meaning in our society and perhaps all societies.' Despite such a negative connotation, places and experiences exist to give people the opportunity to 'escape'. Much research concerning the Dominican Republic has focused on the national sport of baseball. This chapter considers how Haitians use weekend football events to reinforce their sense of community and ethnic identity in a country where they are regarded as outsiders, or as a transient group. In this regard, the sport of football represents an activity where Haitians engage in and create social interactions with other Haitian communities. The research for this study was based in Villa Ascension, a rural village planned and developed by non-governmental organisations to improve living conditions among rural dwellers by promoting community development.

It has been noted that football has become a distraction from feared social inequalities, and allows Haitians to retain links with communities across the northern region/province. This work draws from several conceptual approaches to better understand and reinforce observations pertinent to sense of community (locally) and imagined communities (associated with ethnic identity and social cohesion of Haitians in the region). The content presented in this chapter is based on participant observations and field conversations. Being an inductive study, this work attempts to better understand how Haitians are reinforcing conceptions of an imagined community in the Dominican Republic by organising football events on weekends. Much of the chapter is based on observations of community practice and weekend sporting events. Reflections and quotes from participants are also included throughout for emphasis and context.

Community, identity and social capital

Community, identity and social capital are important concepts to consider when assessing sporting events. Several scholars have referred to Anderson's (1991) notion of imagined communities, where people are bound together through 'horizontal comradeship', of a collective sense of togetherness/belonging. Misener and Mason (2006) argue that sporting events contribute to the creation of community networks, aiding in the development of social capital – encouraging community development. There is a long history of social scientists who have offered perspectives on tangible assets as an important component of social capital. Social capital is especially important to consider when assessing the influence of sports or events on community development because people look for ways to get involved or create a sense of belonging among a group (Atherley, 2006; Misener & Mason, 2006; Saunders & Sugden, 1997; Schwarz, 2009; Tonts & Atherley, 2005). Sense of belonging relates not only to issues of community, but to performances of cultural identity and how people share common beliefs and social values in their everyday life through recreational activities (Carrington, 2010; Ingham & Loy, 1993; MacClancy, 1996; Walseth, 2006).

Building on the literature presented above, conceptualisations pertinent to sense of community are important to acknowledge here as these ideas will assist the framing and interpretations in the subsequent analysis and support the development of social capital. Social capital and discussions of community refer to the binding of people in a particular location to establish a sense of empowerment (Misener & Mason, 2006; Partington & Totten, 2012; Saunders & Sugden, 1997; Schwarz, 2009; Spaaij, 2012; Tonts & Atherley, 2005). While circumstances in each particular locale differ, over the last several decades, academics have debated the idea of community but have consistently argued that people strive to achieve a sense of community (e.g. Castellini, Colombo, Maffeis & Montali, 2011; García, Guiliani & Wiesenfeld, 1999; Hummon, 1990). McMillan and Chavis (1986) present a definition and theory of sense of community based on four conditions: (1) Membership; (2) Influence; (3) Integration and Fulfilment of Needs; and (4) Shared Emotional Connections. Another factor to consider, which relates to some of the contestations at stake in this research, is the notion of boundaries – defined by 'who is in and who is out' (McMillan & Chavis, 1986, p. 10). This is important in a study focusing on Haitians in the Dominican Republic because the Haitians represent different cultural values. Norms introduced by Haitians are regarded as a threat to the Dominican Republic's 'national homogeneity, or national character' (Howard, 2001, p. 156). Such notions of communities and boundaries lead to contested identities, whereas the dominant group (Dominicans) regards the immigrant group (Haitians) as out of place.

Building on this context, it is relevant to understand how immigrant populations create a sense of being in another place. Integration and the fulfilment of needs is brought into focus here because it offers an in-depth perspective into how people challenge their place and role in another setting (Werbner, 1996; Yassim, 2013). Therefore, reinforcement, in the form of a common set of social norms that acts to connect people becomes a 'cornerstone in behavioural research, and it is obvious that for any group to maintain a positive sense of togetherness, the individual–group association must be rewarding for its members' (McMillan & Chavis, 1986, p. 12). García et al. (1999) support this conceptualisation because integration and fulfilment are requirements for promoting a greater sense of community. This perspective acknowledges that there is 'a series of processes ... [that need to be] established that make personal satisfactions possible while collective needs can also be fulfilled' (García et al., 1999, p. 731). Moreover, Hummon (1990) addresses the fulfilment of needs as functional characteristics, referring to a group's interactions, with the intention of associating individuals to strengthen communities. Schools and various other institutions including churches, community halls, pavilions and recreational spaces represent places of integration. Each of these examples allow community members to organise/structure their needs, improve social capital among the group and sustain a stronger sense of community identity (e.g. Atherley, 2006; Harris & Parker, 2009; Partington & Totten, 2012).

A sense of identity therefore depends on shared emotional connections. Perspectives concerning identity in academic research focus on individualism and collective, national and cultural identity on several scales considering the national, regional and local (Harris & Parker, 2009; Jenkins, 2008). What must also be acknowledged are spaces and functions that further define the very sense of identity that connect people through common social practices. García et al. (1999, p. 731) build upon previously addressed conceptualisations, and suggest that when people are met with 'a difficult or painful situation, the emotions are always shared among members of the community.' As noted, Haitians in the Dominican Republic are regarded as outsiders (Augelli, 1980; Howard, 2001) who simply use football as a way of uniting communities to establish their presence and combat social struggles and prejudices in the Dominican Republic and as a way to socially connect with other Haitians. Collective emotions therefore bind a group's sense of identity – supported thought contact/interactions, investments, culture or shared beliefs (García et al., 1999).

Several of these conceptual points will reinforce the discussions above and be further explored in the following case study to guide the understanding that positions why Haitians consistently travel to other communities to participate in 'football on the weekend'. In the analysis, Tuan's (1998) use of escapism will be revisited and considered below along with conceptualisations of staging and performing identities to critically position the importance of football to the construction of a collective social capital among Haitians in the Dominican Republic.

Haitians, football and contested identities in the Dominican Republic

Sport is a reflection and expression of individual and collective identity that takes on different meanings in particular locales. In some places sport is taken for granted because people have access to sport and recreational facilities and/or compete in organised leagues. In other places, sports facilities and/or the opportunity to participate in sport can be limited. The following analysis will tease out some uncertainties while addressing some conceptual developments associated with local sporting events (football matches on the weekend) carried out by Haitians residing in rural areas of the Dominican Republic. Context deriving from notions of sense of community identity, social capital and escapism act to frame some of the understandings associated with Haitians and the significant meaning football has to this transient group scattered across rural communities in the Puerto Plata region of the Dominican Republic. The fieldwork for this case study was conducted mainly in Villa Ascension. The weekend football events observed in this rural community offer insight into the social and cultural fabric of football on the collective identity, or imagined community of Haitians.

Haitians and Dominicans have a long and contested history on the island of Hispaniola (see Augelli, 1980; Howard, 2001). It is beyond the purpose of this chapter to offer an in-depth history of the social struggles in Hispaniola, but the contemporary setting is linked to the legacy of negative connotations and gratitude expressed towards Haitians, who have no rights or legal status (Goodwin, 2011). It is important to acknowledge that in the mid-1900s Haitians were allowed to enter the Dominican Republic on temporary contracts, employed to harvest sugar cane.

The Haitians stayed in remote areas in local blocks or communes constructed by the owners of the sugar cane plantations. Throughout the 1900s, Haitians consistently sought employment opportunities in the Dominican Republic, and based on an agreement between the Dominican and Haitian governments, 20,000 Haitians could enter the country legally each year – but it has also been estimated that as many as 60,000 enter illegally each year (Goodwin, 2011). Having entered on temporary contracts, Haitians were to return to Haiti after harvesting sugar cane. Over the years, especially during periods of recession, Haitians would stay in the Dominican Republic due to the lack of economic opportunity in Haiti. Although social benefits are nonexistent, their legal status is not recognised and issues of discrimination persist, the potential economic benefits act as the main factor that keep them in place.

Community and identity

To overcome the social difficulties and struggles Haitians are met with in the Dominican Republic, they have found ways to unite and express their collective sense of community identity. Football is an important component of Haitian identity, and many participants were quick to refer to football as the national sport of Haiti. Building on these studies, another component to acknowledge is the meanings that weekend sporting events involving other Haitian communities from nearby towns have for connecting Haitians. This reinforces how football acts as a cohesive bond, and many Haitians use the sport and weekend events as a way of uniting Haitian communities distributed across the region. Moreover, this performance of collective identity observed during weekend football events can also be interpreted as a passive form resistance to prejudices, struggles and hardships. Communities and a sense of identity and belonging are often constructed through common associations – and sport has consistently acted as an important variable in this regard. As will be outlined in the participants' quotations below, football is important not only to individuals, but to everyday life in Villa Ascension. As noted, football is regarded as the national sport in Haiti, and while nationalism, from the perspective of imagined communities, does in fact transcend boundaries, the sport of football has to be viewed as taking on a different meaning when Haitians residing in the Dominican Republic gather for football.

Football becomes more than a game, and scholars have noted that sport is an influential component of collective identity, pertinent to political and social issues concerning race and ethnicity (Carrington, 2010; Harris & Parker, 2009; MacClancy, 1996). This was clear when observing Haitian footballers during the week in Villa Ascension and more so when two Haitian communities come together on weekends.

It is not uncommon, or a new phenomenon, that migrant groups use sport to generate a sense of community (Burdsey, 2008; Carrington, 2010; Yassim, 2013). As discussed, we can take sport for granted, but when Haitians gather to participate in and watch football each weekend, whether in Villa Ascension or another community, those who actively perform on the field and those who stood on the sidelines are brought together for a common cause. Footballers often expressed the importance of the sport to their individual identity and their Haitian identity. For instance, participants have noted:

> Football in [Villa] Ascension is so important. If we didn't have this field here then it would be bad because then I could not play football, there would be no place to play. This field is so important in my life and the community. When I play football, I see all the people coming together, even if the people can't play, they just come to see and watch how we play.
>
> (Haitian, age 18)

It [football] is very important for Haitian people. To Haitians people our favorite game is football. Our children, they really appreciate football, you can see this when someone comes to play football – a lot of children come to play football, they just want to practice.

(Haitian, age 26)

All the Haitians are very interested in football. That is why so many people are [always] at the field. Even if they can't play they are interested in watching football.

(Haitian, age 22)

This field is very important for this community because every day, you can't pass a day where you don't see any people on this field. It is the only place you can find all the people.

(Haitian, age 31)

Building on the last comment about the field, in previous research Haitians spoke of the significance of having a field to play football (Wise, 2011). The same field the footballers speak of becomes an events space on weekends. Typically one community is invited, but about once each year, they arrange a tournament and invite a few communities to participate. When observing these weekend football matches, the way they were organised and performed would perhaps be perceived as informal in practice. However, to these Haitians who commonly gathered on the weekends for matches in a host community, such events are very much formal because they represented opportunities for social gatherings between two (or sometimes more) Haitian communities. In relating back to discussions of the field, one week the Haitians spent several days preparing the field for a weekend tournament. They cut the grass with a machete to delineate boundaries, brought in fill dirt to fix holes on the field where puddles had formed and cleared accumulated rubbish. Much time was spent preparing the space for weekend events in a similar manner to how people make arrangements for social gatherings at their homes or in public parks. As argued by Wise (2011), to the Haitians in Villa Ascension the field is a possession, and they take much care and pride in getting the field ready for football. The field in this case is the venue upon which to stage weekend events in Villa Ascension. There is a strong sense of pride associated with the football field here and the footballers, with the assistance of the community, groom the field to prepare it for other Haitian visitors. Based on the observations of the field, this chapter now turns to the weekend football events to discuss how these gatherings unite people, contributing to the promotion of social capital among Haitian communities, locally and collectively.

Social capital

People strive to create a sense of community (Misener & Mason, 2006). Studies on social capital have focused on how communities can develop or create a strong sense of togetherness and belonging through some, or several, intermediary activities – including sport and events. In some cases it is difficult to measure social capital directly, because the focus needs to be directed to how effective an activity is in promoting social interactions. Here the emphasis is put on achieving/fulfilling people's needs through a shared emotional connection. In Villa Ascension, non-governmental organisations have funding programmes to promote and support Haitians in rural areas of the Dominican Republic though community development programmes, mainly by constructing houses. This form of capital, through assistance efforts, is an attempt to improve the quality of life among Haitians residing in rural areas. While it was recognised that homes with good foundations were an initial basic necessity, the organisers also recognised that football was an important social activity to Haitians. Leaders of the non-governmental organisation then designated an area in Villa Ascension for football as a means to promote social capital among community members. Villa Ascension has space designated for football and goalposts are also present, so in many respects they have an existing space designated for football to host such weekend events as compared to other communities. However, when the football team from Villa Ascension travels to another community the Haitians have to compete for the space. In all other observed cases, football had to be played on baseball fields because there is no space designated specifically for football.

The sports landscape in the Dominican Republic is dominated by baseball, but with the influence of Haitians in rural and coastal areas, fooball becomes another layer of identity. Since football is not the dominant or national sport in the Dominican Republic, Haitians do not necessarily have priority access to sports spaces, often resulting in less opportunity. Some of the footballers from Villa Ascension have noted that they prefer to host weekend matches or tournaments because they do not have to compete for space compared to some of the coastal towns and communities where baseball's influence dominates. Although Haitians and Dominicans do live interdependently in Villa Ascension, the space for sport and recreation was designated for football, representing a power shift in this case influenced by the non-governmental organisations that promote community development among the Haitians.

To address the sport of football directly, Haitians often expressed their gratitude towards the importance of football and matches on weekends, for instance:

> A lot of Haitians appreciate football. That's why when Haitians come here they just occupy their minds with sports. You see when they play in Ascension you find many Haitian people even if they can't play football they come to watch. When we are going in Monte Llano, Sosúa, Puerto Plata, Cabarete, they pay for transport and go and watch football.
>
> (Haitian, age 31)

> Yes, [whether we have a game in] Montellano, Cabaret, Sosúa or a game here all the people in these places come to watch football on Sundays. Also, people come on other days to watch football.
>
> (Haitian, age 28)

Each of the quotations above highlight different contexts of social capital, but the central focus is on how football acts as a core signifier of identity that promotes a collective sense of belonging. Another common theme that occurred here was how the Haitians expressed that football acted as a force promoting/ generating togetherness:

> The football field brings the people together ... Sunday afternoons you can see many people on the field; you have to push so you can see the football game. Haitians are very interested in these games. When we have a game to play, the game really unites the people.
>
> (Haitian, age 26)

> Football here is much more important. When I play football I can see all the people come to watch ... men and women, children and adults ... they just come to see. It is different when they play baseball, there are some fans but not much; but during football there are many, it brings the people together.
>
> (Haitian, age 18)

Moreover, this context presented above puts emphasis on the investment and commitment of people's time to football. This is evidence that football generates social capital among Haitians in rural areas. The next section adds another conceptual element to this chapter by discussing how football relates to the notion of escapism for Haitians.

Discussion: escapism

In isolated rural settings such as Villa Ascension, people bond and create a sense of community, or togetherness, through shared associations. Part of the broader socio-political limiting forces involved that directly affect the majority of the Haitian residents in Villa Ascension is the struggle to obtain full-time employment. Collectively, the shared sense of living under similar (economic) conditions generates a sense of community in such rural locales. When visiting Montellano, Sosúa, Cabarete or Puerto Plata with the footballers, the cases symbolise how segregated the country is socially and ethnically. Segregation is common in the Dominican Republic, broadly, because of contestations over civic and ethnic issues concerning nationalism (Howard, 2001). When speaking with some Dominicans in Montellano after a weekend football match, they seemed concerned when they discovered that I was residing in a predominantly Haitian community, even though many people, mostly volunteers, have stayed in Villa Ascension – this also reinforces how Haitians were perceived as the 'other' group.

Power relations in the Dominican Republic are complex, which has a direct impact on people's relations as regards inclusion and exclusion. As it was observed, football's impact on the social relations and interactions of Haitians contributed to increasing their social capital and well-being. The gathering of

Haitians and their common expression of identity through such weekend sporting events offers another critical point of discussion, referring to escapism in relation to the power relations and structures at play in the Dominican Republic. As Tuan (1998) notes, people seek places to escape and find closure. People seek alternative situations when faced with difficulties: they seek places such as malls, amusement parks or community centres where they can do something that moves away from everyday norms, distractions or disturbances. However, such options discussed by Tuan (1998) are not necessarily available in this case, so the eventful gathering of Haitians to enact their community identity is staged and performed through the practice of football.

With football and these weekend events interpreted as a form of escapism, this allows homogeneous groups to make symbolic connections – thereby reinforcing their contribution to the Haitian imagined community. While sports in the Dominican Republic are generally more inclusive based upon an individual's ethnic identity, Haitians and Dominicans do commonly interact in Villa Ascension because of the heterogeneous composition of the community. Dominicans play baseball on the same field on which Haitians play football, and the Dominicans do consistently encourage Haitians to play baseball. Wise (2013) argues that the reason Dominicans try to encourage Haitians to play baseball is to conform them to their national sporting ideals and defend their sense of identity in such rural locales. Haitians were hesitant to play baseball because they felt that this was an attempt by the Dominicans to push their culture and identity on them (Wise, 2013). According to one Haitian footballer (age 18):

> Many Haitians don't like to play baseball. When they play baseball there are some fans, but when they play football you find many people. For the football you find many people coming to the field. For the baseball you only find the Dominicans only watch baseball, when football is played you find all the Haitians appreciate and love football, not baseball.

When Haitians play football, they are the only ones present (with the exception of the researcher). The Dominicans do not take an interest in football, nor do they engage with Haitians during weekend matches. With exclusive groups of Haitians consuming spaces for football events on weekends, the cultural atmosphere becomes inherently and distinctly Haitian. Even though this particular locale was in the Dominican Republic, the interaction among Haitians was a reflection of similar weekend occurrences in Haiti. This (re)creation of space and place in another country reinforces the impact of weekend events on generating a sense of togetherness and reinforces how social capital is achieved among Haitians residing in rural areas. Here, McMillan and Chavis' (1986) conceptual developments reinforce how weekend sporting events establish membership among the group of Haitians, linked to football as a shared emotional connection. In previous studies, the performance of sport allowed Haitians to connect with Haiti, as their home (Wise, 2011). Escapism in this regard reinforces a sense of community and allows Haitians to create an imagined community to link and bond with other Haitians across the Puerto Plata region through the performance of football. Football is not commonly associated with Dominican identity, and therefore, the sport further relates to difference, or uniqueness, by coming together through something that is inherently Haitian, and this performance can be linked to displays of ethnic nationalism.

Conclusions

This chapter has offered some conceptual points of interpretation regarding how locally organised sporting events, if initially perceived as informal, contribute to the social capital and sense of belonging among Haitians in the Puerto Plata region of the Dominican Republic. It is clear that Haitians residing in the Dominican Republic are faced with social hardships and are exposed to prejudice. Football to Haitians is a part of everyday life, and people are brought together through active participation or through watching football matches. What is more important to consider is that Haitians from several communities gather through weekend football events because it gives them the opportunity to connect and escape from the pressures of being the 'other' group in the Dominican Republic. Moreover, football conforms to the imagined Haitian community, and through sport these Haitians are able to (re)create a sense of community allowing them to relate to something familiar by reinforcing their sense of identity. The notion of social capital supported the context of community identity because events and gatherings give people a voice and act to improve social conditions despite the much broader political influences pertinent to struggles concerning race and ethnic identity.

In conclusion, the purpose of this chapter was to assess local community gatherings/events to show and argue the significance and impact football has on Haitians in the Puerto Plata region of the Dominican Republic. It has been argued that more research is needed to assess micro-locale case studies, and this particular study looks at one case from the Dominican Republic. It is important to consider the influence of sport and events on migrant communities, and such conceptualisations of sense of community, social capital and escapism support understandings and observations positioning how transient groups create a sense of being and belonging in different cultural settings. In this case, football events act to reinforce a sense of being Haitian.

References

Alegi, P. (2010). *African soccerscapes*. Athens: Ohio University Press.
Anderson, B. (1991). *Imagined communities*. London: Verso.
Arthur, D. & Andrew, J. (1996). Incorporating community involvement in the management of sporting mega-events: An Australian case study. *Festival Management and Event Tourism, 4*, 21–27.
Atherley, K. (2006). Sport, localism and rural social capital in rural Western Australia. *Geographical Research, 44*, 348–360.

Augelli, J.P. (1980). Nationalization of Dominican borderlands. *Geographical Review, 70*, 19–35.

Bairner, A. (2001). *Sport, nationalism, and globalization*. Albany: State University of New York Press.

Burdsey, D. (2008). Contested conceptions of identity, community and multiculturalism in the staging of alternative sport events: A case study of the Amsterdam World Cup football tournament. *Leisure Studies, 27*, 259–277.

Carrington, B. (2010). *Race, sport and politics*. London: SAGE.

Castellini, F., Colombo, M., Maffeis, D. & Montali, L. (2011). Sense of community and interethnic relations: Comparing local communities varying in ethnic heterogeneity. *Journal of Community Psychology, 39*, 663–677.

Gaffney, C. (2008). *Temples of the earthbound gods*. Austin: University of Texas Press.

García, I., Guiliani, F. & Wiesenfeld, E. (1999). Community and sense of community: The case of an urban barrio in Caracas. *Journal of Community Psychology, 27*, 727–740.

Goodwin, P.B. (2011). *Latin America and the Caribbean*. New York: McGraw-Hill.

Grainger, A. (2006). From immigrant to overstayer: Samoan identity, rugby, and cultural politics of race and nation in Aotearoa/New Zealand. *Journal of Sport and Social Issues, 30*, 45–61.

Harris, J. & Parker, A. (eds). (2009). *Sport and social identities*. Basingstoke: Palgrave Macmillan.

Howard, D. (2001). *Coloring the nation: Race and ethnicity in the Dominican Republic*. Oxford: Signal Books.

Hummon, D.M. (1990). *Commonplaces: Community ideology and identity in American culture*. Albany: State University of New York Press.

Ingham, A.G. & Loy, J.W. (eds). (1993). *Sport in social development*. Champaign, IL: Human Kinetics.

Jenkins, R. (2008). *Social identity*. New York: Routledge.

MacClancy, J. (ed.). (1996). *Sport, identity and ethnicity*. Oxford: Berg.

McMillan, D.W. & Chavis, D.M. (1986). Sense of community: A definition and theory. *Journal of Community Psychology, 14*, 6–23.

Misener, L. & Mason, D. (2006). Creating community networks: Can sporting events offer meaningful sources of social capital? *Managing Leisure, 11*, 39–56.

Partington, J. & Totten, M. (2012). Community sports projects and effective community empowerment: A case study in Rochdale. *Managing Leisure, 17*, 29–46.

Saunders, E. & Sugden, J. (1997). Sport and community relations in Northern Ireland. *Managing Leisure, 2*, 39–54.

Schwarz, E.C. (2009). Building a sense of community through sport programming and special events: The role of sport marketing in contributing to social capital. *International Journal of Entrepreneurship and Small Business, 7*, 478–487.

Shobe, H. (2008). Football and the politics of place: Football Club Barcelona and Catalonia, 1975–2005. *Journal of Cultural Geography, 25*, 87–105.

Spaaij, R. (2012). Building social and cultural capital among young people in disadvantaged communities: Lessons from a Brazilian sport-based intervention program. *Sport, Education and Society, 17*, 77–95.

Tonts, M. & Atherley, K. (2005). Rural restructuring and the changing geography of competitive sport. *Australian Geographer, 36*, 125–144.

Tuan, Y.-F. (1998). *Escapism*. Baltimore, MD: Johns Hopkins University Press.

Walseth, K. (2006). Sport and belonging. *International Review for the Sociology of Sport, 41*, 447–464.

Werbner, P. (1996). 'Our blood is green': Cricket, identity and social empowerment among British Pakistanis. In J. MacClancy (ed.), *Sport, identity and ethnicity* (pp. 87–111). Oxford: Berg.

Wise, N. (2011). Transcending imaginations through football participation and narratives of the *other*: Haitian national identity in the Dominican Republic. *Journal of Sport & Tourism, 16*, 259–275.

Wise, N. (2013). Maintaining Dominican identity in the Dominican Republic: Forging a baseball landscape in Villa Ascension. *International Review for the Sociology of Sport.* doi: 10.1177/1012690213478252.

Yassim, M. (2013). Cricket as a vehicle for community cohesion: Building bridges with British Muslims. *Journal of Islamic Marketing, 4*, 218–227.

9 Pride, identity and authenticity in community festivals and events in Malta

Vincent Zammit

Introduction

Community events have become an important and integral part of the tourism product in Malta. In recent years there has been a number of such events being organised, first by the National Tourism Authority and subsequently by many different local and communal organisations. These have provided the organisers with the possibility of participating in the tourism market, albeit a niche market, wherein they can feel part of an important industry to the local economy; they can also attract tourists to their events and locality, and at the same time give an identity to their own community. Some of the events have taken on the aspect of providing the authenticity of the local community and at the same time it has been an impetus to revive lost traditions. These festivals have been influenced by the highly successful religious feasts that have been organised for decades by the various localities. These feasts are the epitome of pride and identity to the locality.

The varieties of the festivals that have been organised are varied. Besides the religious feasts, there are the national cultural events like the Malta Arts Festival, Fireworks Festival and *Notte Bianca*. Local councils have also started to organise their own festivals, some of which are culturally oriented. There has also been an increase in organising festivals and events connected with the traditional aspects of the locality, like strawberries, pumpkins, bread and pork. This has led to a different kind of activity wherein the revival of old recipes and the introduction of new ones have become the norm. These have become an annual event that helps the community to work together for a successful activity.

This chapter looks at the development of community festivals and events in Malta during recent years, the synergies behind these activities and the plans for further events in view of the fact that Valletta (the capital city of Malta) has been chosen to be the European Capital of Culture 2018.

Tourism in Malta is one of the country's most important money-generating industries. Statistics are always being examined and analysed and reports commissioned in order to make sure that tourist arrivals continue to increase. The success can be gauged by the large number of tourists that visit Malta every year. The latest statistics show that the last four years have registered an annual increase in arrivals. When tourism started to gather pace, the number of visitors in 1969 was 143,748. During 2012 there were more than 1,400,000, and more than 600,000 cruise liner arrivals (NSO, 2012). It is estimated that 2014 would be another record year. Yet, it has been clear for some years that tourism in Malta needed to distinguish itself from typical Mediterranean islands' tourism – the sea, sun and sand mentality.

Malta, being a small island, is also blessed with a large concentration of important archaeological, historical and cultural sites, making the island one of the most culturally densely populated country in the Mediterranean, if not in the world. Yet, the cultural and heritage richness of the island was never very high on the agenda for the tourism authorities, until the trend in international tourism started to change. One of the ever-present popular activities that are held throughout the islands by the locals is the annual religious festivals. At least since 2003, there has been a conscious effort made to increase religious tourism to Malta. The Malta Tourism Authority discussed the possibility of collaboration with the local Church authorities, as it was clear that Malta has a lot to offer (Cini, 2003). During the same event, the Chairman of the Malta Tourism Authority appealed 'for more private initiatives to boost the cultural, musical and culinary events calendar to add more attractions for the visitor'.

Eventually there was a general interest and acceptance that events and festivals organised at different localities could be an important activity for various reasons. Rather than concentrating all tourism activities around the same and usual places, there could be a spread of tourism to other areas still not affected by the industry. At the same time, it would also be in line with what government authorities suggested, that tourism needed to be felt by everyone and as many locals as possible needed to be involved with its success.

Besides the religious activities organised by the local parishes, and with no official intervention and help by the state, the tourism authorities introduced the idea of organising a national historical re-enactment festival. There was no real dilemma in choosing the subject, as the period of the Order of the Knights of St John in Malta is considered one of the golden eras of Maltese history. It is also very spectacular, and as such is the right subject for such an event.

The success of this event led to the organisation of many other efforts by different groups of enthusiasts. One of the reasons behind the success is the participation of volunteers.

What are community festivals?

In Malta myriad festivals are held throughout the year. They can be divided into two different categories: the national and the communal. Some of these can be considered as national festivals, and usually these would be organised by one or another of the government departments. The national festivals are usually tied with a particular theme, and are held at various localities all over Malta. Among the festivals that are organised throughout the year are the Valletta International Baroque Festival (January), the Karnival ta' Malta (February/March), the Fireworks

Festival (April), the Ghanafest – Malta Mediterranean Folk Music Festival (May/June), the Isle of MTV Music Festival (June), the Malta Arts Festival (June), the Jazz Festival (July), the Regatta (September), *Notte Bianca* in Valletta (October) and the International Choir Festival (November) (more information can be found on the festivals' websites; see References for details). These festivals are given a national dimension as they are organised by a central committee, and have the intention of attracting an international audience. This does not mean that the locals do not participate in these festivals; in fact, usually a good percentage of the audience is local. Yet, communal pride is missing, and national pride tends to be foregrounded.

Three of the above-mentioned national festivals can take on the form of communal activity, as there is a competitive element involved. The Fireworks Festival is one of the highlights for the many enthusiasts of fireworks displays. In Malta there are a number of fireworks factories that prepare all the fireworks for the annual feast of their patron saint. The competitive element has always been present, but in recent years this has also been channelled towards participation in this international event. Besides local companies, foreign companies would be competing with their own displays. The fact that there would be more than one local fireworks factory taking part engenders the competitive element among the locals.

The same can be said of the International Choir Festival, which is organised by the Malta Tourism Authority. The participants are both local and international choirs. The participation of local choirs leads to a certain amount of local competition and pride. Yet, this competition is more akin to affiliation rather than to the community, as the members of the choirs come from different parts of the islands.

Another activity that is held in Malta is the Regatta, wherein a number of boat races are held in the Grand Harbour of Valletta. This activity has been held for centuries, and although it is traditionally considered that the event started in the 16th century in commemoration of the victory of the Great Siege of 1565, there is no real documentary evidence to confirm this. Yet, since the 19th century, this event has been held annually, and its popularity has never waned. The competitors hail from a number of seaside cities and villages, and they compete in a number of different boat races, at the end of which the winners are given a shield. This is very competitive and the scenes at the end of the day are usually chaotic and very festive. The winning team is carried shoulder high to their city, and together with the winning boat they would be paraded around the streets of the locality, emphasising the pride of the community.

Although local participants are present, the competitive element as well as local pride is clearly missing, however. These events fall into the sphere of those festivals that have become part of the tourism product. As celebratory events they have been present for a long time, and the only difference is that these might have become more tourist-oriented then before. They have become part of organised domestic and international mass tourism (Picard & Robinson, 2006). These types of festivals are organised by commercial companies. There are wine and beer festivals, organised by the main wineries and brewery of the island. These festivals are held in order to provide free music entertainment, provide food stalls and offer the chance to taste the products of the organising companies. As these festivals are held during the summer months, they are aimed at the locals as well as the many tourists visiting the islands.

These types of festivals can be considered to form part of the actual package and are a tourist attraction in their own right. Modern-day tourists travel in order to participate and be part of a festival. The increase in individual travellers has also helped in the popularity of these festivals and events, as generally these travellers would be more interested in the authenticity of the activities that they visit. The success of these festivals in attracting visitors lies in the way branding is carried out. The successful linking between location and the activity being organised brings in success, and this leads to a better end product (Smith, 2012).

Pride and authenticity in communal festivals

As tourism has been regarded as a good economic activity, various communities have tried to participate in this industry.

Smith (2009) noted that often festivals would serve as a means of reaffirming or reviving a local culture or tradition, and would offer communities the chance to celebrate their cultural identity. Yet, not all communities can actually benefit from tourism. There are certain areas where the main tourist-related activities and business are located. These tend to lose their identity and the authenticity of the place is thus debatable. Other areas tend to be part of the tourist industry

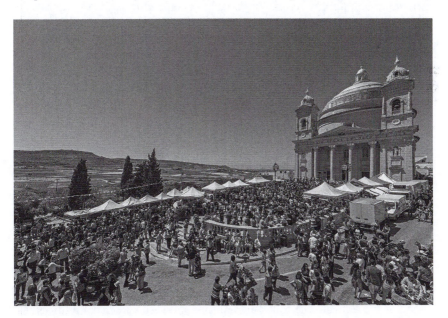

Figure 9.1 Festa Frawli at Mġarr (Malta) (photo credit: Daniel Cilia, 2014)).

activities due to limited visits and activities organised within the community. Yet, there are other areas where tourists very rarely pay a visit or leave any impact on the local community. Due to the small size of Malta it is possible to spread the tourist activity all over the territory. Distances are short and therefore many communities can participate in the economic benefits of tourism. This has led to the development of a number of communal festivals.

Communal festivals have become the latest trend in Malta. There have always been communal festivals as part of Maltese cultural life, but these were purely religious. Since the 18th century, each village has, to the best of their abilities, celebrated a popular festival in honour of the patron saint. With the passage of time, these festivals became more elaborate as fireworks, street decorations and band clubs became an integral part of the whole event. The decorations, both outdoor and within the parish church, became another source of competition, as the various parishes vied to outdo their neighbours. These religious celebrations are still very popular, and throughout the summer there is never a weekend without a feast or two being celebrated. Another religious spectacle is the various pageants and street processions that are held during Holy Week. These have become elaborate affairs and in certain villages hundreds of volunteers participate in these activities (Zammit, 2009).

With the advent of tourism to Malta, and its ever-increasing role in the economic activity of the island, various festivals started to be organised. Following the success of national festivals, it was the turn of the local villages through their local societies and local councils to start organising their own festivals and popular events. The first activities were small and maybe not so well organised, until it became important for community pride to improve the organisation of the events. The organisation of these festivals and events help to generate interest in other local attractions that might not be well known outside the community. According to Gold and Gold (2005), this packaging of events has become the norm, as other attractions and activities will take advantage of the main event.

Pride is very relevant in this concept; it goes hand in hand with identity – the identities that need to be preserved or rediscovered, in order to display the community. This is considered a conscious action, as people need to identify and to preserve their own identity (Harris, 2009).

Neighbouring villages tended to organise their own event in order to show the best of their own culture – real or imaginary. Some of the organisers have carried out research into old traditions, recipes, crafts and other such things that would make them unique in comparison to the other communities. In the meantime, when such events are repeated, certain old traditions and crafts tend to be rejuvenated, and preserved for posterity. In order to imbue the event with more authenticity, the local participants (mostly volunteers) would dress up in old traditional costumes. This is assumed to demonstrate the authenticity of the event, even though one would never see people wearing such costumes outside the period of the festival. The following are some of these communal festivals that are held yearly in Malta:

- A *Strawberry Fair* is held in one of the small villages of Malta, Mġarr. The first ever Strawberry Fair was organised in 2007 and since then it has increased in popularity.[1] Both Maltese and overseas tourists visit the festival, during which there are displays of strawberries – one of their famous local products – and the opportunity to taste different strawberry-based dishes. This has led to a number of new dishes being created, although there has also been an interest in looking at the historical background of the same product. The pride of the local villagers is immense as many volunteers participate in the preparation and organisation of the whole event. The local council encourages this activity as it brings in a lot of visitors to the small village, thus generating economic activity. Of course, visitors to the event will be able to taste more than just strawberries, as other local produce, as well as wine produced by local farmers, will also be on display.

- A former name of the once-rural village of Ħal Qormi was *Casal Fornaro*, meaning the 'village of bakeries'. Before the introduction of modern machinery, the best bakeries for the making of Maltese bread were said to be located at Qormi. There are still a number of bakeries operating there, but nowadays modern technology has taken over the traditional way of making bread. In recent years a number of festivals have been organised, one of which celebrates the making of traditional artisan bread, which has led to the production of typical Maltese bread, opening up of bakeries for viewing, and opportunities for tasting. Qormi has more than one parish, and this led to the establishment of another festival, organised by the second parish. Thus, four annual festivals are organised at Qormi: the *Spring Festival* (April), the *Wine Festival* (August), *Bread Festival* (September) and recently a *Chestnut Festival* was also organised in November. Notices about the various festivals that are organised by different social clubs of the village, but all aided by the local council, can be seen on the Qormi local council's website.

- The small village of Ħal Kirkop has never been considered a place to visit while in Malta. A good number of Maltese would not have ever bothered to visit this village, hemmed in as it is by other larger villages and close to the airport. Yet, in recent years, in May, the village has organised a *Rikotta Festival*. During this festival, the centre of attraction is the rikotta (cottage cheese), focusing on the traditional way of making this cheese, and demonstrating the various foods that can be tasted with the same product. Other activities are also organised around the village, including a visit to one of the farms.

- In the small hamlet of Manikata, a *Pumpkin Festival* is organised annually. The product is synonymous with the area. The festival aims to introduce visitors to the various ways in which pumpkin can be used in cooking, and besides soups one can sample pies, ravioli and even sweets made with pumpkin (Koperattiva Rurali Manikata, 2013).

Figure 9.2 Rikotta Festival, Ħal Kirkop (photo credit: Daniel Cilia, 2014).

Figure 9.3 Żejt iż-Żejtun – the participation of the local villagers brings about a love of the past and reviving old traditions (photo credit: Daniel Cilia, 2014).

- Zejtun is another of the large villages, and its annual festival is inspired by the fact that its name is strongly associated with olives. In September a weekend-long event is organised extolling the importance of olive oil, called *Żejt iż-Żejtun*. The village's association with this very Mediterranean product goes back at least to the Roman period, and one can still see the ruins of a Roman agricultural complex in the grounds of the local school.

All of the above-mentioned communal festivals are agricultural in concept. The importance to the authorities of such local produce is clear, demonstrated by the fact that even the Ministry for Sustainable Development, the Environment and Climate Change has set up a section to help in the organisation of these rural festivities.

Throughout the year the unit organises a number of rural festivals in different localities. Among these one can cite the vegetable fair, the fish festival, the milk festival as well as the wine and grape festival. This has given the necessary impetus to increasing awareness on the part of the local councils and the local population of their own heritage. The participation of the locals indicates an increase in appreciating these traditions and an understanding that these festivals attract a number of local visitors, as well as tourists. Smith, Macleod and Hart Robertson (2010) noted that although many festivals aim to cater primarily for the local community, they succeed nevertheless in attracting tourists, and many new festivals are created with a tourist audience in mind.

With the above in mind, one starts to better understand the organisation of the other type of festivals held in Malta throughout the year. The Malta Tourism Authority organises a number of historical re-enactment events that focus on the rich history of the islands and provide a visual event illustrating this history. The 'In Guardia' and 'Alarme' military re-enactments are held within historical fortifications, which lends more authenticity to the parades, demonstrations of military prowess of the soldiers and the display of arms and armour (Visit Malta, n.d.). These historical re-enactments have become very popular. At Mtarfa, a newly created urban centre, an annual military show is organised, during which enthusiasts parade their armoured cars, weapons and other paraphernalia dating mainly to the Second World War.

The city of Mdina uses its medieval history and architecture as the backdrop to its annual Medieval Festival. During this festival a number of historical re-enactment groups gather in the narrow streets and small squares of Mdina to spend a weekend of living the life of the past. There are groups displaying their prowess in archery, sword fighting and hand-to-hand combat. The same groups can also provide information on the various weapons, the daily routine of a medieval soldier and what the soldiers ate. This activity takes the form of an educational exercise, helping visitors understand better past centuries and the way that our ancestors lived. Other activities with a medieval theme include a display of falconry, medieval music and jousting. This particular festival is very popular with locals, but it also attracts a lot of tourists.

The two harbour cities of Vittoriosa and Senglea offer two other types of local festivals. There is nothing rural in the festivals that are organised here. The spectacular event organised in Vittoriosa when the electric street lighting is switched off for an evening of promenading the medieval streets by candlelight is unique and very popular. It offers an insight into how the people lived in times gone by, before the advent of electricity. Senglea, meanwhile, organises its Maritime Festival, emphasising the maritime heritage of the city. The fact that these two cities are located literally opposite each other, with a narrow creek separating the two peninsulas, does not seem to aid local cooperation in organising just one, much larger event. Pride is an important factor that has led to this local rivalry, and an added impetus for such festivals to continue to be organised.

The organisation of these historical re-enactments has been the catalyst to initiate important restoration and, in certain areas, urban regeneration (Zammit, 2013). From year to year people tend to notice whether there has been any improvements, and it is not the first time that the same localities actually showcase the latest restoration efforts that would have been executed.

Local festivals and the future

The success of the majority of these festivals lies in the number of volunteers that participate. They offer their help without any remuneration and this helps to keep costs down. Local pride is important, as this helps to offset any financial difficulties that might arise if everything needed to be paid. The participation of local councils helps in sustaining the organisation of these events and festivals for a number of years. However, the organisation of even more events similar to those mentioned above would not result in more participation and even more sponsorship, as the ideas might become stale. It is clear that local authorities support these events in order to enhance their importance within the community, to instil pride among the population and to increase financial benefits to the local businesses. It helps to attract tourism to their locality (Raj, Walters & Tahir, 2009). It is also important for the organisers of these events that their offer takes on a wider aspect of their community, so that the benefits would be felt by everyone, or, as it has been said, the visitors would participate in the 'enjoyment of the entire city' (Yan, Zhang & Li, 2012).

A key feature of the festivals mentioned is the focus on food. Gastronomic tourism is increasing, and although it is not yet one of the niche markets for Malta's tourism offering, it can only be enhanced. Gastronomic tourism attracts travellers who are interested in the local cuisine, sampling authentic food and experiencing local ways of cooking, and learning about the whole process (Smith et al., 2010). Food is integral to the destination and its cultural heritage; for the tourist, it is an added attraction. The success of the various communal festivals held in Malta can be ascribed to the fact that food forms an important part of the whole activity, as it attracts locals and tourists alike.

One of the great success stories from the organisation of these events must surely be that of Vittoriosa. The first historical re-enactment event was held in 1995. The local inhabitants immediately took on board the importance of the festival for their locality and, without any prompting, started to take care of their immediate environment. Streets were kept cleaner, and a number of flower pots were installed in the narrow and medieval streets of the city. Although these were meant to last only for the duration of the festival, they are still there, having become a permanent feature.

In 2018 Valletta, the capital city of Malta, will be the European Capital of Culture. This means that a different mentality is required, with new concepts as regards festivals and events. It is also the reason for the regeneration of a number of areas (Raj et al., 2009) that have lagged behind in recent restoration work. Due to the small size of Malta, in 2018 it will not be just Valletta that will be the focus of activities, but rather the whole island. This will be an important boost for national pride. The Valletta 2018 team are aiming to include future generations in their cultural activities; establish and consolidate routes that are the hallmark of the vibrant small city of Valletta; be creative in the conservation of the past while looking at the contemporary scene; and emphasise the importance of the sea as part of national identity of Valletta and Malta (Anon., 2013).

Conclusions

Festivals and events are ingrained in the Maltese national character. Public festivities are an everyday occurrence in Malta, and they are well supported and liked. Given the opportunity to attract more locals and tourists alike to one's village and/or community, many local residents happily volunteer in the organisation of such events. This establishes communal pride within the locality and engenders a better understanding of and respect for one's heritage and traditions.

Authenticity is also part of the whole process. The small and community festivals that are organised by the small localities tend to be very authentic, as they would still be untainted by the tourist demand. Yet their success might also lead to a loss of this authenticity. It is necessary that visitors perceive the event as authentic and genuine (Smith et al., 2010), as otherwise there would be negative feedback. The organisation of festivals that would be geared mainly towards local consumption are usually the more authentic, and these also tend to be the activities that tourists appreciate more (Quinn, 2013).

In recent discourses about the future of tourism, it has been suggested that creativity needs to be the base on which future plans, activities, events and festivals are built. Tourists are bored with the usual products that are offered to them. What the modern tourist is looking for is authenticity, contact with the local community and engagement with the local culture (Richards, 2009). In the same paper Richards argues that rather than just selling the place, tourism can be used to support the identity of the local community, and thus offer and emphasise the local culture to the visitors.

In the recent past, Malta has managed to gear itself towards a more culturally minded tourist product. After the initial involvement of the central authorities, it is now more common to have local communities organising their own festivals, events and other cultural activities, sometimes without the help of the central authorities. More localities are taking the initiative to increase these kinds of activities within their local community and preserve their local traditions. This augurs well for the future of the tourism industry and in the appreciation of local culture.

Notes

1 A short YouTube video can be viewed at: http://youtu.be/X4zIU12xFNU (accessed 1 December 2013).

References

Anon. (2013). *Imagine 18.* Valletta: Valletta 2018 Foundation.

Cini, G. (11 June 2003) Talks with Church to promote religious tourism. *Times of Malta.* Retrieved 19 November 2013, from www.timesofmalta.com/articles/view/20030611/local/talks-with-church-to-promote-religious-tourism.148200#.UovjTqVwZjo.

Ghanafest – Malta Mediterranean Folk Music Festival. (2014). Retrieved 1 December 2013, from www.maltaculture.com/content.aspx?id=185291.

Gold, J.R. & Gold, M.M. (2005). *Cities of culture: Staging international festivals and the urban agenda, 1851–2000.* Aldershot: Ashgate.

Harris, D. (2009). *Key concepts in leisure studies.* London: Sage.

Isle of MTV Music festival Malta. (2014). Retrieved 1 December 2013, from www.isle-ofmtv.com/tv.

Karnival ta' Malta. (2014). Retrieved 1 December 2013, from www.maltaculture.com/content.aspx?id=185279.

Koperattiva Rurali Manikata. (2013). Retrieved 1 December 2013, from www.manikata-farmers.com/news_pumpkinfest2013.html.

Malta Arts Festival. (2014). Retrieved 1 December 2013, from www.maltaculture.com/content.aspx?id=185298.

Malta International Fireworks Festival. (2014). Retrieved 1 December 2013, from www.maltafireworksfestival.com.

Malta Jazz Festival. (2014). Retrieved 1 December 2013, from www.maltaculture.com/content.aspx?id=185294.

Notte Bianca. (2014). Retrieved 1 December 2013, from www.maltaculture.com/content.aspx?id=185301.

NSO. (2012). *Malta in figures 2012.* Malta: Government Printing Press.

Picard, D. & Robinson, M. (2006). Remaking worlds: Festivals, tourism and change. In D. Picard & M. Robinson (eds), *Festivals, tourism and social change: Remaking worlds.* Clevedon: Channel View Publications.

Quinn, B. (2013). *Key concepts in event management.* London: Sage.

Raj, R., Walters, P. & Tahir, R. (2009). *Events management: An integrated and practical approach.* London: Sage.

Richards, G. (2009). Creative tourism and local development. In R. Wurzburger, A. Pattakos & S. Pratt (eds), *Creative tourism: A global conversation* (pp. 78–90). Santa Fe, NM: Sunstone Press.

Smith, A. (2012). *Events and urban regeneration: The strategic use of events to revitalise cities.* London: Routledge.

Smith, M.K. (2009). *Issues in cultural tourism studies.* Abingdon: Routledge.

Smith, M.K., Macleod, N. & Hart Robertson, M. (2010). *Key concepts in tourism studies.* London: Sage.

Valletta International Baroque Festival. (2014). Retrieved 1 December 2013, from www. vallettabaroquefestival.com.mt.

Visit Malta. (n.d.). Retrieved 1 December 2013, from www.visitmalta.com/en/recurring-events.

Yan, Q., Zhang, H. & Li, M. (2012). Programming quality of festivals: Conceptualization, measurement, and relation to consequences. *International Journal of Contemporary Hospitality Management, 24*(4), 653–673.

Zammit, V. (2009). Holy Week at Zebbug (Malta): A cultural and religious experience. In A. Trono (ed.), *Tourism, religion and culture: Regional development through meaningful tourism experiences* (pp. 147–158). Lecce: Mario Congedo Publisher.

Zammit, V. (2013). Case study 3: Urban regeneration and culture – Maltese example. In R. Raj, K. Griffin & N. Morpeth (eds), *Cultural tourism* (pp. 129–139). Wallingford: CABI.

10 The importance of community events in nationalist oriented political environments

The case of the Portuguese *Estado Novo*

Cândida Cadavez

Introduction

> The parades, the festivities, the icons and the rituals are extremely necessary so that ideas remain alive … […] Poor are the ideas that are not lit…. They may be very beautiful and fair, but they will die unless there is a constant trigger bringing them back to life.
>
> (Ferro, 2007 [1932]: 221)

This chapter discusses the importance of community events in Portugal in the early years of the *Estado Novo*, between 1933 and 1940. It is argued that the new political regime deployed different sorts of community festivities and events with a twofold purpose. On the one hand, they served to gather the national population around more formal activities organized with the goal of teaching lessons about the so-called true essence of the 'Nation'; on the other hand, these community events were designed to convey to foreign audiences how Portugal remained a peaceful country where people could enjoy moments of leisure even while conflicts and wars were devastating Europe.

The Portuguese context: *Estado Novo*

Resulting from the establishment of a republican regime in 1910, Portugal underwent a period characterized by a variety of riots, rebellions and uprisings. Indeed, the 1926 National Revolution took as its justification the alleged need to re-establish the social order that had supposedly disappeared during the early years of the Republic. Two years later, António de Oliveira Salazar, who would later become the brain and the face of a new political regime, took office as the Minister of Finance. The year 1933 is broadly acknowledged as the beginning of the totalitarian and nationalist-oriented paradigm that would rule Portugal for the next decades until 1974, the *Estado Novo*.

Despite the *Estado Novo* displaying some of the characteristics of other contemporary European governments, adopting fascist and nationalist discourses, the Portuguese regime insisted on exhibiting itself as a different 'Nation'. So as to achieve that goal, two subjects were recurrently borrowed in order to shape different representations with the aim of portraying this 'new' Portuguese reality. In fact, most of these narratives focused on the idea of a unique Portuguese popular culture and a singular history.

Furthermore, and according to this new ideology, the true essence of the 'Nation' was to be found outside the big cities and in those rural communities where people had managed to retain the original national characteristics and therefore were subject to consideration as valid icons of religiosity, humbleness and hard work. Hence, the artefacts and rituals originating in those non-urban locations came in for high praise by the authorized voices of the *Estado Novo* and set up as good models to follow.

The second favourite subject was the 'Nation's' history, which would tell of heroic deeds performed by brave Portuguese characters. The beginning of Portugal, the era of discovery and exploration as well as independence from Spain would feed into all sorts of stories and re-enactments staged by community events and festivities.

As happened with other political paradigms of this time, propaganda proved a vital tool to the survival and stability of these regimes. In Portugal, propagandist mechanisms began spreading into and controlling ever more areas of society and therefore making recourse to every available tool so that the lessons of Salazar and his way of governing would become known and accepted both by the Portuguese population and internationally. Within this context, popular culture and history were the favourite sources of inspiration for the voices of propaganda to build narratives able to promote and validate the new regime.

As this chapter details, community events and festivities represented a perfect arena for gathering all sorts of audiences in activities that presented and praised the two preferred ideals of popular culture and national history. The regime adopted the organizing of these types of events with the purpose of creating informal and casual events that enabled the conveying of ideological lessons to participants who would mostly react uncritically to what was being portrayed as the true representation of the 'Nation'.

Ferro and the Portuguese propaganda system

The year 1932 was when Salazar was formally introduced to the 'Nation'. António Ferro carried this out in a set of five 'interviews' subsequently published in December of that year by the Portuguese daily newspaper *Diário de Notícias*. Ferro was a journalist and a writer whose main interests also included theatre, literature and politics. He had studied law and served as a government official in the colonies as well as being involved in several public activities and campaigns. However, what may well have drawn the attention of Salazar probably stemmed from Ferro having already published a book called *A Voyage around the Dictatorships*, including interviews with contemporary politicians such as Primo de Rivera and Mussolini, whose ideologies were held in great esteem by the Portuguese politician.

Salazar was apparently pleased with the outcome of the first five conversations he had with Ferro, which had been staged with the objective of informing the 'Nation' about the particularities of the new political paradigm under construction in Portugal. Issues such as censorship, the colonies, anti-parliamentary beliefs, comments about the 'authentic' groups in society and even the arts were extensively covered by the 'interviews'.

Hence, the 1933 nomination of António Ferro as head of the *Secretariado de Propaganda Nacional* (SPN) – National Bureau for Propaganda – did not really come as a surprise. Through to 1949, Ferro would serve as the main architect of the authorized representations of the 'Nation', which also included the organization of community and public events, a widely and deeply praised propaganda tool for exhibiting the supposed essence of the new 'Nation'. Decree number 23:054, dated 25 September 1933, explained the rationale behind this department, perceived as a humble Portuguese version of those ministries of propaganda already existing at the time in other countries. The decree also stated that such a bureau had to prove effective enough to rally the Portuguese population around the moral creeds henceforth deemed to constitute the values of the 'Nation'. This same decree highlighted an apparently urgent need to organize and monitor internal and external Portuguese propaganda, as was then being undertaken by other European regimes, as well as ruling on how public festivities and national and international exhibitions would be organized and staged and thereby implicitly acknowledged as valuable means of both education and propaganda.

The importance of community events and festivities to the regime

In one of his last speeches as the Bureau of Propaganda director, before embarking on a brief diplomatic career in 1949, António Ferro recalled how impressed he had felt when, as a young boy, he participated in public events and festivities taking place in Lisbon. Those were his favourite popular haunts where he would encounter real outbursts of popular happiness and simplicity (Ferro, 1950, p. 9).

António Ferro justified the setting up of the People's Theatre, the touring cinema and all sorts of popular and community activities and events as a strategy to implement the Policy of Spirit. He explained this expression, which would underpin his initiatives as Bureau director, as stemming from an urgent need to consider literature and the arts as important assets to Portuguese society, deserving meaningful protection and official support and attention. These areas represented the favoured ways of exhibiting this authentic essence of the new 'Nation'.

Recreation centres were acknowledged by Ferro as an important means not only to define the best and most natural and spontaneous feelings of the 'Nation' but also to boost Portuguese popular culture and to consolidate national tranquillity and peace (Ferro, 1950, p. 12). Ferro did actually believe that recreation centres represented the spiritual activities of Portugal as well as its prevailing good mood and humour (Ferro, 1950, p. 13). Hence, among others, those centres were to organize popular shows, visits to museums, churches and other monuments, excursions or physical and sporting activities and contests.

Lisbon's Popular Festivities, which still take place in June, were one of the preferred community events held in Portugal's capital city. The festivities were mainly composed of parades and outdoor country dances. *Diário de Notícias* stated in June 1932 that these events were meant 'to cheer the city up and to evoke popular traditions, and should be a task put into practice by those encharged with supervising the national social life' (*Diário de Notícias*, 6 June 1932, p. 1). In that same year, the Parque Mayer management board decided that there should be some outdoor popular activity as part of the schedule of Lisbon's Popular Festivities. This is a neighbourhood located on Avenida da Liberdade, in central Lisbon, where most of the city's vaudeville plays are still performed. As such, Parque Mayer and Leitão de Barros, a film director who had worked with Ferro, decided to invite some recreation centres to participate in a parade that would walk and dance along central Lisbon's Avenida da Liberdade while wearing rural costumes and to the sounds of popular music.

Diario de Lisboa, another contemporary newspaper, stated that this sort of festivity had to aggregate as many national icons as possible and also added that the parade had been a patriotic initiative (*Diario de Lisboa*, 17 June 1935, p. 1). The first popular parades were so warmly welcomed by the population that from 1934 onwards, the City Hall of Lisbon took charge of all the necessary arrangements and promotion. As Daniel de Melo argues, 'the political powers adopted this cultural event and adapted it to their historicist, traditionalist and rural ideology' (de Melo, 1997, p. 300).

In turn, the *Fundação Nacional para a Alegria no Trabalho/FNAT* (National Foundation for Joy at Work) was set up in 1935 and also proved to be an important promoter of community and popular events and festivities. This was a poorer and less ambitious version of similar organizations then existing in Italy and Germany, and whose main purpose was to enable the regimes to organize and structure the free time of workers. A 1935 decree implemented FNAT based on an officially announced need to care for the physical and psychological well-being of the poorest social classes, otherwise unable to afford proper leisure or education. For several decades, FNAT would serve as another surreptitious but effective propaganda tool for spreading new Portuguese values. Excursions and tours would be carefully prepared so that participants gained the opportunity to become acquainted with meaningful locations within the particular ideological framework of the *Estado Novo*. Thus, visitors would preferably travel to iconic Guimarães (a symbol of the birthplace of the Portuguese national identity), Alcobaça (intimately linked with the founding of the Portuguese monarchy and the place where Afonso Henriques was proclaimed king) or Batalha (a monastery built to commemorate the victory of the Portuguese over the Castilians at the Battle of Aljubarrota in 1385). Other favourite activities run by FNAT included visits to public exhibitions of popular culture, artefacts or practices and correspondingly consisted of visits to museums or watching musical parades or similar.

Furthermore, Vala Roberto argues that the Portuguese government of Salazar was clearly a promoter of public festivities dedicated to both nationals and foreigners (Roberto, 2010, p. 42). Anticipating this argument, Ann Bridge and Susan Lowndes, two British visitors to Portugal in the 1940s, stated that the country seemed always to have a reason for celebration and merrymaking (Bridge & Lowndes, 2008, p. 5).

The 1940 Portuguese World Exhibition

As was also then happening in other countries, national and international fairs and exhibitions served as valid tools for representing nations through an apparently casual gathering together of their populations. From the 1933 implementation of the *Estado Novo* through to 1940, Portugal organized and participated in several such events, testifying to how they became a particular favourite of the regime. These events were dedicated to the national community that was correspondingly expected to acknowledge them as moments for exalting, cheering and praising national Portuguese characteristics and virtues. The press would thoroughly cover these fairs and exhibitions, to which the entire population was invited to visit and participate. The 1934 Colonial Fair in Oporto, for example, was mentioned and recommended at every Sunday mass service.

Standing out from the other, whether smaller or larger, similar events happening at the outset of the *Estado Novo*, was the Portuguese World Exhibition, a mega community event that took place in Lisbon and was the iconic moment in the 1940 anniversary commemorations of the nation's foundation and restoration. The six-month celebrations called for a nationwide movement requiring the involvement of the entire population. While much of the rest of the world was engaged in severe conflicts and wars, Salazar was preparing his 'Nation' for a major community event aimed at praising the particularities of a regime that had managed to steer Portugal away from a similar fate.

Different sorts of public infrastructure were built, such as roads, hotels or entire neighbourhoods, and many others, including monuments, museums and even the National Parliament, were restored in order to prepare the 'Nation' to be the perfect stage for hosting these festivities. The organization of the festivities began in 1938 and its thorough planning programme extended to the means necessary to invite/force the population to participate actively in them. The capital launched a public transport network with many excursions held throughout the six months so the entire 'Nation' had the opportunity to attend the Lisbon exhibition.

The Exhibition of the Portuguese World was located in one of Lisbon's most symbolic neighbourhoods, by the riverside in Junqueira, where two monuments dedicated to the Portuguese Renaissance Discoveries are located, Belém Tower and the Monastery of Jerónimos. The vicinities underwent dramatic conversion so the premises occupied were able to host several buildings and exhibition areas that were to display evidence of the underlying justification for Salazar's ideology, i.e. popular culture and echoes of past allegedly heroic deeds from

Portuguese history. Thus, Junqueira became transformed into a representation of the entire Portuguese empire, ranging from its European extent to its African and Asian colonial territories. Small villages were built to serve as stages for 'real communities', temporarily relocated from their home towns to Lisbon, who lived out their daily professional and social routines as if back in their home communities whether in the north of Portugal or in Africa. In addition to the other permanent settings, different types of activities were held daily from June to December and included parades, historical re-enactments and folk music and dance performances.

The Bureau of National Propaganda and António Ferro played a key role not only in the promotion but also in the a priori acknowledged success of this mega community event. Even while the official government intention did not extend to attracting foreign visitors, its guidelines referred to the importance of preparing a warm welcome for those visiting peaceful Portugal. Thus, *Casas de Portugal* staged a massive campaign inviting Europeans to contemplate this majestic event gathering together the whole Portuguese community and occurring at a time when other peoples were in great suffering because of a brutal war. *Casas de Portugal* referred to delegations from the Bureau for National Propaganda. The most active *Casas* were those in Paris and Antwerp and provided all sorts of information about Portugal as a tourism destination and organized cultural events.

As Ferro stated four months before the opening of the exhibition, the event would convince the entire international community that Portugal was then the 'lighthouse of Europe' (Ferro, n.d., p. 8), thereby stressing how the organization of the commemorations had taken on a strong ideological purpose targeting not only nationals but also foreigners. One month before the end of the celebrations, the director of the Bureau for National Propaganda highlighted how the event grew out of a community effort filled with spirituality, love and enthusiasm (Ferro, 1940). On another occasion, when giving a speech entitled 'Lessons from the Double Centenary', he added that the Portuguese population had been the entity responsible for the Portuguese World Exhibition (Ferro, 1941, p. 5). The same document argued that foreign visitors had considered the event as the best they had ever attended before emphasizing how the European conflict had allowed that Portuguese community festivity to shine even brighter (Ferro, 1941, p. 1).

As expected, the official regime voices heard through the newspapers, for example, heralded how much national and international visitors had supposedly learned from the Portuguese World Exhibition and how much the whole 'Nation' had been involved.

Conclusions

> The popular joy is like running water.
> You cannot either command or organize it.

(Ferro, 1950, p. 11)

But why would community events and festivities be such a favoured propaganda tool for a regime like Salazar's? From an ideological and propagandist point of view, these activities represented a preferred means of informally imposing feelings of happiness upon the Portuguese population. The whole 'Nation' would thereby learn about the features of an old, authentic country and be grateful for a political leader who had spared Portugal from severe conflicts. Besides, as António Ferro uttered on behalf of the regime, those community events allowed different layers of society to mingle in joyful, natural and simple moments, as had happened during the 4th International Congress of Theatre and Music Criticism, in 1931 (Ferro, 1950, p. 11).

Furthermore, foreigners witnessing those events and the way the national community participated in them were to understand the singularity and uniqueness of a 'Nation' carefully protected from evil and that enabled its celebrations even while the rest of the world suffered.

Propaganda lives on in the most diverse strategies as long as it continues to prove its efficacy, preferably in surreptitious forms. Community events certainly do still represent casual and informal moments in which groups gather and are open to uncritically accepting disguised and hard-to-identify ideological messages.

References

Bridge, A. & Lowndes, S. (2008). *Duas Inglesas em Portugal: Uma Viagem pelo Portugal dos Anos 40*. Transl. Jorge Almeida e Pinho. Lisbon: Quidnovi Viagens. (Original work published 1949)

de Melo, D. (1997). *Salazarismo e Cultura Popular (1933–1958)*. Dissertação final de Mestrado em História dos Séculos XIX e XX (secção séc. XX). Faculdade de Ciências Sociais e Humanas, Universidade Nova de Lisboa.

Ferro, A. (1940). Fundação António Quadros, Caixote 015B, Envelope XV.

Ferro, A. (1941). 'A Lição dos Centenários'. Fundação António Quadros, Caixote 016, Crónicas, Artigos AF.

Ferro, A. (1950). *Sociedades de Recreio: Política do Espírito*. Lisbon: Edições SNI. (Original work published 1949)

Ferro, A. (2007). A Política do Espírito. In A. Ferro, *Entrevistas a Salazar* (pp. 225–229). Lisbon: Parceria A.M. Pereia. (Original work published 1932)

Ferro, A. (n.d.) 'Faltam quatro mêses…'. Fundação António Quadros, Caixote 016, Crónicas, Artigos AF.

Roberto, J.V. (2010). *Anos 30: Um Estado Novo em Portugal*. S/l: Editora Planeta DeAgostini, S.A.

Newspapers

Diario de Lisboa, 17 June 1935. Year 15. No. 4526.
Diário de Notícias, 6 June 1932. Year 68. No. 23815.

Legislation

Decree number 23:054, dated 25 September 1933.

11 'Something greater than the sum of its parts'

Narratives of sense of place at a community multicultural festival

Kelley A. McClinchey

Introduction

Exploratory studies have concluded that festivals can contribute to sense of place and community (e.g. De Bres & Davis, 2001; Derrett, 2003; Quinn, 2003) but how festivals contribute, for whom, and to what degree are deeper questions that need attention. Little is known about community cultural festivals in multi-ethnic urban areas and cross-cultural differences have not been studied systematically (Getz, 2007, 2010). While community festival researchers have analysed perspectives of community residents, festival visitors, and festival organizers (Gursoy, Kim, & Uysal, 2004; Nicholson & Pearce, 2001), little attention has been paid to festival exhibitors, especially the non-profit exhibitors whose motivation for participation goes beyond economic gain (Mosely & Mowatt, 2011). The purpose of this chapter is to investigate how festival exhibitors perceive a sense of place and whether a community multicultural festival contributes to these perceptions.

Place meanings and community festivals

Community festivals' contribution to place-making, place marketing and urban regeneration is well documented but the exploration of sense of place, its complexity, and its connection to festivals is only just emerging. Much of the research involving festivals relates to place marketing, destination image, and place promotion (e.g. Schöllmann, Perkins, & Moore, 2000; Snepenger, Murphy, Snepenger, & Anderson, 2004; Williams, Gill, & Chura, 2004; Young, 1999). While these studies make a valid contribution to the study of place as it relates to these topics, little is known about the complex meanings of place and how they are impacted by festivals specifically.

Much of the research that does exist is exploratory and any detailed examination of the concept of sense of place is limited. A study by De Bres and Davis (2001) examined group and place identity of a regional festival in Kansas. While not specifically defining or investigating place meanings, De Bres and Davis discovered that commoditization of culture through tourism and festivals may lead to cultural misrepresentation. However, they do see this as a minor issue compared with the benefits to sense of place and community. Similarly, Quinn (2003) examined place identity in connection to the Wexford Festival Opera in Wexford, Ireland. Quinn argued that there is a need to deepen our understanding of the interconnections between festival-tourism activity and the social and cultural contexts within which it takes place. Derrett (2003), in a case study of four cultural festivals in Australia, explored sense of place as it relates specifically to tourism, community involvement, and a sense of community. Derrett used a historical perspective of a floral festival, hemp festival, beef festival, and a New Year's Eve celebration as well as stories from individuals and groups to provide testimony. She concluded that community cultural festivals can be shown to provide a sense of place for residents and increase their sense of community by offering connections, belonging, support, empowerment, and participation. Derrett, recognizing the explorative nature of the study, commented on the need for more empirical research on festivals and sense of place.

A gap also exists in the research on understanding the role multicultural festivals play in contributing to place meanings in general and with regard to exhibitors or visitors of multi-ethnic backgrounds specifically. Although not addressing meanings of place directly, Shukla (1997) discussed the production of Indian ethnicity in the United States through a close examination of the Cultural Festival of India, an event that took place in New Jersey during 1991. The festival presented a general and extravagant vision of India for Indian as well as non-Indian Americans and was seen as a type of 'imagined community' for members of the Indian diaspora (Shukla, 1997). On the other hand, Chessell (2002) explored the role of Italian festivals in Australia's outdoor Mediterranean-style public spaces in authenticating a cosmopolitan sense of place. While not specifically defining a sense of place or examining it in detail, Chessell discussed these places of 'imagination' through data concerning people's experiences of places of ethnic difference, attendance patterns, geographic dispersal, and identification with Little Italy (Chessell, 2002).

Because multicultural festivals occur in communities with high proportions of immigrants, socio-political processes may impact perceptions of the festival and senses of place. Again, while not specifically analysing sense of place, Jeong and Santos's (2004) study discussed the conflicts that exist among globalization, tradition, and place identity with regard to the Kangnung Dano festival in Korea. The authors suggested that festivals can act as political instruments and promotional products reconstructing regional identities due to contested meanings of place. Louie (2000) also explored relationships between identity and mobility in terms of an ethnic festival. Louie's exploration called into question the underlying existence of a shared Chinese identity and whether the festival created a better understanding of place. In another case, Chacko (2009) compared and contrasted the politics of identity and the spaces and places where ethnic group-specific festivals such as Chinese New Year and the Ethiopian New Year (Inqutatash) are celebrated in Washington, DC. Chacko (2009) suggested that festivals can be bridging events that underscore home and host cultures and identities. Immigrants use memory and traditions from the home country in conjunction with American practices to mark festival spaces as simultaneously ethnic and American places. These studies discussed place meanings as a social benefit of community events but sense of place perceptions were not examined specifically. There has yet to be any research on the sense of place perceptions of multi-ethnic festival exhibitors and how a multicultural festival contributes to these meanings.

Community cultural festivals offer those of other cultural backgrounds a glimpse into the lifestyles and traditions of ethnic culture. Traditional festivals in Asian cities offer a reassuring presence for various migrant groups who fashioned hybrid social/cultural identities while also providing opportunities to forge new conceptions of place and self-identity (Chang, 2005). While several academic studies have acknowledged place meanings such as place identity, attachment, and sense of place in relation to community and ethnic festivals, research thus far has been exploratory. Investigating sense of place perceptions and the role of festivals in contributing to sense of place deserves explicit attention. A more thorough examination of sense of place and its application to urban community experiences from other literature is needed.

Sense of place

While sense of place is perceived as a broad and holistic concept (Butz & Eyles, 1997; Hay, 1998a; Hummon, 1992; Manzo, 2005), there is some question about how it relates to other concepts such as place attachment and place identity (Manzo, 2005). Sense of place has been compartmentalized into measurable dimensions such as place identity, attachment, and dependence (using different places in our everyday experiences) (Jorgensen & Stedman, 2006). Place attachment is an emotional bond or affective bond that develops between people and places at both the individual and community level on a daily basis (Altman & Low, 1992; Hidalgo & Hernandez, 2001). Place identity, on the other hand, is the contribution of places to one's self-identity – self-identity being rooted in many facets of everyday life (Hull, Lam, & Vigo, 1994). The relationship among these three concepts garners much attention in terms of understanding how we derive meaning from places, how we interact with place, and how these phenomena can be measured. Sense of place, therefore, may be about more than definable and measurable constructs and more comprehensive such as is perceived through the term a *sense of place*.

The symbolic, emotional attachment and personal and social identity people have with places is a phenomenon that geographers have understood for some time and it continues to interest researchers from a variety of disciplines. In particular, Relph (1976) devised various notions of 'insiderness' and 'outsiderness' based on people's level of experience with place. Insiders feel at one with a place and have deep experiences with place whereas outsiders feel alienated or perceive place as little more than the background or setting for activities. Relph defined a sense of place as originating from lived experience, understanding the intangible essence of a place, experiencing place as an insider. Tuan (1980) perceived that an individual develops a sense of place by knowing the place intimately and reacts to it emotionally; the place becomes significant to the individual. Steele (1981) discussed how sense of place is the particular experience of a person in a particular setting (feeling stimulated, excited, joyous, and so on); reactions that are brought forth by the features of the setting and aspects the person brings with it. However, Tuan (1980) differentiated sense of place, which is a conscious experience, from 'rootedness', which is an unconscious experience. He described how sense of place can be achieved and maintained but rootedness cannot: one must have lived in a place for a long time. Hummon (1992) suggested that sense of place involves both an interpretive perspective on the environment and an emotional reaction to it.

These emotional reactions to place centre on how places connect us with our senses. Lynch (1976) explained how we use patterns of sensations to understand the *quality of a place*. Lynch described quality of place as how we see, feel, smell and hear, and use these sensory cues. These are important affective and cognitive components of the physical space and are referred to as sensual geographies (Rodaway, 1994). Rodaway explored in great detail how the use of our senses through perception of the world aids our understanding of geographical experience at individual and social levels, in different historical, cultural, and technological contexts. Rodaway referred to the duality and ambiguity in the concept of 'sense', as in 'making sense' which refers to order and understanding and 'the senses' which refers to the sense modes – touch, smell, taste, sight, and hearing. What are the ways that community festivals influence our sense of place and to what degree?

Sense of place in urban space

There has been a lot of research on how individuals establish sense of place in urban areas. Several different methods have been applied to investigate these perceptions. A major focus in empirical analysis is on exploring how individuals and groups establish place meanings. Sense of place can be influenced by ecological (physical landscape), social (relationships with others), and ideological (prevailing social and economic systems) elements (Eyles, 1985). Through a case study analysis of Towcester, England, Eyles devised 10 sense of place categories including social, apathetic-acquiescent, instrumental, nostalgic, commodity, platform/stage, family, way of life, roots, and environmental. For example, individuals with a social sense of place regard the place where they reside as important because it facilitates relationships with family and friends, whereas a nostalgic sense of place is the product of recalling past sentiments related to place. An instrumental sense of place is when individuals find meaning in the place as it offers them amenities such as shops and employment opportunities and an environmental sense of place is when people find personal connections to the physical environment. In a later study, Butz and Eyles (1997) compared the senses of place experienced in Towcester to those in Shimshal, Pakistan. An ecological sense of place existed in Shimshal and not in Towcester, likely because the small agricultural community found a closer relationship with the natural environment than did residents in Towcester.

Findings from both case studies revealed that sense of place is the product of social interaction mediated through individual subjectivities, and an individual's sense of place is unlikely to be stable or unitary (Butz & Eyles, 1997).

Shamai and Ilatov (2005) also discussed the concept of sense of place as being a combination of the physical (environmental) and social (as well as personal) interactions in a place. The sense of place of Israeli-born and immigrant groups living in Israel were measured using a uni-dimensional scale that would try to capture the concept in a direct and straightforward way (Shamai & Ilatov, 2005). This study showed that most respondents in both groups had similar patterns of positive feelings towards the place where they live. Shamai and Ilatov (2005) argued that a more complicated measurement scale for such a complex concept may not be the answer. It is further suggested that the measure of sense of place be tailored to each case and that the variety of methodological tools are only an advantage that widens the scope of sense of place.

While measurement scales and quantitative analysis on sense of place dimensions are important, other studies in urban geography applied qualitative methodologies to analyse sense of place. For example, Billig (2005) applied an ethnographic analysis of women living in six new developments to identify the behavioural and affective variables that make up local sense of place. Hargreaves (2004) examined sense of place by analysing survey respondents and identifying the social narratives, symbols, and concepts informing their view of place. 'Local narratives tell us less about "history" and more about how people construct their sense of place and cultural identity' (Bird, 2002, p. 519). Hargreaves (2004) discovered that communities with an awareness of place exhibit habitual patterns of movement around familiar and significant objects in the construction of both individual and social identity which in turn produces a more positive sense of place.

Phenomenology and ethnography are used to analyse sense of place to provide a rich understanding of complex phenomena that are not easily interpreted through objective measurement (Relph, 1976). An analysis of Cowichan Valley residents' mental maps on Vancouver Island showed that residents also defined their place largely by the valley's topography and regular trips within the valley (Hay, 1986 in Hay, 1998b). Research on residents' sense of place is continued by Hay (1998a, 1998b) through a cross-cultural focus on Maori and European-descent respondents in New Zealand. Hay (1998a) uses three contexts – residential status in the place, age stage, and development of the adult pair bond – to examine the development of sense of place. Social survey methods showed trends across the sample using descriptive statistics while the methods of phenomenology and ethnography enabled a more intuitive, reflective assessment. Residential status and social belonging were identified as important towards an increased intensity of sense of place (Hay, 1998b). Interactions were found among place and pair bonds (marriage); however, a stronger sense of place was most evident among those who were raised in the place and had spent most of their lives there (Hay, 1998a).

Socio-demographic and political variables are also factors that have been shown to impact a sense of place. Taylor and Townsend (1976) explored the sense of place perceptions of residents within four towns in England. It was found that the extent of experience (i.e. length of residence) that an individual had with the particular place influenced their perception of place. For example, those over the age of 65 expressed a stronger sense of place. As well, Garcia-Ramon, Ortiz, and Prats (2004) discovered weak senses of place of a common public space through the perceptions of three groups of women (non-immigrants, European immigrants, and non-European immigrants) living in Barcelona, Spain. Changes existed over time with regard to the local women's senses of place due in part to the influx of immigrants into the area.

'Sense of place is not *an* or *the* authentic quality of a place waiting to be recognized by the more observant among us, but a social construction perpetrated by someone or some group with a particular interest' (Williams, 2002 p. 354). Even though some scholars question the level at which sense of place is a social construction (e.g. Stedman, 2003; Williams, 2002), others are determined to explore how power relations impact individual's and group's senses of place especially in urban space (e.g. Keogan, 2002; Manzo, 2005; Twigger-Ross & Uzzell, 1996; Becker, 2003). Becker suggested that a combination of political dimensions including social relations, class, gender, race as well as geographic and historic circumstances influence emotional experiences with place.

Similarly, Manzo (2005) utilized a grounded theory approach to the in-depth interviewing of 40 residents of New York City in order to address a range of specific variables such as sex, race, ethnicity, marital status, parenthood status, sexual orientation, income, and residential mobility and account for the holistic sense of both the positive and negative meanings associated with different places.

Even though Manzo (2005) investigated place identity, she also related the socio-political underpinnings of our emotional relationships to places, particularly the impact of gender, race, class, and sexuality. For some, the metaphor of home aptly fits their experience of connection, stability, and belonging. For others, the metaphor of journeying may be more useful as people's stories about significant places in their lives describe their particular journey in the world, as important and meaningful places can act as symbolic milestones in their life journey (Manzo, 2005).

Mazanti and Ploger (2003) focused on the political symbolic construction of place (outside understanding/construction) and urban residents' social construction of place (inside understanding/construction). Mazanti and Ploger suggested that a sense of place can be seen as being related to the individual experiences as well as the collective experiences and memories tied to places people have lived in as well as to other places. The analysis reveals how urban residents, even those seeming to live in deprived urban neighbourhoods, create meaningful place identities, conceive their place of residence, and use their place in everyday life (Mazanti & Ploger, 2003). Everyday experiences of a place are what often signify a difference between an 'insider' understanding of a place and an 'outsider' understanding of a place. It is important to acknowledge these deeper understandings of sense of place as a social as well as a cultural construction and the multiple dimensions that influence an individual's overall sense of place.

Sense of place is a concept that, according to the research discussed here, can be examined through complex multi-dimensional constructs or through simply analysing it holistically, thereby deciphering its many components. The in-depth research on sense of place from multiple discipline areas such as urban studies, environmental psychology, and ethnic and racial studies can be a valuable contribution to the investigation of sense of place in the context of community cultural festivals. Community festival studies would benefit from embracing stronger conceptual understandings in order to determine how, and for whom, festivals contribute to sense of place. This chapter demonstrates how some of these methodological and conceptual contributions can be applied to a multicultural festival in downtown Kitchener, Canada.

Method

The Multicultural Festival in Kitchener is one of many festivals and special events established in 1967 to mark and celebrate Canada's Centennial. It is a two-day festival occurring on the third weekend in June for the past 44 years and is located in Victoria Park, a public park in downtown Kitchener. The festival is an open-gate festival and attracts day visitors to the downtown core from the surrounding region. There are four components to the festival: international cuisine, traditional folksong and dance, artefacts for sale from around the globe in an international marketplace, and community participation.

Personal interviews with not-for-profit ethno-cultural/community group leaders provided an in-depth analysis allowing rich descriptions and experiences to emerge (Chacko & Schaffer, 1993; Fredline & Faulkner, 2000; Higham & Ritchie, 2001). A total of 25 out of 33 key informants agreed to participate in the interview. Semi-structured and open-ended questions guided festival exhibitors in their story-telling and allowed respondents to answer in their own terms regarding festival perceptions, senses of place, and return travel to countries of origin (Table 11.1) (Bailey, 2000; Basch et al., 1994; Bryman, 2001; Gustafson, 2001; Hay, 1998b; Hidalgo & Hernandez, 2001; Jorgensen & Stedman, 2006; Manzo, 2005; Mazanti & Ploger, 2003; Mountz & Wright, 1996; Quinn, 2003; Schöllmann et al., 2000; Shamai & Ilatov, 2005; Werbner, 1999; Young, 1999). Data were synthesized into themes both by the frequency of representative phrases and by interpreting the values, meanings, and experiences of the stories as shared. Narratives have the potential to help researchers understand what

Table 11.1 Questions relating to sense of place

- What do you think it means to have a 'sense of place'?
- Do you think the festival plays a role in contributing to a sense of place? If so, how?
- Do you feel you have a sense of place for any place(s) in particular? Of which place (s)? Why?
- Are there any (other) place(s) that are meaningful to you? If so, which place(s)? What makes them meaningful?

---

festivals mean to ethnically diverse individuals in relation to their lived experiences (Glover, 2004). Sequential, systematic coding in all qualitative data analysis is the pivotal link between collecting data and developing an emergent theory to explain data (Charmaz, 2009; Glaser & Strauss, 1967). The organization and subsequent analysis was performed with the assistance of NVivo 8 software. Names of key informants were changed to protect anonymity.

Festival exhibitors' sense of place

Through qualitative coding of the responses to the above questions the following themes emerged explaining what festival exhibitors perceived is the meaning of a sense of place. There were 43 total excerpts searched in NVivo for relevant themes.

Belonging

Several of the respondents perceived that a sense of place meant a *sense of belonging*, a *place to belong* or where *you feel you belong*. Sandra, a school teacher and Scottish dance instructor explained: *To feel that you belong, that you're valued, that you have something to contribute.* Andrea also explains how her work gives her a sense of place: *my work, for 31 years, I feel like I belong there.*

Festival exhibitors perceived a sense of place as being connected with the themes of *belonging* and *identity* which was further conceptualized through the themes of *attachment, duality of place, roots/origins/back home* and *rootedness/like home/comfortable.* Holloway and Hubbard (2001) commented that generally people attach meanings to place, feel a sense of belonging to place and that place plays an important role in the formation of our identities. Hargreaves (2004) also referred to sense of place as a feeling of belonging. This sense of belonging related to what Relph (1976) described as insiders feeling at one with a place and having deep experiences with place as well as the intangible essences of a place. These respondents had a sense of place for places they experienced as an insider. As the festival exhibitors described why they found certain places meaningful their comments related to knowing the places intimately and reacting to

Table 11.2 Meanings of a sense of place

Meanings of a sense of place	Frequency	(%)
Belonging	8	19
Identity	7	16
Attachment	6	14
Dual identity, duality of place	6	14
Roots, Origins, Back home	5	12
Rooted, Like 'home', Feeling comfortable	4	9
Difficult to articulate		

them emotionally (Tuan, 1980). As Steele (1981) discussed, sense of place is the experience of a person in a particular setting (feeling stimulated, excited, joyous) and the reactions brought forth by the features of the aspects of the setting.

Attachment

Places were also meaningful because festival exhibitors identified with the place by feelings of attachment. Twigger-Ross and Uzzell (1996) discovered that those that were not attached to the Docklands neighbourhood in London were more attached to some other place. Hidalgo and Hernandez (2001) found in their study that social attachment was more important than physical attachment; however, in this study respondents identified with places both socially and physically. These connections to the physical and social environment of a place compare with Eyles' (1985) typology of senses of place and Shamai and Ilatov's (2005) definition of a sense of place. Eyles (1985) categorized sense of place into 10 categories. Sandra very quickly mentioned her attachment to out west and could describe some aspects of why she finds it meaningful but it was personal. She found it difficult to really explain why:

> Out west in Saskatoon. I do really miss it. A sense of, well, I feel good in wide open spaces, I have a strong attachment to the west. I don't know why, well, maybe because when I lived there, my friends were nice to me, there was fresh air and sunshine and open spaces. I've lived in Waterloo for many years but I am not attached to the city.

Karen, who very clearly understood the term, found it difficult to articulate how she finds meaning in places:

> The places that have meaning to me and that I can relate to also have a sense of place. My next door neighbour continues to visit New York City for the same reasons. She also says that NYC 'has a heartbeat'. I find it fascinating that she longs to experience this, but continues to live in a bland suburb where you can't really walk to much of anything. I have struggled to verbalize the difference for me between living in Milwaukee and living here, but my friend who moved from Kitchener to Vancouver recently nailed it on the head. She said in relation to her experience now living in Vancouver that she feels like she is 'part of something greater than the sum of its parts'. She did not feel this living in Kitchener, even though she was quite an active member of the community. I felt the same way living in Milwaukee, and have lost that living here.

Much like what Manzo (2005) discovered in her study on residents of New York City, the places festival exhibitors found meaningful were not extraordinary but were places where they had strong feelings of belonging, identity, and attachment. Few respondents talked about their neighbourhoods and only a few mentioned the city. But more importantly, references to particular places were holistic such as Croatia, Turkey, Canada, Jamaica, and Australia. Hidalgo and Hernandez (2001) found that residents were more attached to the city or house as opposed to the neighbourhood. Hernandez, Hidalgo, Salazar-Laplace, and Hess (2007) suggested that it is because the neighbourhood lacks symbolism while the city is heavily charged with content and meaning. In contrast, natives born in the Canary Islands showed more intense links with the island and the city rather than the neighbourhood and more so than non-natives. Moreover, the concept of a clearly defined region such as a country with borders to differenti-ate it from nearby places enables us to experience a sense of place and have a place identity. Residents or those rooted in place may have a stronger place attachment and identity (Hay, 1998b; Tuan, 1980). Hay (1998a) and Taylor and Townsend (1976) concluded that length of residency is an important factor in determining a stronger sense of place due being rooted in that place.

Roots, origins, back home

The concept of 'roots' or feeling 'rooted' related to identity but in the context of being connected to one's country of origin. This may have been felt through an actual physical connection or a place that made one feel like they were going back home, like with Andrea and the German club she belongs to, *The — Club. It's my heritage and my culture, my parents belong and this feels I've connected to my German heritage and roots – Like I have left but gone back.* Social net-works and personal histories also contribute to stronger senses of place. Second, festival exhibitors were rooted in their country of origin or had a sense of place for 'back home' because of the deep emotional experiences associated with it. Tuan (1977) differentiated sense of place which is conscious experience from rootedness which is an unconscious experience. He described how sense of place can be achieved and maintained but rootedness cannot, one must have lived in a place for a long time and become deeply ingrained within that place.

In these particular narratives, it was less about length of residency and more about memory, emotion, and personal connection that led festival exhibitors to base their sense of place on needing to connect with one's roots. Eyles (1985) referred to this as nostalgic sense of place, which is the recalling of past senti-ments related to place. However, nostalgia is sometimes perceived in a negative connotation as one may be remembering a place during a mythical time or as it once used to be. But this is not the case in these respondents' experiences. Their senses of place and connecting to one's origins, roots, or to back home were deep, emotional, personal, individual, and at times difficult to articulate. The theme of *difficult to articulate* in trying to answer why someone has a sense of place for a particular place was felt by others as well. Clearly, people know they are attached to a particular place, but they may not know why. They simply say 'it is part of who I am' or 'it is who I am'.

When I asked Sonia from Jamaica if she had heard of the term or knew what it meant, she did *not really know it*. But after I explained the commonly held definition of the term, she then described that she had a sense of place for specific places:

> Yes, home, back home; even though I've lived here longer than I have lived in Jamaica. Home will always be Jamaica. I'll tell you why. Here I'll never be me but when I return home I always feel I am who I am [pauses]. I can be me. [pauses] No one can take it away. [pauses] I can't really explain it, it's too deep [pauses] I mean, I hope that's good, it's just – too deep. [and] ... Canada – I've spent most of my years here. Kitchener, it's beautiful, I love Kitchener. I've lived in Waterloo before but yeah I like Kitchener. It's comfortable living in the community.

Albert, originally from Zimbabwe, perceived a sense of place to be about *belonging*, because *it enables newcomers and immigrants to fulfil two homes to remind them about life.* This understanding is best described by his personal narrative for how he finds meaning in a few different places:

> Yes – related to Texas – it reminded me more of Africa than anywhere, I could talk to everyone. It is where I got my hat that reminds me of a South African hat [he has worn the hat to the interview but has removed it out of polite courtesy as we are inside a coffee shop]. It was a wealthy area with cattle and horses. In KW I have a strong connection with the religious group it was a stronger factor in having a sense of place. I am able to connect with the 'white mothers' – is what the women in the religious group are called – I feel at home here. I think it is because they show similarities of what you know, where your origins are based, what in it is the cultural attraction that gives you a sense of belonging and sense of pride? For Africa – it is where my origins are based.

Rooted, like home, feeling comfortable

Another theme that emerged related to this concept of being rooted. It coincided with one's 'roots' but in a different way. This concept of being rooted had to do with feeling comfortable, meaning if someone either spent a lot of time in a place or had lots of family and friends then they felt more rooted to that place and thus more comfortable. Peter, who has lived in the KW region his whole life, is rooted to KW:

> A place to feel safe, probably a place, where there is more understanding and people are accepting of some differences. Definitely, Kitchener-Waterloo – I was born here and lived here my whole life. My kids and grand kids are here. I worked in the community. I went to UW.

In this particular study, home was an important theme but it emerged in two very different contexts. In one, home was perceived as having a sense of place for one's origins, roots, and being 'back home' in the country of origin. In the other, it is perceived as a sense of place for a place that is comfortable, a place to be rooted for a long time or with family and friends, being 'home'. Tuan (1980) suggested that rootedness, an unconscious experience, was different than a sense of place, a conscious experience. However, the perceptions of these respondents brought to light that even the concept of being 'rooted' has multiple meanings. Manzo (2005), through interviews with New Yorkers of varying gender, race, class, and sexuality, discovers the metaphor of home for some means stability, connection, and belonging, while for others it is more about journeying. Therefore, the metaphor of home in this study is with a sense of belonging and identity with one's roots, country of origin, and being 'back home'. The metaphor of home also connects with the feeling of stability and connection to a place that is comfortable and where one has spent a lot of time; perhaps feeling, as Relph (1976) described, as an insider. Manny, born in Turkey, explained how a sense of place really meant comfort and ease of expression, even though he described this in two places:

> To express yourself comfortably – just be comfortable and relaxed where you are. Here. I grew up here. I am able to express and live both my cultures at the same time without suppression by anyone I feel more liberal here than anywhere else. It feels more like home here than anywhere else. Other people feel that way too. Turkey – the way my family was raised – the culture from there – when I go live there I live there I live the culture – the general community – When I am there I feel part of the Turkish community.

This concept of being rooted and comfortable related to an individual's connection with their ethnic community that led to a feeling of bonding. Krystina, born in Croatia, described this with assurance:

> Yes absolutely, I have a sense of place with the Croatian community – a sense of bonding. It's fun, we talk about our parents. We are all first generation so our parents seem all the same [Croatian immigrants]. This house, Croatia, Australia; my whole family is from Croatia and Australia. I have family there and they mean the world to me.

Duality of place identity

The difference between the concept of 'home'/being 'rooted' and 'back home'/ one's 'roots' also emerged through the notion of a dual identity or duality of place. Some ethno-cultural group leaders described having a sense of place for two places; these two places were, one, the country of origin and, two, where they live currently. There is a personal, emotional connection with both places due to feelings of attachment and identity. This notion of a dual identity and duality of place has not been addressed in previous literature on sense of place. It relates to the meanings of place for people of different ethnic backgrounds and the complexities they must experience in remembering past experiences plus adapting and adjusting new place identities. Samuel, from Bulgaria, described a duality of identity and place but also describes it as being very individual:

> Well, something is always missing. But it changes – when you are happy where you are its mostly home but then when you become disappointed it is like you are in limbo. We have dual citizenship – I've been here almost 20 years so I feel we've built a home here but when you are in one place or the other you miss them both. Sometimes I think about going back home one day to Europe and think maybe we should have stayed.

While Sophia perceives that a sense of place means a sense of belonging, she describes in more detail what her perceptions are in relation to her own experiences:

> For example – my son is Canadian – he has nothing to do with Romanian culture except having visited Romania and eaten a few Romanian dishes. He is responding to his own reality that he has a Romanian heritage. But it is difficult enough for children born outside Canada and then having a dual identity.

Marvin, a Sri Lankan Canadian, explained how it is important to instil a sense of place for the next generation since they are really living in two different worlds:

> Our own community is a sense of place for our children who are here. You see a sense of place for us is two different worlds – we need to be in touch with 2 different worlds but for kids sense of place is here we need to introduce the sense of place for the other place. There is always a possibility things will erode but it depends on the people who participate in our culture/arts.

The concept of a hybrid identity, whereby migrants adopt or share the cultural identity of their country of origin and present country of residence, is often referred to in discussions relating to immigrants, place identity, and mobility processes (e.g. Chacko, 2009; Chang, 2005). However, the concept of a hybrid identity is one that seems driven from above, or a researcher-led descriptive, rather than one coined by the immigrants themselves. 'Hybrid' conjures up perceptions of equality, sinuosity, and even acceptance that both identities are equal and shared. Yet, the term that emerged in this research was a dual identity; one that conjures up images of complexity, contested identities, sometimes confusing and conflicted senses of place.

Sense of place and the festival

Festival exhibitors were asked whether they thought the Multicultural Festival contributed to a sense of place. Some of the respondents said *yes*, but the

Table 11.3 Themes for how the festival contributes to a sense of place

Themes for contributing to a sense of place	Frequency	%
Individual	6	27
Awareness	5	23
Valuing identity	4	18
Sustain culture	3	14
Cultural exchange	2	9
Attachment	1	5

majority of comments were *I guess so, I think so, it depends on the people, a little bit, to people who want it to, it probably does,* and so on. Festival exhibitors gave some suggestions as to *how* they perceived the festival contributes to a sense of place. Table 11.3 shows the themes that emerged from respondents' answers. There were 22 excerpts searched for the themes.

The role of the festival in contributing to a sense of place was viewed by some respondents as not substantial or significant. It really depended on the individual perceptions of each particular festival visitor. As Lou from China remarked:

> It depends on the people. For tourists, they might say, I just come to see the festival and there is no sense of place for me in Waterloo. For long term residents yes, maybe, we know in June every year there is the festival and we mark it on the calendar.

Past research on festivals and sense of place has been exploratory and limited. Derrett (2003) suggested that festivals can contribute to a sense of place by offering connections, belonging, support, empowerment, and participation. De Bres and Davis (2001) also mentioned that commodification of culture through the tourism aspects of the festival is a minor issue compared to the benefits of sense of place and community. The results of this study conclude that festivals may contribute to a sense of place, but not necessarily substantially. It may for some. The role of the festival in contributing to a sense of place was not significant; more so the festival acted as a space for the exchange and communication of culture, a connection that festival exhibitors needed to maintain throughout the year in order to connect to broader meanings of place and identity. The festival allowed festival exhibitors to value their own ethnic identity, maintain their cultural traditions, and increase the awareness of their culture.

Festival exhibitors explained ways the festival contributes to a sense of place. For instance, the Multicultural Festival enables people to value their ethnic identity. Karen stated:

> Yes, because the festival altogether has a very diverse population it is not isolated. There is an opportunity to feel not alone that you are not the only one from this culture. That someone else prays like this or dresses like this.

People attend festivals in order to not feel like an Other or an outsider but instead to be reminded of how much they are the same. They identify with themselves at the festival because they are reminded of their past relationships of family and friends much like them. Specifically, Kyle and Chick (2007) interviewed inform-ants at an agricultural fair with quite homogeneous ethnic backgrounds in order to investigate social constructions of sense of place. These fair-goers were direct descendants of the original German, English, and Irish settlers. Despite having similar backgrounds and having lived in this central Pennsylvania rural region for multiple generations, informants' place meanings relating to the broader fair-ground were quite varied (Kyle & Chick, 2007). Place meanings were either most often associated with connections with family and close friends or defined by previous place experiences at the fair; the social experiences at the fair bonded these informants to the place.

On one hand, this quite homogeneous group had similar meanings attached to the fair in so far as their meanings related to a closely knit social world of family and friends. Sandra commented that festival participation contributes to valuing one's cultural identity: *I think that when you participate you want to com-municate who you are, and when you hear the applause you feel valued.* Increas-ing the awareness of cultural groups through the festival can also contribute to a sense of place. Manny said:

> I think so. People who have – well it gives minorities opportunities to show-
> case and it can seem – Gives them a feeling that I belong – bring in pride
> and in nation themselves. For example, for more recent immigrants like
> Serbian and Croatians it allows them to express themselves. It gives them
> belonging.

Comparisons with literature about other ethnic festivals can only be made in broad terms since previous research has not directly analysed sense of place but discusses its relationship to other issues. The Cultural Festival of India provided an extravagant vision of India for Indian as well as non-Indian Americans – it can be seen as a type of imagined community (Shukla, 1997). Jeong and Santos (2004) suggested that festivals can act as political instruments and promotional products at the same time as reconstructing meanings of place. Therefore, the Multicultural Festival may be an imagined multicultural community where polit-ical desires envision a cohesive, inclusive multicultural society without conflict. This works for the festival space, but may be a mythical place since deeper aspects of culture, more authentic types of foods and cultural traditions are not present. Even though it is an aestheticized space for consumption promoted for 'mainstream' community enjoyment, it contributes to the positive place experi-ences for ethnic migrants as it gives them motivation and pride in ethnic culture and reason to sustain it. The Multicultural Festival contributes to a sense of place by helping to sustain culture. Albert commented that the festival gives groups a reason to continue practising the traditions they know best and allow for the opportunity of showing them to others. While Marvan explained that the festival contributes to a sense of place by giving children the confidence to hold onto their ethnic traditions:

> We always try to maintain a balance between western culture and preserving our culture. We really want to maintain good values. Yes, we will be exposed to western culture at some time but we need to help our next generation. Most of our artists were born here. We give these children a confidence and give them their culture. They socialize with their group and don't have to feel isolated.

In other examples relating to festivals, Chacko (2009), Louie (2000), and Shukla (1997) discussed how festivals contribute to immigrants' place identity. While these examples illustrate how festivals may contribute to a sense of place identity for immigrants and transnationals, how these individuals or collective groups conceptualize a sense of place or find meaning in places is not acknowledged. Quinn (2003, 2005) concluded that arts festivals in Ireland can contribute to a sense of place identity and pride in place for residents even if they do not attend the events. However, representations of high, low, and popular culture are distinguished from each other by the festivals and thus by the residents which are social constructions contributed to by the festival itself. These strong place connections engendered by the festival depend, almost ironically, on the festival's relationship with other places (Quinn, 2003).

On a similar note, the Multicultural Festival also provides opportunities to sample a variety of ethnic foods from around the globe. As the food cooks there are scents wafting and floating from food tent to food tent. Sounds of musicians playing traditional instruments and singing are heard throughout the festival grounds. Festival exhibitors wear traditional fashions during performances and also sell crafts and artefacts from around the globe. The festival's sensuous geographies are plentiful. For Andrews (2005), sense of place connects, not only to the five senses as Rodaway (1994) suggested, but to how the body is used to establish a sense of place. This connected to Albert specifically in that he wears his hat on a daily basis to remind him of the two places he finds most meaningful, Texas and South Africa. Likewise, as the dance performers wear their traditional costumes and move their bodies in the traditional ways for the dances during the festival, or play their instruments, they use their bodies to embody the culture and places they maintain ties with. Tasting food, listening to music, going through the motions of cooking, dancing, and socializing is embodying a sense of place for the place of ethnic origin all within the festival space.

In addition to sustaining culture, the Festival enables ethnic group members to exchange culture, which may contribute to a more positive sense of place. More importantly, the Multicultural Festival enables ethno-cultural groups the opportunity to, simultaneously, be more attached to their ethnic heritage while also connecting more closely to Canadian culture within the urban space.

Conclusion

The results of this research have demonstrated that the Multicultural Festival has contributed to varying conceptualizations of the meaning of a sense of place for festival exhibitors: those that participate in the festival. Festival exhibitors' individual senses of place differed greatly in terms of which places they found meaningful but how they found meaning in these places was quite similar. Festival exhibitors value places that give them a sense of belonging, contribute to their identity through place attachment, and feeling comfortable, rooted, or connected to one's roots. While the festival itself may not contribute greatly to a sense of place for Kitchener it connects multi-ethnic festival exhibitors with their own interpretations of place, whether it is for the city itself or somewhere else. That somewhere else often referred to their country of origin. This was because the Multicultural Festival allows multi-ethnic festival exhibitors as ethnic group leaders/members to connect with their country of origin through the ethnic foods, music, and cultural performances they showcase at the festival. These connections may be unique to multi-ethnic or ethnic events rather than a finding that is revealed through other types of festival experiences. The festival brought up feelings of nostalgia and memory and reconfirmed the pride, identity, and attachment individuals have to places they already find meaningful.

The Multicultural Festival also contributed to maintaining and exchanging culture; important contributions to people's individual sense of place even if it is difficult to articulate or even to comprehend. This was especially important for festival exhibitors who were trying to teach sense of place for their country of origin to their children through their performances and experiences at the festival. The festival is one small part of a bigger set of pieces that fit together to contribute to establishing sense of place. Some of these pieces include ethnic group activities, festival and event participation, ethnic and mainstream community involvement, and maintaining connections with the culture and tradition of their country of origins. Due to the lack of research that currently exists on how festivals contribute to sense of place it is difficult to draw comparisons or make connections. Therefore, the degree to which community festivals contribute to sense of place, how, and for whom is still worthy of more attention in future festivals research.

References

Altman, I., & Low, S. (1992). (eds). *Place attachment*. New York: Plenum.

Andrews, H. (2005). Feeling at home: Embodying Britishness in a Spanish charter tourist resort. *Tourist Studies, 5*(3), 247–266.

Basch, L., Glick-Schiller, N., & Szanton Blanc, C. (1994). *Nations unbound: Transnational projects, post-colonial predicaments, and de-territorialized nation-states*. Langhorn, PA: Gordon and Breach.

Becker, G. (2003). Meanings of place and displacement in three groups of older immigrants. *Journal of Aging Studies, 17*, 129–149.

Billig, M. (2005). Sense of place in the neighbourhood, in locations of urban revitalization. *Geojournal, 64*, 117–130.

Bird, S.E. (2002). It makes sense to us: Cultural identity in local legends of place. *Journal of Contemporary Ethnograpy, 31*(5), 519–547.

Bryman, A. (2001). *Social research methods.* Oxford: Oxford University Press.

Butz, D., & Eyles, J. (1997). Reconceptualizing senses of place: Social relations, ideology and ecology. *Geografiska Annaler, 79B*, 1–25.

Chacko, E. (2009). *Spaces of celebration and identity: Ethnic festivals in the public spaces of Washington, DC.* American Association of Geographers Annual General Meeting, Washington, DC.

Chacko, E., & Schaffer, J. (1993). The evolution of a festival: Creole Christmas in New Orleans. *Tourism Management, 14*, 475–482.

Chang, T.C. (2005). Place, memory and identity: Imagining 'New Asia'. *Asia Pacific Viewpoint, 46*(3), 247–253.

Charmaz, K. (2009). *Constructing grounded theory: A practical guide through qualitative analysis.* London: Sage.

Chessell, D. (2002). *Italian festivals in Australia's Little Italy's: The use of public spaces in Italian–Australian commercial precincts to create a cosmopolitan 'sense of place'.* Events and Place Making: Proceedings of International Event Research Conference, Sydney.

De Bres, K., & Davis, J. (2001). Celebrating group and place identity: A case study of a new regional festival. *Tourism Geographies, 3*(3), 326–337.

Derrett, R. (2003). Making sense of how festivals demonstrate a community's sense of place. *Event Management, 8*, 49–58.

Eyles, J. (1985). *Senses of place.* Warrington: Silverbrook Press.

Fredline, E., & Faulkner, B. (2000). Host community reactions: A cluster analysis. *Annals of Tourism Research, 27*(3), 763–784.

Garcia-Ramon, M., Ortiz, A. & Prats, M. (2004). Urban planning, gender and the use of public space in a peripheral neighbourhood of Barcelona. *Cities, 21*(3), 215–223.

Getz, D. (2007). *Event studies: Theory, research and policy for planned events.* Oxford: Butterworth-Heinemann.

Getz, D. (2010). The nature and scope of festival studies. *International Journal of Event Management Research, 5*(1), 1–47.

Glaser, B.G., & Strauss, A.L. (1967). *The discovery of grounded theory: Strategies for qualitative research.* New Brunswick: Aldine Transaction.

Glover, T.D. (2004). Narrative inquiry and the study of grassroots organizations. *Voluntas: International Journal of Voluntary and Nonprofit Organizations, 15*(1), 47–69.

Gursoy, D., Kim, K., & Uysal, M. (2004). Perceived impacts of festivals and special events by organizers: An extension and validation. *Tourism Management, 25*(2), 171–181.

Gustafson, P. (2001). Meanings of place: Everyday experience and theoretical conceptualizations. *Journal of Environmental Psychology, 21*, 5–16.

Hargreaves, A. (2004). Building communities of place: Habitual movement around significant places. *Journal of Housing and the Built Environment, 19*, 49–65.

Hay, R. (1998a). Sense of place in developmental context. *Journal of Environmental Psychology, 18*, 5–29.

Hay, R. (1998b). A rooted sense of place in cross-cultural perspective. *Canadian Geographer, 42*(3), 245–266.

Hernandez, B., Hidalgo, M.C., Salazar-Laplace, M.E., & Hess, S. (2007). Place identity and place attachment in natives and non-natives. *Journal of Environmental Psychology, 27*(4), 310–319.

Hidalgo, M.C., & Hernandez, B. (2001). Place attachment: Conceptual and empirical questions. *Journal of Environmental Psychology, 21*, 273–281.

Higham, J.E., & Ritchie, B. (2001). The evolution of festivals and other events in rural southern New Zealand. *Event Management, 7*, 39–49.

Holloway, L., & Hubbard, P. (2001). *People and place: The extraordinary geographies of everyday life*. Harlow: Pearson Education Ltd.

Hull, R.B., Lam, M., & Vigo, G. (1994). Place identity: Symbols of self in the urban fabric. *Landscape and Urban Planning, 28*(2–3), 109–120.

Hummon, D.M. (1992). Community attachment: Local sentiment and sense of place. In I. Altman & S. Low (eds), *Place attachment*. New York: Plenum.

Jeong, S., & Santos, C. (2004). Cultural politics and contested place identity. *Annals of Tourism Research, 31*(3), 640–656.

Jorgensen, B.S., & Stedman, R.C. (2006). A comparative analysis of predictors of sense of place dimensions: Attachment to, dependence on, and identification with lakeshore properties. *Journal of Environmental Management, 79*, 316–327.

Keogan, K. (2002). A sense of place: The politics of immigration and the symbolic construction of identity in Southern California and the New York metropolitan area. *Sociological Forum, 17*(2), 223–253.

Kyle, G., & Chick, G. (2007). The social constructions of sense of place. *Leisure Science, 29*, 209–225.

Louie, A. (2000). Re-territorializing transnationalism: Chinese Americans and the Chinese motherland. *American Ethnologist, 27*(3), 645–669.

Lynch, K. (1976). *Managing the sense of a region*. Cambridge, MA: MIT Press.

Manzo, L.C. (2005). For better or worse: Exploring multiple dimensions of place meaning. *Journal of Environmental Psychology, 25*, 67–86.

Mazanti, B., & Ploger, J. (2003). Community planning: From politicized places to lived spaces. *Journal of Housing and the Built Environment, 18*, 309–327.

Mosely, M., & Mowatt, R. (2011). Re-conceptualizing and re-positioning festival exhibitors within tourism research. *International Journal of Event and Festival Management, 2*(3), 254–270.

Mountz, A., & Wright, R. (1996). Daily life in the transnational migrant community of San Agustín, Oaxaca and Poughkeepsie, New York. *Diaspora, 6*, 403–428.

Nicholson, R., & Pearce, D. (2001). Why do people attend events: A comparative analysis of visitor motivations at four south island events. *Journal of Travel Research, 39*, 449–460.

Quinn, B. (2003). Symbols, practices and myth-making: cultural perspectives on the Wexford Festival Opera. *Tourism Geographies, 5*(3), 329–349.

Quinn, B. (2005). Changing festival places: Insights from Galway. *Social and Cultural Geography, 6*(2), 237–252.

Relph, E. (1976). *Place and placelessness*. London: Pion.

Rodaway, P. (1994). *Sensuous geographies: Body sense and place,*. London: Routledge.

Schöllmann, A., Perkins, H.C., & Moore, K. (2000). Intersecting global and local influences in urban place promotion: The case of Christchurch, New Zealand. *Environment and Planning A, 32*(1), 55–76.

Shamai, S., & Ilatov, Z. (2005). Measuring sense of place: Methodological aspects. *Tijdschrift Voor Economische En Sociale Geografie, 96*(5), 467–476.

Shukla, S. (1997). Building diaspora and nation: The 1991 Cultural Festival of India. *Cultural Studies, 11*(2), 296–315.

Snepenger, D., Murphy, L., Snepenger, M., & Anderson, W. (2004). Normative meanings of experiences for a spectrum of tourism places. *Journal of Travel Research, 43,* 108–117.

Stedman, R.C. (2003). Sense of place and forest science: Toward a program of quantitative research. *Forest Science, 49,* 822–829.

Steele, F. (1981). *Sense of place.* Boston, MA: CBI Publishing Company, Inc.

Taylor, C.C., & Townsend, A.R. (1976). The local 'sense of place' as evidenced in northeast England. *Urban Studies, 13,* 133–146. doi: 10.1080/00420987620080281.

Tuan, Y. (1977). *Space and place: The perspective of experience.* St. Paul: University of Minnesota Press.

Tuan, Y. (1980). Rootedness verses sense of place. *Landscape, 24,* 3–8.

Twigger-Ross, C., & Uzzell, D.L. (1996). Place and identity processes. *Journal of Environmental Psychology, 16,* 205–220.

Werbner, P. (1999). Global pathways: Working class cosmopolitans and the creation of transnational ethnic worlds. *Social Anthropology, 7,* 17–35.

Williams, D.R. (2002). Leisure identities, globalization, and the politics of place. *Journal of Leisure Research, 34*(4), 351–367.

Williams, P.W., Gill, A.M., & Chura, N. (2004). Branding mountain destinations: The battle for 'placefullness'. *Tourism Review, 59*(1), 6–14.

Young, M. (1999). The social construction of tourist places. *Australian Geographer, 30*(3), 373–389.

12 Open house food catering

Does it destroy local culture and traditions? A perspective from Malaysia

Azilah Kasim, Mohamed Azlan Ashaari and Shahrul Aman Sabir Ahmad

Introduction

Community events are known to be laden with traditional and cultural elements. However, in some parts of the globe, community events are fast losing those essential elements due to modernization and adoption of new life values. This chapter provides a perspective from Malaysia on the issue of whether or not professional food catering in *kenduri*, or open house events, help to destroy local culture and traditions. It looks at weddings and *Hari Raya Aidilfitri* to compare the traditional open house concept, where food preparation is considered a personal (involving only the family and local community members) affair, with the modern open house concept where professional food caterers are hired to serve guests.

The concept of open house is quite unique to Malaysia. It is a tradition practised by Malaysians of all races. It is an act of 'opening one's door' to receive in your house, to welcome friends, family and neighbours or guests from everywhere and all walks of life to help one celebrate a traditional celebration (Knowledge Corp, 2005). In Malay tradition, for example, *kenduri* refers to traditional and cultural practices for special occasions such as circumcisions, completed study and understanding the Qur'an, instruction in *silat* (Malaysian martial arts) or some other discipline, and at religious celebrations like *Hari Raya Aidilfitri* and *AidilAdha* (two major Muslim religious celebrations for the Malay community in Malaysia). As for weddings or *kenduri kahwin*, the open house is more than just a manifestation of joy for the wedding couple and their relatives but also functions to invite the community to join the happiness of the newlyweds and their families. This gives substantial standing and meaning in the people's living principle. It also provides a community framework or platform of ethnic tradition, custom, practices, norms and culture.

According to Sook-ja (2007), an open house or *kenduri* really is a valuable traditional practice in the social culture because it is a form of expressing gratitude to the community, family, relatives and friends over a joyous occasion such as a wedding, *berkhatan* (circumcision of young boys in a family), *berendoi* (welcoming of a newborn), etc. Hence, organizing an event like open house plays an important role in transferring and sustaining tradition, culture, custom and civilization from one generation to another in a community. The *kenduri* plays a role of community announcer to the neighbourhoods and publics via a chain of occasions including the open house arrangement, serving food to the guest, reception of the guest and so forth. Hence, it creates a landscape that enhances the level of social interaction between community spheres and the hosting family.

Open house catering is an activity where an open house event hires a professional catering company to take care of aspects such as food planning, preparation and serving for the guests. Traditionally, these aspects are the sole responsibility of the host who will seek the help of family members, relatives and friends to come and work together. Today, hosts will often seek the service of an open house caterer and leave the planning and execution of food services to them. An open caterer can be a person or company providing food services by cooking the food either at its own site or off-site such as at a hotel, wedding ceremony, religious event or other location (Hard, 2014).

An open house caterer's scope of services ranges from providing lunch and dinner to complete-service catering. Presently, open house caterers and their workers play an important role in the food service industry. Open house caterers provide many different levels of service depending on the type of open house event but usually include one of these four principles:

1   Prepare and cook food at own site (caterer's place to cook food) and deliver food to other location, a so-called out-station location.
2   Prepare and cook, deliver and serve food at the event site.
3   Provide full-package catering services such as food preparation, logistics, entertainment, hospitality, staff or workers, decoration, cleaning services and so forth.
4   Take on the role of event manager, providing a full set of services ranging from providing food, venue selection and so forth to providing hospitality services and Master of Ceremonies (MC) duties.

Most of the open house events need to be in line with an event theme or event colour arrangement. As a catering company or being known as specialist open house event company, they require talent, skills and knowledge on how to prepare food and drink, decorations, event creativity and innovativeness; the most important thing is to ensure that any services offered for open house events are excellent and attractive. Based on those circumstances, many open house catering companies have transformed their business from just preparing food and drink into a full-service commercial model generally known as event planning. Catering companies are also expected to take on all the tasks and responsibilities of the open house host, not only on food and drink preparation but also with respect to decorations such as table settings, lighting and so forth.

The main objective of open house caterers is to satisfy the clients' needs and requirements in all aspects related to open house from preparing food and drink to providing excellent hospitality services; most of all, serving delicious and delightful food is a major point of focus. With an appropriate and perfect atmosphere, professional open house caterers with excellent knowledge and expertise can make an open house event distinctive and unforgettable. The pricing for catering services is normally on a head-count basis. However, additional items such as lighting, musicians, master of ceremonies, fire licences and so forth are not included in the head-count pricing, so the total price could be much higher.

Objectives and purpose

Community events are known to be laden with traditional and cultural elements. The wedding ceremony, for example, is among the most significant and fundamental of the religious and social cultural tradition. According to Sneizek (2005), the wedding ceremony involves processes, procedures and a substantial number of meanings that are significant towards forging social community relationships and bonding. Typically, wedding ceremonies are stimulated by custom, culture, tradition and religious practices and differ greatly between ethnic, social and national groups. In the Malay culture in particular, the wedding ceremony is traditionally known as a special occasion in the chain of social and community networks. Hosts often spend all their savings, time and energy to organize a meaningful *kenduri* or open house that adheres to all cultural aspects of the event.

However, in some parts of the country, community events can be seen to be changing in terms of practices due to modernization and adoption of new life values. This chapter provides a perspective on this by looking at the issue of food preparation in community events in Malaysia. Specifically, it discusses the current tendency to hire professional food caterers in *kenduri* or open house events and how this can destroy local culture and traditions. This issue is deliberated from the perspective of the Malay tradition relating to wedding ceremonies and religious celebrations such as *Hari Raya AidilFitri* and *Hari Raya AidilAdha*.

The open house culture in Malaysia

From the context of national unity, open house culture and tradition is quite a unique aspect of the Malaysian lifestyle. All Malaysians as well as tourists are treated with open house feasting events throughout the nation during religious celebrations such as the *Hari Raya AidilFitri*, Chinese New Year, *Deepavali* and *Hari Raya AidilAdha* holidays.

Corporate companies and government bodies also organize open houses during these community events and festivals. The events are usually held in halls or open grounds where tents are pitched. They would invite all the staff, family members, their clients and local communities to attend the open houses. There are also open houses by the prime minister or even His Majesty the king. Besides that, the Ministry of Tourism and Culture will usually hold open houses during major festivals such as *Hari Raya Aidilfitri*, Chinese New Year, *Deepavali*, Christmas, *Gawai* and *Keamatan*. These open houses are usually held on a grand scale in various parts of the country. There will be showcases of cultures and dances from various communities during such events. Tourists who visit the country during any the festive season are welcome to attend any of the open houses, especially those given by the prime minister or the king or by any government bodies. Tourists who have attended these open houses have been impressed by how Malaysians from various cultures and religions celebrate festivals together in harmony. Having the opportunity to meet and shake hands with the prime minister or the king is definitely beyond their expectations while enjoying the mouth-watering dishes served for the occasion and watching the dances performed for the festivals.

The attraction of the open house concept in Malaysia lies in the opportunities it offers for openness, togetherness, moderateness and inclusiveness of the community towards others. For instance, during *Hari Raya AidilFitri* open house, we can see Chinese and India communities pay an annual visit to their Malay friends' houses, smartly dressed in traditional attire, and Malaysian-Chinese and Indian families will also bring along a gift hamper. They can be neighbours, perhaps a part of the family, friends or anybody from the community.

Nowadays, the culture and tradition of open house in Malaysia has expanded into national heritage and culture, with many local political leaders including the prime minister holding an open house event during the festive celebrations. The prime minister's open house, held in the new capital city of Putrajaya, draws crowds from all races, such as Malay, Chinese, Indians, and all walks of life and segments of society. Even though racial polarization exists in Malaysia as in every multiracial society, the culture and tradition of open house events and celebrations on the ground do play a role in encouraging the Malaysian spirit of *muhibbah* or respect and tolerance towards other communities' ways of life.

Open house in community events also plays a role in enhancing tourism in Malaysia. The intangible characteristics of the open house tradition formed an integral part of the promotional activity to attract foreign tourists to visit Malaysia in conjunction with Visit Malaysia Year 2014. For example, tourists who attend the *Hari Raya Aidilfitri* open house event at one of the *kampong* in Malaysia can observe a harmonious spirit among the people in *kampong*, and will be fascinated by the socializing element of preparing meals. No amount of brochures and pamphlets can convince tourists or citizens alike that peace, harmony, neighbourliness and collaboration during the open house is real, compared to living and experiencing the open house celebration they discover that Malaysia is unique and full of diversity of culture and tradition. Even in the non-Muslim community, when they organize an open house, they will serve halal food for their Muslim friends to show their respect during the celebration of Chinese New Year, *Thaipusam*, the *Deepavali* festival of lights, the *Gawai Ka'amatan* festival, Christmas Eve and so forth. Normally in the *kampong*, people or villagers will assist, collaborate and contribute whatever items are needed for preparing food and drink to the host of open house in order to ensure the success of the event. This is a real example of how the Malay community in Malaysia inculcate the culture and tradition of the open house rooted in Islamic teachings from some 1,400 years ago; they not only preach respect, tolerance and harmony but actually practise it.

Wedding ceremonies kenduri *in Malaysia*

As a multicultural country, Malaysia has its own methods of conducting this special social cultural practice, regardless of tradition, ceremonies and rituals that differ according to religious belief, nation and location. With multiracial ethnic groups in Malaysia including Malay, Indian, Chinese, Kadazan, Iban and others, despite participating in necessities such as education, the economy and so forth, they are free to practise their own religion and organize open house events such as religious festivals, marriages and so on. The wedding ceremony open house is the key element in the success of mutual public relationships in Malaysia.

In Malaysia, ethnic groups such as the Malay community has unique cultural practices in each level of the wedding ceremony tradition, beginning with the initial level such as arrangements for the wedding day. In its traditional sense, a *kenduri kahwin* or wedding open house in the Malay community is also a platform for community collaboration and teamwork. Malay wedding ceremonies must adhere to the principle of Islamic teachings by adhering to Malay traditions. The processes involved in traditional Malay wedding practices comprise various levels, starting with coordinating activities, pre-wedding activities, activities on the wedding day itself and the post-wedding activities. It includes a series of events as follows:

1   pre-wedding day: *Majlis Merisik* (famously known as a spying activity);
2   pre-wedding day: *Majlis Pertunangan* (engagement event ceremony, also known as a promise that ties for future marriage);
3   the wedding day: *kenduri* (the wedding day);
4   either on the pre-wedding day or on the wedding day: *Majlis Akad nikah* (solemnization or validation of ties between bride and groom);
5   the wedding day: *Adat Bersanding* (seat on the wedding platform or stage);
6   the wedding day: *Majlis santapan beradab dengan raja sehari dan pasangannya* (wedding meal with bride and groom);
7   after the wedding day: *Kenduri timbal balik* (wedding open house either at groom's house or bride's house).

All of these traditional practices are vital in order to ensure the marriage and wedding event meet the objective of the community; organizing an open house demonstrates that the couple has been married. Open house is the only platform for the Malay community to engage in developing strong ties among relatives and the surrounding community. Open house hosts need to understand that food is an important element; in times past, most of the older generation perceived it as the highest success factor in the Malay wedding open house. Activities such as food arrangement, preparation and processing via cooking and so forth are influenced by the Malay traditions and customs in matrimonial ceremonies; in the village or *kampong* areas, it is a community affair with every person within the community collaboratively spending their time in helping the wedding open house host. This encompassed all kind of activities ranging from cooking to serving the food to the guests of the wedding open house.

Hari Raya Aidilfitri kenduri

Among all the community events and festivals in Malaysia, *Hari Raya AidilFitri* is arguably the most joyously celebrated because of the Malay majority in the country. This community event reinforces the messages of ritual and spiritual value and the rejuvenation of moral behaviour after the end of *Ramadhan*. The month of *Ramadhan* is the month in the Islamic calendar during which all Muslims are required to fast from sunrise until sunset.

Traditionally, *Hari Raya Aidilfitri* is a community celebration, aimed at strengthening the relationship or *Tali-Silaturrahim*, manifested by performing prayers to the Almighty God *Allah SWT*, visiting the *masjid* or mosque, *surau* and relatives' mausoleum and attending gatherings with family, but the most important activity is open house. In Bahasa, *Hari* translates as day and *Raya* as religious festivity. It is also known as *Hari Raya Puasa* because in Bahasa Malaysia *puasa* means fasting. After fasting in *Ramadhan*, many Muslims will schedule activities such as the social follow-up and community activities in the month of *Syawal* via organizing open house events for the *Hari Raya* celebration.

Among the major explanations for the wonderful style of open house is the well-known integration of Malay-Muslim traditions and cultural practices. Even with the current rate of urbanization, modernization and suburbanization, Malay community members continue to uphold and celebrate traditional events such as *kenduri kahwin* (open house for wedding ceremony) and *Hari Raya*.

They will *balik kampong* (return to one's place of birth) in droves to visit parents, families and relatives during the special festive gathering and holidays, which effectively strengthens the relationship and close bonds between families and establishes the culture of open house in the context of Malaysian society.

On the first day of the celebrations, most Malay men usually wear traditional Malay costume in cheerful, beautiful colours. These include *Baju Melayu*, a long-sleeved shirt beautifully designed in soft smooth cotton, or a silk shirt worn with trousers, a round-style formal collar, and a skirt-type sarong known as *Kain Sampin* and expensively made of a *kain songket* girdle tight around the waist. Also, a black velvet hat known as *songkok*, *ketayap* or *kopiah*. For a particularly fierce appearance, men may wear a Malay warrior-style, or *panglima*-style, complicated three-sided headpiece known as *Tengkolok* to complete the look. Women will wear equally colourful, beautiful Malay garment called *bajukurung*, which is a loose-fitting full-length dress. These kinds of clothes are part and parcel of the open house tradition and culture in Malay community.

The traditional foodways for open house in the Malay community

A vital part of the Malay open house tradition is the opportunity for community bonding offered by the attractive prospect of enjoying delicious and superbly presented food during the festive events. Appropriately, *pesta* is the Malay expression for a party, not unlike the Spanish word *fiesta*. Mohamed (2008) defined open house in Malay culture and tradition as a community network especially for the villagers who spend their time and energy helping the open house host in activities like arranging foodstuff, cooking and distributing food to people. During the occasion, most women of the house will stay up all night planning and preparing food for their families, friends and guests, showing their skills and knowledge of traditional Malay dishes. In big events such as weddings, community members of the village will show their respect for one another while mingling and socializing during the feast preparation. Traditional delicacies of the day, such as *daging rendang*, delicious *satay* served with rice dumplings, popularly known as *ketupat nasi* and *ketupat pulut* and wrapped in coconut-leaf pouches, or *lemang* which is made by cooking glutinous rice in a rod-lined bamboo, will be prepared.

When preparing a special dish during festivals to be served to family and friends, the best dish with the best ingredients will be used. It will be served on the best plates and bowls that are usually kept in a display cupboard, reserved for special occasions only. Only the best quality and freshest ingredients will be used in preparing the dish because it will be consumed by someone we love and care about. No pre-prepared 'ready meals', with high salt, sugar and preservatives content, will be used. Extra effort will be taken to ensure the dish turns out perfectly since it is usually prepared once a year only. It will also be enjoyed greatly by everyone knowing that it was prepared with so much care, thought and effort. Children and the young generation who helped in preparing the dish would be excited to explain to their friends and family how they helped. This creates a personal touch and interest in preserving the recipes.

During the open house, everyone is welcomed warmly, including strangers who happen to be passing by. This tradition has been successful in getting people together irrespective of background and religion, making it a valuable heritage that needs to be preserved. The tradition of families preparing food and drink for the guests is a long-established culture passed from one generation to another. It is the true concept of the open house tradition – one that does not cost much money, but prospers on social harmony, peace and relationships.

Is modernization of food preparation by open house caterers destroying the culture and tradition of open house?

Professional food catering is a relatively new but booming business in Malaysia. In many ways, it represents the modernization of foodways or food preparation culture in local community events and festivals.

Many hosts now prefer hiring caterers to prepare and serve food and drink for their guests. A number of reasons could be attributed to this new trend: (1) time

– the modern family has both husband and wife as the breadwinners. After a long day at work, women are less inclined to bear sole responsibility for all the household tasks such as cooking. Therefore hiring professional caterers is the perfect solution for this type of family; (2) money – since both husband and wife work, the household income has doubled, thus making hiring a professional caterer much more affordable; (3) less attached neighbours – modern communities in Malaysia tend to live in neighbourhoods where members are less connected with one another due to lack of time to socialize.

A professional food caterer will therefore take on the following tasks and responsibilities in organizing an open house on behalf of the host:

Before the events start

1   event planning
2   venue selection
3   determine time of the event
4   determine the number of guest and prepare invitation cards
5   menu selection
6   prepare food and beverages
7   prepare venue decoration
8   ensure venue cleanliness.

During the events

1   cooking process
2   serve the food and drinks
3   hospitality
4   event management
5   cleanliness.

After the events end

1   clean the venue
2   receive feedback from host and their guests
3   event post-mortem.

When most people refer to a 'caterer', they mean an open house caterer who has staff to serve food at dining tables or stand at self-service buffet tables ready to assist. The food may be prepared entirely on site at the open house, or the caterer may have an option to bring prepared food in and apply the final touches at the open house. The on-site staff are only responsible for setting up the dining area, hospitality and serving the guests, but not for preparing the food. These types of services are typically provided at banquet halls, conventions centres and wedding ceremonies.

As professional caterers are business people, it is logical to assume that their planning and execution of food preparation may be influenced by prioritizing cost over quality due to the need to make a profit. Nutritional values and authenticity of ingredients may take a backseat. Preservatives may be desired to ensure the food lasts longer throughout the day, while some items may be reused at the next event elsewhere in the quest to cut costs. In short, most professional caterers could not afford to 'cook from the heart' and add personal touches that would be expected from family and/or community members in the traditional food preparation for an open house event.

The concept of the open house caterer has really had a significant impact in changing the culture of the open house concept in the Malay community. The old traditional concepts of open house, such as matrimonial and religious celebrations and foodways practices that have long been associated with the Malay community that lives in rural areas, are hardly seen due to the penetration of the new concept of professional open house catering services. It has significantly affected the old tradition and culture of the open house, particularly in the Malay community. The influence is not limited to urban communities, but is slowly creeping into the lifestyle of the rural communities as well.

Another criticism of the practice of hiring open house catering professionals is the sheer wastage of excess foods that is often observed from either (1) the open house host's attempt to show off their higher standard of living, or (2) poor planning and overestimating the number of guests that will arrive. The first tendency is inconsistent with the Malay tradition, which holds to the teaching of Islam to be moderate and to provide to the poor or less fortunate. However, the present-day open house catering focuses instead on the aim to establish chains of linkage with corporate acquaintances, customers, local authority personnel and other distinguished guests. There is a tendency to show off status symbols of individual prestige and fortune such as the new extension to the large private house, the modern, urban look of interior design, as well as the ability to feed and entertain hundreds of friends and relatives for days on end. To be precise, nowadays, many open house organizers will hire an open house caterer in order to show off their status and wealth rather than organize an open house through the spirit of neighbourliness and collaboration within the community.

Open house food catering also changes the values associated with food preparation brought about by modernization. Darnton (2013) refers to foodways as the cultural, social and economic practices relating to the production and consumption of food. According to Gillette (1997), several behavioural changes are taking place in the way of people cook and eat traditional food. Modernization has had a significant impact on everyday eating habits and also on traditional events such as the open house by means of adjusting the preparation and consumption patterns of food. Most notably, modernization relates to the concept of 'convenience' (Buckley, Cowan & McCarthy, 2007; Warde, 1999). In modern life, many people prefer the convenience of fast food due to their hectic lifestyles and the time constraints of daily routines. This scenario also affects local cultures and traditions with more open house caterers adopting innovations and technological developments that bring new activities to the food and beverage production process.

No doubt the demands of modernization force societies to change many aspects of their social culture. In this case, the arrangements of Malay festive open house foodways from the traditional *gotong-royong* style (helping each other) to the hiring of professional caterers demonstrate that alterations and transformations occur in Malay culture as well. In today's wedding open houses, for example, wedding foods are now served buffet-style by placing food on a long table or sideboard from which guests help themselves, instead of the traditional way of four or five people sharing a *dulang* (tray) of traditional dishes.

Li, Yin and Saito (2004) warn that many traditional and conventional food practices, cultures and traditions are on the verge of being lost because of the modernization that has undoubtedly also brought many advantages to food businesses, particularly in rural areas. They suggest that modernization of food production be embraced. However, one key aspect of traditional food practices that will be lost by adopting modernized food production (as offered by professional food caterers) is the meaningful bonding opportunities that strengthen relationships and community integration. Sani (1999) argues that wedding and other *kenduri* foodways provide the power to improve harmony and strengthen people's alliances within a community group. When all villagers participate regardless of their social background and class in preparing foodstuff, they nurture the culture to assist each other and collaborate. It also illustrates food as a relationship tool not only for the family but for the *kampong* or village community.

Professional food catering for community events also calls into question safety and cleanliness when preparing food, especially in large amounts. When the foods are prepared at home by family members, the ingredients used and how they are cooked are known. However, with professional caterers, the client must rely on the caterer with regard to the quality and taste of the food prepared. There have been several cases where people have died and others have been poisoned by the food consumed at open houses, either festivals or weddings. Three people died and 65 others were hospitalized after consuming food at a wedding in Sg Petani, Kedah (*The New Strait Times*, 1 October 2013), while another 25 people were made seriously ill by food poisoning in Tangkak, Johor (*The Star*, 12 April 2012). Such reports are of very serious concern for both the caterers and the function hosts, especially when there are deaths involved.

Often, professional caterers prepare food at a location other than the open house site. This means that cooked food must transferred via some mode of transport, thereby enhancing the possibility of contamination from factors such as dirty containers and incorrect temperatures. As Worsfold and Griffiths (2003) has proposed, the caterer needs to be familiar with the area in which they will be serving the food because climate conditions can affect food quality. Keeping and serving food at the right temperature, making sure the utensils being used for the food service are clean at all times and choosing good quality ingredients from reputable suppliers also help to ensure the guests do not get sick from consuming the food. Especially the service staff who are serving the food must be clean. Clean uniforms (some caterers have uniforms for their service staff so it is easier to identify them among the guests), clean hands and nails and a generally clean appearance would also help prevent food-related sickness among the guests. The location where outdoor catering takes place also has a role in ensuring the safety and hygiene of the food. Serving halal food should also be a major concern when hiring a caterer. Generally, if a Malay caterer is hired, they will serve halal food. Special attention must be given when organizing a function in a hotel or restaurant that does not have halal certification from the local Islamic food certification agency, JAKIM.

Professional food catering also changes other elements in organizing an open house. For example, for a wedding, it can influence selection of venue, venue decoration, time of the event, theme of the open house and so forth. Hence many open house hosts prefer to have professional caterers organize their event. Modernization has given huge opportunities to professional open house caterers to expand their business to new levels as part of Malaysia's economic growth.

On the other hand, the professionally catered open house concept has the potential to erode quality communication, caring attitudes, social relationships and social bonding among community members. These values are very much upheld in the traditional open house food preparation concept, and are still practised in some rural Malay communities today. In other words, among the functions of open house in the traditional context is to act as a mechanism for forging relationships among people within a community and society. However, the current trend of hiring professional open house food caterers means that the open house is slowly losing this important function. If allowed to continue, a community may lose its sense of togetherness and teamwork with its members gradually becoming more self-centred, selfish and individualistic. This may have negative ramifications on the lifestyle of the future generations; particularly those who live in urban areas who may never have an opportunity to experience the real meaning of their own culture and traditions.

Conclusion

In conclusion, it is evident that while modernization can and does improve many aspects of our daily life, modernization can also reduce the mutual integration, *esprit de corps* and the neighbourly spirit that is a long-established feature of Malay community culture and traditions. This is evident within the context of the open house concept in community events and festivals such as wedding ceremonies and *Hari Raya Aidilfitri*, particularly in term of food preparation for open house activities.

The practice of open house culture and traditions, especially in the preparation of foods for matrimonial and *Hari Raya* celebrations, for many generations has been a platform for social communication and integration between members of a community that strengthen the social bond or relationship. Nevertheless, modernized lifestyles have brought about transformations, modifications and changes in every dimension of people's lives including in the preparing of food, which has transformed open house culture and traditions. Indeed, recently adopted open house food practices via the hiring of professional food caterers who introduce a modern approach to the preparation of foodstuff can negatively affect the local traditions and cultures of inculcating community bonding and social relationships.

It is vital that the Malay community conserves their culture and tradition of social bonding practices, because the more communities embrace the concept of modernism, the more elements of community culture and tradition can be eroded, leading to selfishness, individualism and community disintegration. While we acknowledge the need to embrace modernity in the future, we also need to preserve our culture and not let modern ways swallow our cultural identity and traditions.

References

Boon, P. (2013, 12 August). Open house traditions, a valuable heritage. Retrieved from www.theborneopost.com/2013/08/12/open-house-tradition-a-valuable-heritage.

Buckley, M.C., Cowan, C. & McCarthy, M. (2007). The convenience food market in Great Britain: Convenience food lifestyle (CFL) segments. *Appetite, 49*, 600–617.

Darnton, J. (2013). Foodways: When food meets culture and history. Michigan State University Extension. Retrieved 5 March 2013.

Gillette, B.M. (1997). *Contemporary Chinese Muslims (Hui) remember ethnic conflict: Stories of the late 19th century 'Hui Uprising' from Xian.* Paper presented at the Association for Asian Studies meeting, Chicago, IL.

Hard, R. (2014). *Catering.* Retrieved from http://eventplanning.about.com/od/event industrytermsae/g/Catering.htm.

Knowledge Corp. (1996–2005). *Malaysia's festivals.* Retrieved from www.geographia. com/malaysia/festivals.html.

Li, L.T., Yin, L.J. & Saito, M. (2004). Function of traditional foods and food culture in China. *JARQ, 38*(4), 213–220.

Mohamed, A. (2008). *Simbolisme makanan dalam perkahwinan Melayu* [food symbolism in Malay wedding]. Unpublished manuscript. Bangi: UniversitiKebangsaan Malaysia.

New Straits Times (2013, 1 October). Food poisoning leaves 3 dead, 65 warded. Retrieved from http://news.asiaone.com/news/malaysia/food-poisoning-leaves-3-dead-65-warded.

Sani, F.M. (1999). *Pengantin dan belanja besar* [Brides and big spending]. Selangor Darul Ehsan: Al-Islam.

Sneizek, T. (2005). Is it our day or the bride's day? The division of labour and its meaning for couples. *Qualitative Sociology, 28*(3), 215–230.

Sook-ja, Y. (2007). Traditional Korean wedding food. *Koreana*, 19–23.

The Star (2012, 12 April). Pupil dies after food poisoning from nasi lemak. Retrieved from www.thestar.com.my/News/Nation/2012/04/10/Pupil-dies-after-food-poisoning-from-nasi-lemak.

Warde, A. (1999). Convenience food: Space and time. *British Food Journal, 7*, 518–527.

Worsfold, D. & Griffith, C.J. (2003). A survey of food hygiene and safety training in the retail and catering industry. *Nutrition and Food Science, 33*(2), 68–79.

13 Religion, community and events

Rev. Ruth Dowson

Introduction

The typology of community events and festivals would be incomplete without some reference to the role religion plays, both within the local community and in building a community of its own. An aim of most mainstream religions is to engage with and include a wider community. This chapter examines the role that churches and their associated events play within a specific community, whether in a geographic location or more widespread.

The Anglican Church has a geographic delineation, with local parishes making up regional dioceses, which in turn combine to form a province. In both urban and rural settings, the Church of England has over 16,000 churches, set in parishes that cover every inch of the country, within 42 dioceses that make up the two provinces of Canterbury and York, each with its own Archbishop. In addition to weekly services held mainly on Sunday mornings, voluntary work is undertaken for churches. Church members contribute 23.2 million hours every month in volunteering outside church activities, within their own communities, more than for any other organisation.[1]

While connections between church and 'events' may not initially be apparent, in addition to the range of projects and services within local communities, many churches' energies are focused on events, from fetes, to community days, to music events and conferences for clergy and laity. Such events might be held within the church buildings, whether for church members or the wider community, and include involvement in community-led events and the provision of resources – such as venues – for use by the local community for their events.

This chapter draws on empirical research (Dowson, 2012) undertaken over the period May–July 2012 into the role of events in building community and influencing the culture of religious organisations (in this case, churches). By exploring the role of events in church culture, this research developed from an academic awareness of the growth of events as part of popular culture generally, in the United Kingdom and elsewhere (Bowdin, Allen, O'Toole, Harris & McDonnell, 2011), and personal observations of a (possibly related) level of increase in events in a range of churches. I have examined the ways in which different churches use events to transmit, express and develop their own cultures and communities, as well as new ways of 'being church'. My research focused on three churches, selected because although all based in one Yorkshire city, they are diverse in terms of size and demographic membership, because their approaches attempt to include those who do not attend church and because they each use different types of events in different ways as part of 'being church'. The three churches include a large independent church that uses its buildings as a commercial conference centre, an Anglican village parish church adjacent to an urban priority area and a city-centre Anglican fresh expression immersed in issues of justice. In this chapter I argue that the use of events by churches enables the development of a sense of community, whether within their own locality, within their church or in a community connected to the church and its ethos or interests.

Events and life in the 21st century

The dramatic explosion of events into our way of life, evidenced by their growth as part of popular culture, in the United Kingdom as elsewhere (Getz, 2007), provides over 0.5 million fte jobs (Goldblatt, 2008) in a diverse industry (People1st, 2010). Also in the United Kingdom, a plethora of public cultural events, combined with international sporting and music events, result in an environment in which events thrive, at local, national and international levels. Media coverage of events, particularly in the Internet era, significantly influences and affects public experience: one Sunday in July 2012 included the Wimbledon men's tennis final, the British Formula 1 Grand Prix and the 'T in the Park' music festival, only weeks before the London 2012 Olympics. Despite the overwhelming impact of the Internet, experiential marketing is foundational to the strategic approaches of many organisations today, as they seek to engage customers' senses, inspire them to action and build relationships (Varey, 2002, p. 36), and events are key to this development, both for communities and for organisations such as churches. This growth in events is mirrored across mainstream religions, whose associated events have emerged from seasonal, life cycle or celebratory religious origins.[2]

Theoretical basis of church, events and community

Tillich's assessment of 'the religious significance of contemporary culture' (Lynch, 2005, p. 30) connects church culture into the values and beliefs of wider society, and in meeting social and community needs. A question arises here: is the church imitating 'art' by providing and participating in different types of events, as a means of building that community which is so sought after by wider society? We might see that imitation emerge through conferences, or music events, exhibitions, social events or even protest, turning 'occupation into something that is beautiful, something that brings community together, something that calls for love and happiness and hope' (Chomsky, 2012, p. 122).

Durkheim's proposition that society finds its formational basis within 'religious enactments' (Morrison, 2006, p. 271) placed 'festival' in a central role, while Turner asserted that 'When a social group, whether it be a family, clan, village, nation, congregation or church, celebrates a particular event or occasion … it also "celebrates itself"!' (Turner, 1982, p. 16). Meanwhile, according to Hermkens (2007, pp. 347–364), festivals 'express dedication' and 'provide a contemporary arena in which various identities are actually embodied and expressed visually'. And Goldblatt's (2008, p. 5) definition of a 'special event' as 'a unique moment in time celebrated with ceremony and ritual to satisfy specific needs' was indeed inspired by Turner's observation that 'every human society celebrates with ceremony and ritual its joys sorrows and triumphs' (ibid., pp. 5–6).

A structuralist, Turner's definition of ritual stemmed from a recognition of life as 'performance – as literature, as theatre, as storytelling, as game, as a movie script or scenario, or as a symphonic composition' (Abrahams, 1969, p. vii). In this vein, events are clearly in line with those activities that describe the ways in which people celebrate with each other, doing life together as a group, forming community. Turner's anthropological roots lay in van Gennep's analytic framework that identified structure in ritual: beginning with 'separation from the everyday' into a 'ritual world removed from time and space' (ibid., p. ix). Whereas previously, community had been described from a structural perspective, including religion as one of the 'agreed-upon systems', cultural ethnographers such as Turner focused on the performative elements of a community and identified their shared 'understandings and experiences' (ibid., p. viii) as expressed through celebrations. While Durkheim viewed religion as fundamental to the creation of society (Morrison, 2006, p. 271), Turner (1969, p. 6) argued that 'rituals reveal values at their deepest level' within group settings. He noted the difference between observing another's ritual performance and reaching 'an adequate understanding of what the movements and words mean to them', i.e. to the participants in the performance (ibid., p. 8). In this context, it is therefore argued that church events provide such an expression, making it possible to interpret events as performative texts that communicate, within the community as well as without, the wider meaning of that community.

Hofstede's (2003) dominant concept of cultural criteria measured countries like the United Kingdom as high in individualism (as opposed to collectivism) (Brooks, 2009). And from an historical perspective, the Enlightenment brought about the rise of individualism in relation to Western society, as the individual overcame the 'dominance of social institutions' (Morrison, 2006, p. 13). However, while community and group identity are formed through a range of influences, including leadership (Smith & Peterson, 1988), and thus culture emerges, it is clear that culture is not static, as asserted by Hofstede, but that it changes over time (Sivakumar & Nakata, 2001), and that cultures also have internal heterogeneity (Tjitra, 2011). While Hall's rival theory (Sivakumar & Nakata, 2001) explored the source and boundaries of 'identification' (Hall, 1981, p. 232), the variety open to the individual in terms of choice of church allows the individual to choose a church and its community, to fit not only their theological tradition or worship style, but also their personality, political beliefs, values, geographic location and other explicit or implicit preferences.

Cultural analysis attaches several levels to identifying organisational culture: first, according to Schein (1996, p. 434), observation from within an organisation aids understanding of the meaning of and interrelationship between communication and behaviours. Second, values shared within the organisation are recognised as being influenced by leadership; and third, 'basic assumptions' demonstrate what is 'taken-for-granted' within the organization (ibid, p. 437). Hence the rationale behind the strength of an individual's identification with their chosen church is of interest – to what extent do churchgoers identify with their church community and its events, as part of what defines and classifies themselves (Foreman & Parent, 2008, p. 225)?

Event Studies and religious events

Within Event Studies, 'religious' events are associated with ceremonial, ritual and pilgrimage, providing an opportunity for developing a typology of religious events. For example, Getz (2012, p. 41) cites 'festivals', 'religious rites', and 'pilgrimage' within 'cultural celebrations', but lists 'rites of passage' and 'weddings' as 'private functions', while 'concerts' fall within 'arts and entertainment'. However, the central role of 'festival' was identified by Durkheim's proposition that society finds its formational basis within such religious enactments. Thus, as events are 'sociologically important in characterising and understanding modern societies' (Roche, 2009, p. 3), creating and developing a sense of community, it should not be surprising that the external levels of events activity might be reflected in the levels of church events activity.

Church and culture

In the United Kingdom and across the developed world, a weakness of church culture is that it may not easily relate to the outside world, sometimes preferring 17th-century language, practices and rituals that defy understanding by those outside the walls of the church building – and by some within. Thus, in 21st-century Britain, church can seem to much of the population to be 'an alien culture' that those not acquainted with it may view as having 'seemingly bizarre components and interrelations' (Turner, 1969, p. 2). The academy is challenged to recognise the difficulty of viewing from within (emic) (Collins, 2005), as compared to the view from without the church. Being fluent in the language, customs and texts of an individual church, adherents may take for granted the understandings and assumptions of those 'outside', particularly if they are 'unchurched', rather than 'dechurched' (Stearns, 2010, p. 153). Thus the impact of cultural change – or contextualisation – enables the creation of a new 'group identity' (Shorter, 1994, p. 30) or community, visible from outside the church, that is recognised within the church and responded to by the church. The diversity of life in the United Kingdom today suggests a review of the wisdom of continuing the classical 'perfection' of a traditional church that does not recognise the ethnic and sociological plurality that now exists. The Second Vatican

Council reflected such a sentiment, concluding that 'the church has been sent to all ages and nations and, therefore, is not tied exclusively to any race or nation, to any one particular way of life, or to any customary practices, ancient or modern' (Shorter, 1994, p. 32). This argument underpins the creation of new ways of being church, ways that are relevant for the growing millions of Christians in Latin America or Africa, enabling authenticity in each context without losing the centrality of shared faith. This argument applies equally in the United Kingdom as elsewhere, and whether events enable churches to provide 'just a religious version of the surrounding culture' (Tomlin, 2008, p. 77) or whether they contribute to the creation of their own counter-culture, such activity draws people together into community, cultivating a shared life together.

In 2009, the Church of England published its 'mission-shaped' strategies, having thoroughly reviewed external factors affecting the UK population, from demographic and social changes to new leisure activities, and proposed a new agenda, enabling churches to engage with parishioners in 'fresh' ways (Archbishops' Council, 2009). The considered aim of this innovative activity was:

> to create environments in which culturally authentic experiences of God and worship are possible, a quest driven by the subcultural identities of members but also distinguished by a ritual and ecclesiological experimentation inspired by pre-modern church tradition as much as by ideas associated with post-modernity.
>
> (Guest, 2007, p. 44)

This initiative had its challenges, theologically (Guest, 2007, p. 44), and the Church of England responded with its own thoughts (Croft, 2008), including those who see fresh expressions as what the church should *be*, rather than what it should be *doing*: 'The fundamental task of mission is to bear witness to Christ – to be, if you like, "fresh expressions" in the world of God's living Word. (Not fresh expressions of the church!)' (Loveday Alexander, cited in Baines, 2011). Such reflections recognise that 'God's Spirit can be at work in the old centres too' (Alexander, 2008, p. 145), that traditional church continues to have value, while others argue for a continually evolving process of change (Croft, 2008) that enables people to belong (Davie, 2008) to a loving community.

Church studies

The field of church studies developed in the 1980s with the purpose of identifying the 'nature, status, social and theological significance of Christian congregations'. Early researches by Hopewell (1987) in the United States, and in Scotland by Dowie, utilised an ethnographic methodology, 'to access the identity or culture of specific congregations' (Guest, 2007, pp. 17–18), applying theological approaches to the results. Hopewell (1987) focused on the development of narrative, the story of the church community as a subculture, each one rich in its own meaningful ritual and symbolism. Guest (2007, p. 19) argues that a church community begins to engage with people in its own context, first by building 'shared traditions' and 'internally-constructed discourses', through interaction between its own members, before stepping outside the church building. However, such community development is less likely to happen if people only attend a service for just one hour on a Sunday; instead, such community/ network/relationship-building requires people to share everyday life, and for the church to facilitate such activity (Tomlin, 2002). What Hopewell (1987, p. 15) referred to as the 'mere baggage ... [of] events whose sanctity is obscure' today finds meaning within that shared ritual, knitting together a human community.

History of church events

From a historical perspective, church events activity has evolved to meet a range of purposes, and has been influenced by significant developments over the past 50 years. In the charismatic movement, Roman Catholics met in 1968 at Notre Dame, Indiana, and Anglicans in Guildford in 1971 (Clark, 1984, p. 49). During the 1980s, John Wimber's 'Signs and Wonders' conferences brought new spiritual experiences across the world.[3] In the same decade, a British Council of Churches ecumenical programme, 'The People Next Door', saw 80,000 people participate across the United Kingdom in small Bible study groups (Clark, 1984, p. 58). This might be seen as a precursor to the now global events-based Alpha course that annually boasts millions of participants and features on UK public transport advertising each autumn.[4] Core to building community was the nurturing aspect provided by small groups 'in which individuals can most readily experience what it is to be, and to be known, as whole persons ... hold[ing] together people's deep need for significance and for solidarity' (Clark, 1984, p. 73). These small group developments took church membership beyond one-hour Sunday church, building community in an age where, increasingly, many people no longer lived in the same area where they had grown up, and thus lacked local connections and relationships that provided support in earlier generations. A notable aim of small groups recognised in 1980 by Roman Catholics was to provide 'nurturing ... to strengthen ... fellowship and gain support and enlightenment in a way impossible through congregational gatherings' (Clark, 1984, p. 86). Thus, the limitations surfaced of local community formation being achieved through church services alone.

The emergence of large-scale UK Christian events began with Billy Graham's evangelistic crusades in 1954, attended by 1.3 million people over three months (Guest, 2007, p. 24); 30 years later, over one million attended his 'Mission England' mass rallies. But whether these meetings were merely 'public spectacles' (ibid., p. 24), or had any measureable impact in terms of numbers attending church, at the time they achieved 'media coverage and public visibility' (ibid., p. 25), in stark contrast to larger Christian events (one million-plus attendees) that regularly occur today across the southern hemisphere. In the 1970s, Christian festivals emerged, from the overtly political arts-based Greenbelt, to the activist evangelical Spring Harvest aiming to 'equip the church for action'. By 2012, festivals were

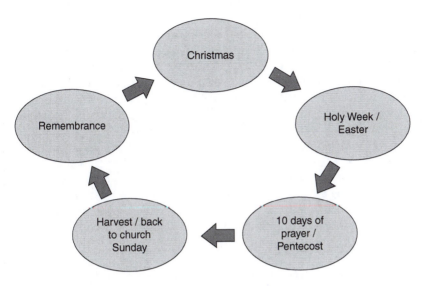

Figure 13.1 Seasonal festivals and events in the church year.

openly paraded as 'the new church', supported by the publication of guides to organising Christian festivals (Share Jesus International, 2011).[5]

Within its mission strategy, Sheffield Diocese propose an annual cycle of process evangelism, based on the Five Marks of Mission (Diocese of Sheffield, n.d.). Following the liturgical year, it contains three identified seasons, of 'sowing, nurture and deepening' (ibid.), using thematic hooks, shown in Figure 13.1, to direct the focus of teaching, integrated within supporting events activity (ibid.). However, Bishop Steven Croft (2012) argues that the methods used (such as events), are secondary; what is central is a double listening to and theological reflection on scripture and culture. In this scenario, events become an overt 'peg' on which to hang outreach and discipleship.

The results of this study support the argument that the evolution of an events programme – whether purposely undertaken or not – can construct a framework that enables those outside the church to begin to establish whether or not they wish to learn the language – and provides an opportunity from those within churches to develop their multilingual skills.

Building community through church events

The research undertaken with the three churches in the study provided insights into a range of issues that relate to the use of events in building a sense of community, and a feeling of belonging – both to the church as well as to the local area. Overall, 22% of respondents heard about their church through a family member, with another 36% invited through a friend, while some 10% cited specific pastoral/event-related reasons, such as baptisms, confirmations, weddings and funerals for first attending their church, and almost 20% said it was due to receiving a personal invitation from a church leader, or (for the suburban village church) because they were living in the neighbourhood. Engagement within the local village parish community is a key aspect of events activity, and the pastoral dimension vital (Pravera, 1981, p. 251). While one church leader saw events as 'sort of stepping-stones, never an end in themselves' (Dowson, 2012), the focus of events activity is within the locality, and their purpose is to bring the local community into the church as a first step on what might become a journey of faith, and into discipleship. Hence the village church developed a structured annual programme of events that combines with the 'transitional moments in life' (Dowson, 2012) such as weddings, funerals and baptisms, and used the resources available to the church to provide pastoral care, but this programme was underpinned by consistent evangelistic opportunities. In contrast, leaders of the large independent church recognised that although a similar approach had been dominant for their predecessors, they themselves had moved beyond such measurement:

> Before, we put on evangelistic events, and got people in. Whereas we've switched it around and said, no, we have to have a social gospel. So let's just help people. Let's do good to all men. And ok, they might not get saved, in the first, second, third, fourth, fifth, sixth contact, but, they've got a good impression of God, they've got a positive impression of the church. Stick that on your Engel scale!
>
> (Dowson, 2012)

Belonging and church events

When asked why they chose to attend a specific church, for the village Anglican church, its geographic location within its neighbourhood was far more important than the tradition of the church. A feeling of being 'at home' in all three churches is relevant, implying that many participants found an environment, culture and style of church that suited their personal circumstances or values (Lee & Sinitiere, 2009, p. 163). Asked whether they feel they belong to their church, 90% responded positively, across all churches. Identity with the church was also demonstrated by a 'pride in telling others' shared by 89%, while some 93% agreed that their church provided a stable community to which they belong. These responses all indicate a strong sense of belonging, of identification as members of the church community.

The large independent church studied builds on inherent linkages of place, thereby assuming the 'social spatio-temporal' (Urry, 2002, p. 154) characteristics of a global mega-event for those people attending its regular international conferences, whether they live locally, or travel from across the United Kingdom or the world, generating 'moments of co-presence' (Urry, 2002, p. 154) and community both on-site and online. Thus many churches increasingly use technology to normalise events activity, to develop and enhance the existence of community 'out of time and place' (Urry, 2002, p. 11) and thereby in practice 'dissolving the boundaries between what is [religious] ... production and what is commercial' (Urry, 2002, p. 77). Despite a collective aversion to the term, the description of 'ritual' within the independent church as 'family, community, a shared life' (Dowson, 2012) is demonstrated beyond modern liturgical limits (Clark, 1984) by the existence of the 'Sunday night family' (Dowson, 2012). Each week, photographs are posted online using the Instagram App, of a group of people from the church, as they share life together – whether rolling down a grassy hill or snugly warm by the fire. The mediatisation (Urry & Larsen, 2011) of the ritual of this community-within-a-community has also become part of the Sunday night/Monday morning ritual for observers, drawn into community online. And the important role of small groups in relationship-forming is underlined here (Clark, 1984, p. 73), whether those groups are self-selecting and informal, or organised through the church as life groups or home groups.

For the village church, 'people here very much have that village mentality – [this] is their church, even though some of them don't come anywhere near' (Dowson, 2012). The exceptions are times such as funerals, Remembrance Sunday and the annual village-organised Christmas Market, when over 1,000 people flood into and through the church on one day, providing further evidence of events engagement within the village community.

Types of events and their purposes

In analysing church events activity within the research, two lists were compiled: first, of different event types encountered within the three churches studied, found in the top half of Table 13.1. The second comprised a range of purposes of church events, separate from specific event types, in the lower half of the table.

However, through the research, it was discovered that any one event might have several purposes, which could include 'spiritual' and 'social' aspects, along with 'pragmatic' or even 'secular' areas, such as marketing (say, to specific demographics), reputation management and fundraising. Yet where does evangelism sit within such a framework, for it is as surely related to marketing as it is to spirituality? And while an evangelistic event may take many different forms, there are various different events that include an evangelistic purpose or outcome. How does the 'spiritual' aspect of 'fellowship' relate to the 'social' perspectives of 'building community', or 'doing life together' in an outworking of the shared values of religious communities? The multiplicity of event purposes and outcomes impacts on a clarity of purpose for every event, but is complicated by the dynamic relationships between the different categories of purpose, and between the events themselves, as religious organisations seek to communicate the stories, symbols, rituals and beliefs that combine to form a culture that engages with the surrounding community, and forms a community in and of itself. These considerations have led to the categorisation of event purposes within a range of identified groupings, shown in Figure 13.2.

Table 13.1 Event types and purposes

Event types

Christian basics courses (e.g. Alpha) Top of Form	Christian city-wide missions	Christian conferences
Christian family courses (e.g. The Marriage Course, How to Drug-Proof Your Kids)	Christian festivals (e.g. Greenbelt)	Christian music events
Christian prayer meetings	Christian residential events (e.g. Soul Survivor, Spring Harvest)	Discussion groups
Flower festivals	Interfaith (prayer) meetings	Local fetes
Men's group	Occupy movement	Other Christian events not associated with your church
Political meetings or campaigns	Protests and demonstrations	Seasonal (church year)
Small groups (e.g. life groups, home groups) Youth eventsBottom of Form	Women's group (e.g. Mothers' Union)	Worship events

Event purposes

Catechesis	Change and transformation (of individual, community and society)	Civic (Remembrance Day)
Commercial activity	Discipleship	Ecumenism
Educational	Evangelism and mission Top of Form	Fundraising
Governance	Forming group identity	Holiness
Initiation	Interfaith	Learning
Life cycle (baptisms, weddings and funerals)	Liturgical	Networking and growing sustainable networks
Nurturing	Pastoral	Social
Raising social justice issues	Relationship building within the church	Relationship building with the wider community
Reputation building (of leaders)	Reputation building (of the church)	Ritual
Teaching	Worship	

Governance	Spiritual church activity	Internally-driven events	Community focus	External organisations hiring facilities for events
Corporate governance	Catechesis Discipleship Holiness Initiation Life-cycle Liturgical Ritual Seasons Worship	Fundraising Networking and growing sustainable networks Social justice		Commercial activity Community-based activity
	Change and transfomation Education Evangelism and Mission Forming group identity Learning Nurturing Pastoral Relationship-building within the church Ritual Reputation Teaching		Ecumenism Interfaith Relationship-building within wider community Civic events	

Figure 13.2 Groupings of identified event purposes (© R. Dowson, 2012).

Church members' involvement in events

Given a list of 26 mainly event-related activities across the churches, respondents were asked to identify whether they had participated in or organised such an activity, either as an individual or as a member of their church.

The top 15 categories, shown in Table 13.2, are ranked according to the highest levels of response. On average, respondents said they participated in 7.2 of the activities listed as part of their church, and in 4.8 activities as individuals. For involvement in organising these events, there was an average of 3.4 activities per person as part of the church, with 2.2 activities as an individual. Overall, the average number of activities was 17.7 per respondent. This demonstrates a high level of events activity by individuals, both within the church and independently from the church. While some events may be occasional or one-off (flower festivals, for example), others are regular activities, whether seasonal (Alpha) or annual (Christian conferences). There were some surprises, such as the evidence of politicisation in all the churches.

A leader explains the importance of events as a feature of one church's life:

> You do tend to monitor people based on their attendance at events, so you observe that someone has not been coming. And actually that percolates

Table 13.2 Participation in events-related activity (%)

Events activity	Participate with church	Participate as individual	Organise with church	Organise as individual	Overall rating
Small groups	65.3	27.8	27.8	22.2	1
Worship events	59.7	25.0	22.2	8.3	2
Other Christian events: with my church	38.9	20.8	27.8	19.4	3
Discussion groups	52.8	12.5	22.2	11.1	4
Prayer meetings	50.0	23.6	13.9	9.7	5
Alpha	41.7	12.5	31.9	9.7	6
Local fetes	40.3	25.0	20.8	9.7	7
Youth events	31.9	16.7	29.2	16.7	8
Christian conferences	33.3	15.3	23.6	8.3	9
Non-Christian events	23.6	23.6	13.9	18.1	10
Christian music events	26.4	26.4	13.9	5.6	11
Women's groups	34.7	8.3	18.1	6.9	12
Christian residential events	23.6	29.2	5.6	8.3	13
Festivals	19.4	25.0	6.9	9.7	14
Podcasts	19.4	29.2	6.9	2.8	15

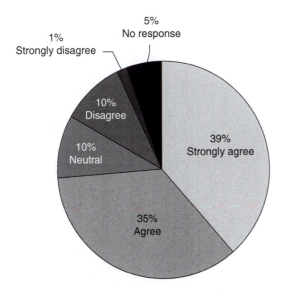

Figure 13.3 Church-related activity and events are part of my everyday life.

right down to small groups ... what are our values in terms of the services, the meetings, the events? Would they have to be purposeful? Why would people turn up to something which did not have a clearly defined purpose, was adding value? So we tend to put our emphasis there, let's make sure, let's plan well, let's talk to God about each event, let's get the elements in there, let's be open. Try and keep it fresh. So I think the 'events' as you're describing them, are a massive part of it.

(Dowson, 2012)

Therefore, it is not surprising that when asked whether church-related activity and events were part of their everyday life, overall, 74% either agreed or strongly agreed, as shown in Figure 13.3.

However, high levels of activity may not always be healthy, and despite the invitation to 'Go ahead, inconvenience me' (Scanlon, 2009), one church leader almost rebukes the constant busyness of those who fill their calendar with going from one event to another (Scanlon, 2011).

Values, events and community

The cultural centre of the three churches is based around relationship: the values of the churches and of individuals were identified from the research questionnaire.

In Figure 13.4 the Wordle™ reflects the responses for each church. One of the key values expressed that applies across all three churches is being 'welcome', though the challenge exists in making this a reality rather than an aspiration. The

Independent church

Village church

Figure 13.4 Church values.

about acceptance all believe belong caring **centred**

Christ **church** communion community course equality freedom *god* good

honest important inclusive Jesus **justice** JustSpace

learning liberation light local loved me mission moaning most others salt **social**

we welcome

Fresh expression

Figure 13.4 Continued.

values are part of what makes up the identity of each church, and for each one, its members have strongly identified with the church and its community.

Conclusion

In conclusion, each church in the study had a distinct culture, and each community was different; yet in all three churches, research participants were strongly committed to and identified themselves with their own church as a community, as well as within the community of their local geographic area. The focus of the role of ritual in church activity, when viewed through the lens of the three participating churches and the literature, is based around relationships; shared values within each church demonstrate an intention to welcome and to build close relationships within the church and into wider community. For some churches, 'serving' at events has an explicit purpose in building community and showing commitment. Small groups facilitate the care of those within them, bringing meaning to shared understandings and experiences, whether formally organised or not.

Ritual can become a dividing barrier between people (and churches), but it can also offer depth of meaning and solace. Events can and do offer opportunities to build new relationships and strengthen existing ones; they can provide possibilities to involve those within and those outside the church – whether unchurched or dechurched. The role played by events in taking the church beyond one hour on a Sunday is to support the building of relationships and encourage a sense of belonging to a community, as well as reaching out beyond the gates of the church.

Notes

1 See www.churchofengland.org/about-us/facts-stats.aspx (accessed 25 January 2012).
2 For more information, see www.royal.gov.uk/HMTheQueen/TheQueenandspecialanniversaries/TheQueensDiamondJubilee2012/TheQueensDiamondJubilee2012.aspx; www.bbc.co.uk/sport/0/tennis/18755331; www.formula1.com/races/in_detail/great_britain_872; www.bbc.co.uk/music/events/ehxzp6; www.london2012.com (accessed 11 July 2012).
3 www.northlondonvineyard.com/Articles/20012/North_London_Vineyard/Welcome/John_Wimber_and.aspx (accessed 22 July 2012).
4 www.htb.org.uk/alpha.
5 See http://uk.cfan.org/History.aspx; www.greenbelt.org.uk/about/history; www.springharvest.org/our-history (accessed 7 June 2012); www.bathandwells.org.uk/diocese/news/story/447 (accessed 11 July 2012).

References

Abrahams, R.D. (1969). Foreword. In V. Turner (eds), *The ritual process: Structure and anti-structure*. New Brunswick: Aldine Transaction.

Alexander, L. (2008). What patterns of church and mission are found in the Acts of the Apostles? In S. Croft (ed.), *Mission-shaped questions: Defining issues for today's Church*. London: Church House Publishing.

Archbishops' Council. (2009). *Mission-shaped parish: Church planting and fresh expressions in a changing context* (2nd edn). London: Church House Publishing.

Baines, N. (2011). What the Church is really for. *Musings of a Restless Bishop*. Retrieved 10 July 2012 from http://nickbaines.wordpress.com/2011/01/13/what-the-church-is-really-for.

Bowdin, G., Allen, J., O'Toole, W., Harris, R. & McDonnell, I. (2011). *Events management* (3rd edn). London: Butterworth Heinemann.

Brooks, I. (2009). *Organisational behaviour: Individuals, groups and organisations* (4th edn). Harlow: Prentice Hall.

Chomsky, N. (2012). *Occupy*. London: Penguin Books.

Clark, D. (1984). *The liberation of the Church: The role of basic Christian groups in a new re-formation*. Birmingham: The National Centre for Christian Communities and Networks.

Croft, Bishop S. (2012, 3 April). Seminar, Yorkshire Ministry Course Easter School. Whitby: Sneaton Castle.

Croft, S. (ed.). (2008). *Mission-shaped questions: Defining issues for today's Church*. London: Church House Publishing.

Davie, G. (2008). From obligation to consumption: Understanding the patterns of religion in Northern Europe. In S. Croft (ed.), *The future of the parish system: Shaping the Church of England for the 21st century*. London: Church House Publishing.

Diocese of Sheffield. (n.d.). *Growing the Body of Christ: A strategy for growth for the Diocese of Sheffield 2011–2021*. Retrieved 12 July 2012 from www.sheffield.anglican. org/index.php/growth-strategy.

Dowson, R. (2012). *The role of 'events' in church culture: An examination of three Bradford churches*. Unpublished master's thesis. Sheffield: University of Sheffield.

Foreman, P.O. & Parent, M.M. (2008). The process of organizational identity construction in iterative organizations. *Corporate Reputation Review*, 11.

Getz, D. (2007). *Event studies: Theory, research and policy for planned events*. Oxford: Butterworth Heinemann.

Getz, D. (2012). *Event studies: Theory, research and policy for planned events* (2nd edn). Abingdon: Routledge.

Goldblatt, J. (2008). *Special events: The roots and wings of celebration* (5th edn). Hoboken, NJ: John Wiley & Sons.

Guest, M. (2007). *Evangelical identity and contemporary culture: A congregational study in innovation*. Milton Keynes: Paternoster.

Hall, E.T. (1981). *Beyond culture*. New York: Anchor Books.

Hermkens, A. (2007). Church festivals and the visualization of identity in Collingwood Bay, Papua New Guinea, *Visual Anthropology, 20*(5), 347–364.

Hofstede, G. (2003). *Cultures and organisations: Intercultural co-operation and its importance for survival – Software of the mind*. London: Profile Books.

Hopewell, J.F. (1987). *Congregation: Stories and structures*. Philadelphia: Fortress Press.

Hull, J.M. (2006). *Mission-shaped church: A theological response*. London: SCM Press.

Lee, S. & Sinitiere, P.L. (2009). *Holy mavericks: Evangelical innovators and the spiritual marketplace*. New York: New York University Press.

Lynch, G. (2005). *Understanding theology and contemporary culture*. Oxford: Blackwell Publishing.

Morrison, K.L. (2006). *Marx, Durkheim, Weber: Formations of modern social thought* (2nd edn). London: Sage.

People1st. (2010). *Labour Market Review of the Events Industry*. Uxbridge: People1st. Retrieved 12 October 2011 from www.businesstourismpartnership.com/pubs/ Labour%20Market%20Review%20of%20the%20events%20Industry%20January%20 2010.pdf.

Pravera, K. (1981). The United States. *Christianity & Crisis, 41*(14), 251.

Roche, M. (2009). *Mega-events and modernity: Olympics and expos in the growth of global culture*. London: Routledge.

Scanlon, P. (2009). *The 15 Revolution: Go ahead, inconvenience me*. Bradford: Abundant Life Publishing.

Scanlon, P. (2011). *Momentum* (CD). Bradford: Abundant Life Church Publishing.

Schein, E.H. (1996). Defining organizational culture. In J.M. Shafritz & J.S. Ott (eds), *Classics of organization theory* (4th edn). Fort Worth, TX: Harcourt Brace College Publishers, 1996.

Share Jesus International. (2011). *The Church has left the building: How to run a community festival – Guide for festival organisers*. London: Share Jesus International.

Shorter, A. (1994). *Evangelization and culture*. London: Bloomsbury.

Sivakumar, K. & Nakata, C. (2001). The stampede towards Hofstede's framework: Avoiding the sample design pit in cross-cultural research. *Journal of International Business Studies, 32*(3), 555–574.

Smith, P.B. & Peterson, M.F. (1988). *Leadership, organizations and culture*. London: Sage Publications.

Tjitra, H. (2011). *Best practices in cross-cultural research: Quantitative research methodologies*. Retrieved 18 July 2012 from www.slideshare.net/horatjitra/best-practices-in-crosscultural-research.

Tomlin, G. (2008). Can we develop churches that can transform the culture? In S. Croft (ed.), *Mission-shaped questions: Defining issues for today's Church*. London: Church House Publishing.

Turner, V. (1969). *The ritual process: Structure and anti-structure*. New Brunswick: Aldine Transaction.

Turner, V. (ed.). (1982). *Celebration: Studies in festival and ritual*. Washington, DC: Smithsonian Institute.

Urry, J. (2002). *The tourist gaze* (2nd edn). London: Sage Publications.

Urry, J. & Larsen, J. (2011). *The tourist gaze 3.0* (3rd edn). London: Sage.

Varey, R.J. (2002). *Relationship marketing: Dialogue and networks in the e-commerce era*. Chichester: John Wiley & Sons Ltd.

14 'Taste'-ing festivals

Understanding constructions of rural identity through community festivals

Jessica Pacella, Jodie George and Rosie Roberts

Introduction

The importance of rural festivals as an aspect of regional identity and economic sustainability has gained significant research interest over the last decade (Bell & Jayne, 2010; Brennan-Horley, Connell & Gibson, 2007; Gorman-Murray, Darian-Smith & Gibson, 2008). These studies have articulated the importance of rural festivals in the construction of place-identity, and much of the contemporary research problematises rurality as merely the geographical foil of the urban (see Cloke, Marsden & Mooney, 2006). This research, however, builds upon this by addressing the significant negotiations of the meaning of 'taste' that take place during festivals. This chapter draws upon findings from a research project that examined three regional festivals across South Australia during 2012 and 2013. These included the Port Lincoln Tunarama Festival, the Kangaroo Island Arts Feast and the Gorgeous Festival held in McLaren Vale. Specifically, this chapter seeks to focus primarily upon the Gorgeous Festival, an event held over one day and night, celebrating the food, wine and music of the region located on the Fleurieu Peninsula, approximately 40 km from Adelaide. In particular, this chapter explores the intersections between taste and class at regional festivals to better define what the researchers have termed 'festival capital', in which all the different consumptive elements of the festival brand themselves to particular audiences and communities.

Given South Australia's position as a global stakeholder in wine production, and the importance of McLaren Vale's brand image as one of the premiere wine regions in both the state and the country, this festival provided a rich space in which to examine the impacts these identity-driven events have on community members and tourists who attend. Additionally, it seemed fitting, given South Australia's own branding of being known as 'the festival state', that we draw our focus to festivals located in rural parts of the state given its underrepresentation in festival literature. As festival spaces may be understood to promote multiple dimensions of community identity, and given that the Gorgeous Festival is privately owned and operated by two local community members, the execution of this festival, in the eyes of the greater McLaren Vale community, is quite significant.

Traditional notions of rurality and the 'country town' were somewhat abandoned during the Gorgeous Festival. Events such as the Tuna Toss and the Keg Roll Competition, while lauded and celebrated at the Tunarama Festival, would more than likely be subject to ridicule at Gorgeous. Rather, this festival addresses the significant intersections of rural 'taste', where what you consume is just as important as where you consume it. Given that there exists assumptions about the poor quality of food in regional areas due to their distance from urbanised and more densely populated areas where high-quality food is more readily abundant and that rural locations are not usually marked as cultural or culinary 'hot spots', the Gorgeous Festival in particular gives us the ability to expose the more complex relationship that exists between taste and class at rural festivals, and how this symbiosis has the capacity to rebrand and reshape what rural means.

The Gorgeous Festival is able to provide the experience of rural exclusivity, which is arguably a relatively new phenomenon in the realm of human geography studies given that much of the research around rural areas and their globalisation is around the proliferation of primary resources such as wheat and minerals (Woods, 2009). Interestingly though, McLaren Vale has never been reliant on traditional agriculture as its primary industry. Since its European colonisation from the early 19th century, wine making and the planting of vineyards has been the dominant industry in this area. Other literature, meanwhile, suggests that in the rural context, out-migration is an ever-present problem, and that staging festivals are indeed a way to revitalise country towns, especially from an economic standpoint (Walmsley, 2003). What this festival is able to capitalise on is its ability to attract people with high disposable incomes through the promotion of the celebration of particular tastes – in particular the sampling of 'boutique wine and gourmet food', relying on a cultivation of the senses.

Research methods

All three festivals chosen by investigators were similar in that they each shared common threads of relationships to food, wine and music. But each of these festivals were diverse in terms of their distance to capital cities, the level of community involvement, age of the event itself and the intended target audience. However, each festival played upon different understandings of the term 'rural'. It was in these differences that a richer and more complex picture of community identity can begin to emerge.

In addition to participant observation and a discourse analysis of promotional material, and in order to be able to critically analyse a rich array of material, researchers conducted informal, semi-structured interviews with both festival organisers and festival participants. We interviewed the festival organisers first, prior to the event, and asked them questions relating to their professional background; involvement with the festival, including its history and future directions; the aims of the event; how they thought the festival might be improved; the demographic appeal of the festival; how they feel the festival contributes to the local community; and to describe a favourite memory of the event. The interviews with the organisers ranged from approximately 1.5 to two hours in duration.

We also randomly selected participants while at each festival. We asked festival participants to describe their favourite aspects of the festival; how they thought the festival might be improved or expanded; who they thought the festival was for; what a typical 'festival goer' might look like; who might not attend the festival; what impact the festival might have on the local community; and, if they had visited the festival before, to describe a favourite memory.

This mixed-methods approach provided researchers with a lens through which to examine the complex entanglements surrounding notions of the rural, and how these tensions can manifest in different representations of local performance.

Gorgeous Festival

> 'We didn't want the cheapest wine available ... we didn't want hotdog and doughnut vans...'
>
> (interview with Gorgous Festival organisers, 2012)

Most participants recognised the emphasis placed on food and wine at the Gorgeous Festival and that it was not ordinary 'festival food' where you might expect to encounter a lot of fast-food vans selling deep-fried chips, giros or hotdogs. The quotation above, taken from an interview with the festival organisers, speaks quite specifically to what they knew they had no desire to see at their festival. In their interview they had also commented on how other festivals or day events that came through the region outsourced food and drinks. So rather than use what was locally available, the organisers saw what was essentially an exploitation of their location, where others were capitalising on a particular brand appeal of McLaren Vale, but not engaging with local vendors. 'They would just come in ... and move on' (Festival Organiser, 2012). At the Gorgeous Festival, food was provided by local restaurants that used largely local produce. However, these vendors are all upmarket restaurants in the McLaren Vale region where on their full menus you can find the starting price for an entrée to cost approximately AU$25 (£13.50) and a main price to start at AU$35 (£18.90). The festival organisers commented on the fact that when they approached local restaurants they were initially met with some resistance and recounted that a number of restaurants had said to them, 'well ... we don't really do that kind of thing'; where 'that kind of thing' came to mean serving archetypal 'festival' food from catering tents. The implication was that, in addition to these local food vendors having little experience of creating their complex menu options to be consumed on such a large scale, festivals that feature music traditionally have a limited gastronomic cultural capital, and as such may do a disservice to the 'boutique' restaurant brand these local vendors have created. But the Gorgeous Festival organisers themselves placed high importance on terms such as 'boutique', 'premium end' and would serendipitously capitalise on the revival of the 'slow food' movement in many capital cities in Australia (particularly Adelaide) while, at the same time, skirting the more parochial ideas surrounding rural food.

> The true basis of the differences ... is the opposition between the tastes of luxury (or freedom) and the tastes of necessity. The former are the tastes of individuals who are the product of material conditions of existence defined by distance from necessity...; the latter express, precisely in their adjustment, the necessity of which they are the product.
>
> (Bourdieu, 1984, p. 177)

What this quotation from Bourdieu helps to explain is how, in a very European sense, this festival still draws upon the idea that 'culinary sophistication has been a highly sensitive marker of social distinction' (Newman & Gibson, 2005, p. 86). Considering that the menu items at this festival consisted of lobster medallion with blue swimmer crab and prawn ravioli in a lobster bisque, freshly shucked Kangaroo Island oysters, Argentinian char-grilled beef short ribs, goat shoulder curry, char-grilled corn with chipotle and parmesan, pulled pork sandwiches, chorizo, pickled onion and romesco panini or artisan cheese platters, it is clear that this festival is capitalising on the attendees' literal consumption of taste, which is acting as an inadvertent mirror of class. In this way, as private, personal tastes are made public through festival attendance, participants revealed their own 'festival capital', and a participation in a resistance to the globalisation of food. This refinement of taste is then, arguably, a political act. As Woods has argued:

> As traditional resource-exploitation-based rural economies have declined, the reinvention of rural localities as 'playgrounds' for visitors and in-migrants can be a relatively attractive option to local actors compared with the alternative futures. Consequently, the politics of globalization in rural amenity resorts are not the politics of local resistance to globalization, but rather a local politics in which the terms of engagement with globalization are negotiated and contested.
>
> (Woods, 2009, p. 369)

There are concerns that such a neo-liberal influence over food politics can lead to an overly moralistic understanding of how we eat food where 'the privileged have taken on the congratulatory mantle of self-reflexivity in eating at the expense of those others who are said to lack the cultural capacities to know that local, organic, slow food *tastes* better' (Probyn, 2011, p. 100). Slow food as a mode for acquiring cultural capital is nothing new (see Brunori, 2006; Donati, 2005; Sassatelli & Davolio, 2010; Tregar, Arfini, Belletti & Marscotti, 2007), but in this case, it knowingly acts in resistance and opposition to the global, or rather, non-local.

Figure 14.1 Char-grilled beef short ribs (image provided by Tony Lewis).

On the event website, the food is described as 'lovingly hand-picked to show-case the talent of local and notable McLaren Vale eateries, that utilise fresh regional produce ... at the festival there's not a hot dog van in sight!' (Gorgeous Festival, 2013). Terms such as 'lovingly hand-picked' carry with them a certain romantic sentimentality that still surrounds some contemporary imaginings of rurality and localism. However, at the same time, while the food at this festival is drawing upon the nostalgic charm of the 'small town' where there is an expectation to find things 'hand-made' or 'hand-picked', there is also a reinforcement of the quality of produce, and urbane cosmopolitanism on the other. The assertion that there will be 'not a hotdog van in sight' featuring on the event website, and reinforced in the interview with the organisers themselves, is demonstrative of a new brand of rural identity. In this respect, fast food at this particular festival would not only be considered tremendously out of place, but would also be, for those who would choose to eat it, politically and culturally isolating.

A comparison may be drawn with the Tunarama Festival where, interestingly, fast food was in abundance and items such as hotdogs, deep-fried seafood, hot chips, soft-serve ice cream, cotton candy and jam doughnuts were all readily available and, indeed, sought after. These food vendors were set up in a children's carnival atmosphere next to rides such as a ferris wheel on the esplanade of the Port Lincoln beach. In this context, this food experience is not considered out of place as the Tunarama Festival, as a whole, quite heavily plays on an archetypal version of rurality that is struggling to move out of a romanticised nostalgia for a time long past; a naive charm.

Many of the Gorgeous Festival participants we interviewed made similar comments about the food, in that it was atypical of other festivals they had attended; something that excited them to come to the event; and, as one participant mentioned, 'because of the location and the menu it's more of a mixed group ... so it's not young teeny-boppers'. We had noticed that the majority of

Figure 14.2 Hand-shucked Kangaroo Island oysters (image provided by Tony Lewis).

participants seemed to range in age from mid-20s to over-50s, suggesting that to attend this festival a participant would certainly require at least a moderate level of disposable income greater than that required of a traditional music festival located in a capital city where incidental expenses throughout the day would be less expensive. Unsurprisingly, this level of disposable income is often age-related, where a person has either completed some form of tertiary education and is no longer casually employed, or has spent a number of years in full-time employment. It is interesting that for some festival goers, this event was made more attractive by its economic exclusivity.

Perhaps this return to slow food illustrates the current position of authentic experiences within tourism literature given that 'authenticity', at least in the experience economy, has so often dominated the debate. Perhaps this is because the relationship to food is not one of curiosity stemmed from the exotic 'other',

Figure 14.3 Lobster medallion with blue swimmer crab and prawn ravioli in a lobster bisque (image provided by Tony Lewis).

but rather a far more primary, gluttonous connection. It is not 'excess', but rather, as argued above, an amorphous, sensory experience where consuming taste is suggestive both of putting something delicious, gourmet and 'lovingly hand-picked' in your mouth and of refinement. Rather, this festival is not a place where the authenticity debate plays out, but in its place is a movement towards a sophisticated hedonism.

> 'It's not come here pre-loaded and buy your chemicals on-site … it's not that kind of festival … it's more just enjoy the vibe.'

The promotional materials for the Gorgeous Festival feature in its background image a depiction of green rolling hills, streaks of sunshine emerging from behind orange and purple clouds painted in soft watercolour. This imagery of an idyllic countryside evokes a European pastoral rural ideal, especially given its soft tones that exude a 'vibe' of 'handmade' and 'artisanal'. This furthers the relationship this festival seeks to forge between slow food and rural locales. It is interesting that a number of locals that were interviewed, when asked if they were a 'local', considered themselves to be so even though they did not live in the township of McLaren Vale itself. Some lived at the furthest stretch on the southern side of the Adelaide city limits, in close proximity to McLaren Vale but still a part of the Adelaide metropolitan area. As a research team, we questioned why festival attendees would claim to be 'local' when in fact they were not. The festival organisers themselves commented on what they considered too much urban sprawl, and the potential loss of place.

> I think it's unfortunate the government approved all that housing at Seaford Heights. [McLaren Vale] is increasingly encroached upon by urban sprawl. I think the recent McLaren Vale protection bill is a really healthy thing … I think limiting the size of McLaren vale, essentially putting a ring around it, [is a good thing]. It feels regional when you're in it, it doesn't feel urban. It feels very much like we live in a country community.
>
> (Gorgeous Festival organisers, 2012)

Perhaps a part of wanting to maintain distance from the city of Adelaide for McLaren Vale is important in maintaining its status as an escape; separate from the more densely populated city as a place to relax and unwind. Festival goers themselves seemed to revel in this 'vibe' and recognised how this festival was different from many others. As the displayed quotation above suggests, this festival was not a place where 'party drugs' such as ecstasy and amphetamines were to be consumed by a large proportion of the audience as can be the case at many other music festivals, where people are routinely searched prior to entry and police sniffer dogs are used extensively. A majority of participants similarly commented on this festival as being a relaxing day, rather than a 12-hour music marathon. Many were happy that the festival started later in the afternoon (at approximately 2 p.m.), as it gave them time to visit the local farmers' market in nearby Willunga, and other surrounding attractions. The day itself started off with cooking demonstrations by a local chef. But even when attendees arrived at the festival site, most people seemed to be lounging on the grass in areas shaded by the trees, eating food and drinking wine. The festival organisers also commented on how they did not want the sound to be too loud so as to make it impossible to have a conversation. Having this space marked out as different seemed to physically and emotionally affect those who attended (Nelson, 2009). Indeed, how a space is laid out and presented to an audience seems to affect how they consume it. One participant noted that 'there's no little kids running around in fluoro tops … it's a little bit like Womad but not quite as hippie'. (Womadelaide is a five-day festival held over the Easter long weekend located on the northern parklands of Adelaide's CBD.) It is a 'world music festival' and is often stereotyped in local newspapers as a 'hippie event' and Adelaide residents often refer to this festival as 'Womad'. Indeed, the 'hippie' atmosphere was less pronounced and in its place was a garden-party/picnic atmosphere created by white picket fences (to separate the VIP area), wine barrel tables scattered around the venue and wooden sail umbrellas. This is a far more sophisticated and exclusive representation of the 'rural idyll' (Cloke, 2006) that often operates under the guise of a more simple and rustic imagined space. Festival goers seemed to be expecting this level of sophistication, rather than a more parochial execution of 'rural'. Indeed, this festival, while taking place in a rural area, is one that actually invites a sensory gluttony due to knowledge of the area as the premium end of the wine industry. The promotional material made it quite clear that there would be music with both 'gorgeous premium wine' and 'gorgeous gourmet food', thus ensuring that the relationship between taste and place is reinforced.

Conclusion

Place and taste are still important areas of research. This is especially so with regard to how to place contemporary and complex understandings of modern rurality. What these different festival spaces have given us is a lens through which to re-examine and look much more closely at how rural locations within South Australia have worked to create specific and highly cultivated identities that have a very explicit appeal. What the Gorgeous Festival offers in particular is a confluence of local identity and culture, but is directly aimed at those wishing to celebrate a very particular kind of cultural capital. The Gorgeous Festival is an amalgam of cultural party, food and wine festival atmosphere and gentrified rural landscape that draws upon romanticised European pastoral ideals. In particular, the festival's focus on slow food and the senses acts as a way for attendees to literally consume 'taste' where, on the one hand, its identity is firmly entrenched within this newly realised rural exclusivity, but on the other provides a recognisable, more cosmopolitan tourism for the urban dwellers who can 'escape to the country', though they really only escape to the city they know.

References

Bell, D. & Jayne, M. (2010). The creative countryside: Policy and practice in the UK rural cultural economy. *Journal of Rural Studies, 26*, 209–218.

Bourdieu, P. (1984). *Distinction: A social critique of the judgement of taste.* London: Routledge.

Brennan-Horley, C., Connell, J. & Gibson, C. (2007). The Parkes Elvis Revival Festival: Economic development and contested place identities in rural Australia. *Australian Geographical Research, 45*(1), 71–84.

Brunori, G. (2006). Post-rural processes in wealthy rural areas: Hybrid networks and symbolic capital. In T. Marsden & J. Murdoch (eds), *Between the local and the global: Confronting complexity in the contemporary agri-food sector* (pp. 121–145). Oxford: Elsevier.

Cloke, P. (2006). Conceptualising rurality. In P. Cloke, T. Marsden & P. Mooney (eds), *The handbook of rural studies* (pp. 18–28). London: Sage.

Donati, K. (2005). The pleasure of diversity in slow food ethics of taste. *Food, Culture and Society, 7*(2), 117–132.

Fonte, M. (2006). Slow food's presidia: What do small producers do with big retailers? In T. Marsden & J. Murdoch (eds), *Between the local and the global: Confronting complexity in the contemporary agri-food sector* (pp. 203–240). Oxford: Elsevier.

Gorgeous Festival. (2013). *The festival.* Retrieved 12 September 2013 from http://gorgeousfestival.com.au/about/festival.

Gorman-Murray, A., Darian-Smith, K. & Gibson, C. (2008). Scaling the rural: Reflections on rural cultural studies. *Australian Humanities Review*, 45.

Nelson, K.B. (2009). Enhancing the attendee's experience through creative design of the event environment: Applying Goffman's dramaturgical perspective. *Journal of Convention and Event Tourism, 10*(2), 120–133.

Newman, F. & Gibson, M. (2005). Monoculture versus multiculinarism. In D. Bell & J. Hollows (eds), *Ordinary lifestyles: Popular media, consumption and taste* (pp. 82–98). Maidenhead: McGraw-Hill.

Probyn, E. (2011). Swimming with tuna: Human-ocean entanglements. *Australian Humanities Review, 51*, 97–114.

Sassatelli, R. & Davolio, F. (2010). Consumption, pleasure and politics: Slow food and the politico-aesthetic problematization of food. *Journal of Consumer Culture, 10*(2), 202–232.

Tregar, A., Arfini, F., Belletti, G. & Marscotti, A. (2007). Regional foods and rural development: The role of product qualification. *Journal of Rural Studies, 23*, 12–22.

Walmsley, D.J. (2003). Rural tourism: A case of lifestyle-led opportunities. *Australian Geographer, 34*(1), 61–72.

Woods, M. (2009). The local politics of the global countryside: Boosterism, aspirational ruralism and the contested reconstitution of Queenstown, New Zealand. *GeoJournal, 76*, 365–381.

15 Swiss and Italian identities

Exploring heritage, culture and community in regional Australia

Leanne White

Introduction

This chapter examines a community festival known as the 'Swiss and Italian Festa' that is held annually in the popular tourist towns of Daylesford and Hepburn Springs in Central Victoria, Australia. The chapter ties in with some of the key themes of this book, including 'culture, authenticity and meaning of local community events'; 'the evolution and life cycle of local community events'; 'community events as tourist attractions'; 'the role and importance of community events'; and 'community hospitality, foods and wine'.

The Swiss and Italian Festa was first staged as a small community event in 1992. Since then, it has evolved to become a 12-day event with a focus on heritage and culture attracting around 14,000 attendees (Laing & Frost, 2013, p. 327). The festival incorporates a variety of aspects and activities such as music, food, wine, the arts, heritage displays, street parades and sporting events. The Swiss and Italian Festa has become the largest celebration of the region's cultural heritage. Like many community festivals, it relies on an enormous amount of good will and commitment from a very small group of committed volunteers.

The chapter examines the interconnections between an established and popular community festival, tourism, tradition and identity in Australia's leading spa tourism area – Daylesford and Hepburn Springs. Gammon has argued that heritage has the ability to 'guide and cement national identities' (Gammon, 2007, p. 1). When exploring our past, we are delving deeper into both our own heritage and that of the nation. Underlying this suggestion is the proposition that heritage is a 'cultural and social process' that is 'ultimately intangible' (Smith, 2006, p. 307). With this in mind, this chapter aims to explore the ways in which the often intangible concept of heritage is imagined, and will examine the decisions made by those associated with this festival to make that case.

By focusing on Swiss and Italian heritage in this region, we can rethink our understanding and 'awareness of the role' that heritage plays 'in our everyday lives' (Waterton, 2010, p. 206). For the individual celebrating the festival, heritage becomes somehow embodied and personified by their own experiences and those of others – along with the many photographs of the experiences that may be taken and shared. If we understand heritage as a process that constructs meaning about the past, then the construction of this brand of heritage in Daylesford and Hepburn Springs is illustrative of this process. It is, essentially, a construction of a form of heritage based on stories, memories, reports and photographs that have been documented and passed down through the generations by family and friends. Contrary to popular notions of heritage that situate it as 'object-based', this example offers an interpretation of heritage that builds on the work of Smith, Waterton, Gammon and others.

Community festivals are widely celebrated around the world and many people are becoming increasingly interested in the roots or cultural underpinnings of the festivals they choose to attend. This chapter considers the distinctive role of the Swiss and Italian Festa in sustaining social cohesion in a regional community. However, as other researchers (Van Winkle, Woosnam & Mohammed, 2013) have explained, more research needs to be undertaken to clarify the exact nature of the relationship between festival attendance and sense of community. While it is possible to examine the phenomena of community festivals and their associated rituals and traditions in mutually exclusive ways, the chapter explores the concepts in a combined manner and examines how particular rituals built on tradition may help develop distinctive identities and ways of thinking – particularly for those who engage in the festival activities.

Falassi (1987, p. 4) argues that festivals modify our normal sense of time with various ritualistic movements that are carried out from the beginning to the end of the festival. This modification creates a so-called 'time out of time' – with a respectfully observed temporal dimension devoted to each key activity. Celebrations can indeed place our 'normal' sense of time in something of a holding pattern while festival (atypical) time is taken to focus on others – especially family and friends. Festivals usually consist of a number of ritual acts or rites. The rites that form key functions in the Swiss and Italian Festa are: rites of conspicuous display, rites of conspicuous consumption and rites of exchange (Falassi, 1987, pp. 4–5). As Falassi contends, an unavoidable element of many festivals is conspicuous consumption. As such, linking with this community festival and the culinary heritage of the region, three local businesses are also worthy of further examination. They are: the Old Macaroni Factory, Lavandula and Lake House.

Following this introduction, some background will be provided on the popular towns of Daylesford and Hepburn Springs. The Swiss and Italian heritage of the region and this distinctive community festival are then explored. Three businesses, out of the many that trade (to a greater or lesser extent) on their Swiss and Italian traditions, are briefly examined before some conclusions are drawn.

Daylesford and Hepburn Springs

Daylesford and Hepburn Springs in regional Victoria were founded in 1852 and 1837, respectively, and boast a combined population of around 3,500. The towns are located approximately 120 km north-west of Melbourne. Daylesford is named after the town of the same name in England, while Hepburn Springs is named after Captain John Hepburn who discovered the mineral springs in 1836, having travelled from Sydney to settle in the area. Hepburn claimed that the area was the most attractive he had seen and he planned to spend the rest of his life there.

The local tourism board promotes the towns with the words: 'famous twin villages built on gold, fertile soils and mineral water … in the foothills of surrounding state forests, these boutique towns are dedicated to indulgence and wellbeing' (Daylesford and Macedon Ranges Tourism, 2011, p. 38). The population grew rapidly with an influx of thousands of miners following the discovery of gold in the 1850s. Gold was discovered in 1851 at the Jim Crow diggings and by 1855, a substantial number of people had settled in the area. Many thousands of Chinese and European settlers (including around 2,000 from the border regions of Italy and Switzerland) were attracted to the cool climate, ample mineral water and the prospect of finding gold.

Timber and agriculture were also key ingredients that attracted new settlers to the area, especially after much of the gold supply had been exhausted. Indeed, a committee of residents, headed by Dr Francesco Rosetti, petitioned the government to protect the mineral springs (effectively thought of as liquid gold to the newly arrived migrants) from being ruined by excessive mining. As a result, the Hepburn Mineral Springs Reserve was created in 1865 (see Figure 15.1).

Figure 15.1 Entrance sign to the historic Hepburn Mineral Springs Reserve.

Prior to the discovery of gold in the region, the Dja Dja Wurrung indigenous people lived in the area. The local tourism visitor guide respectfully acknowledges the original inhabitants of the land: 'The region that centres around Daylesford and the Macedon Ranges has been a gathering place for thousands of years. A sacred place for aboriginal nations since time began' (Daylesford and Macedon Ranges Tourism, 2011, p. 3).

Like many rural communities, the railway line has played an important role in the development of tourism in the region since the 1880s. During this period, Daylesford was promoted with the slogan 'Delightful Daylesford' (Davidson & Spearritt, 2000, p. 76). The depression of the 1890s adversely affected the region – as it did in many parts of the world. The appeal of the area increased during the early 20th century as affluent Melbournians were lured by the supposed healing powers of the mineral springs. As a tourist destination, Daylesford and Hepburn Springs went through a period of stagnation in the 1960s and 1970s. A resurgence of the area occurred slowly from the late 1980s.

With its emphasis on health and wellness, mineral water, heritage, fine food, wineries, art galleries, festivals and more, the historic towns are considered the perfect weekend destination for many Melbournians. The Daylesford and Hepburn Springs area can boast 72 mineral springs. This represents 80% of Australia's mineral springs and the highest concentration in the Southern Hemisphere. As a result, Daylesford authorities promote the town as the 'Spa Centre of Australia'. Not to be outdone, the neighbouring town of Hepburn Springs claims to be the 'Spa Capital of Australia'.

The pursuit of indulgent weekends away has led to a rise in 'wellness tourism' for the towns. Over the past couple of decades, the area has recaptured the popularity that it enjoyed as a spa destination during the Victorian era when tourists flocked to the town to 'take the waters' (bathe in the warm mineral springs). With more than 100 day spa and health/wellness businesses in the area actively embracing the concept and offering services such as spa treatments, relaxation, massage and various holistic therapies, it comes as no surprise that 'wellness in all its forms is the mainstay of the economy' (Robertson, 2008, p. 8). The diversity of offerings in the region is exceptionally varied.

In addition to the Swiss and Italian Festa, Daylesford and Hepburn Springs hold a number of popular festivals and events, including the Lavandula Lavender Harvest Festival, the Highlands Festival which attracts people of Scottish descent, the Words in Winter Festival which celebrates writing, and the 'Chill Out' Festival for gay couples and lesbians – Australia's second largest gay and lesbian event after the Sydney Mardi Gras.

Daylesford received international coverage by topping a worldwide list of 'funky towns' in 2005. The British Airways *High Life* in-flight magazine awarded the town the coveted prize, explaining that Daylesford has a reputation for diversity and tolerance (Kurosawa, 2005, p. 1). Offering more than 300 accommodation options, the region is deliberately marketed as satisfying a wide range of interests and target audiences. The area's success as a tourist destination owes much to its social diversity.

Swiss and Italian heritage

As outlined above, around 2,000 migrants from the border region of Switzerland and Italy decided to settle in the area in the mid 19th century. The reasons why these settlers chose to leave their homeland included poor crops, unemployment, hunger and political unrest (Gervasoni, 2005). The journey to Australia in the 1850s took around 3–4 months. When steam power was introduced in the 1860s, the journey was shortened to about a month.

Some of the names of the families who settled in the area were Pozzi, Morganti, Tomasetti, Perini, Righetti, Milesi, Gervasoni, Vanzetta and Rodini (Carlson, 1997). As Carlson argues, these Italian-speaking settlers were important because they were effectively the first significant group of non-English speakers to settle in Australia. They paved the way for greater acceptance of all migrants and helped shape Australia's tolerant multicultural society.

Italian-speaking Swiss and northern Italians (along with their descendants) have had a significant impact on the way in which the towns of Daylesford and Hepburn Springs have developed over the past 160 or so years. The Swiss-Italians (as they are often referred to) campaigned to preserve the mineral springs (in danger of being damaged due to excessive gold mining) and ensured that the health-giving waters would continue to flow for future generations. Among other achievements, they established vineyards; built impressive stone mansions, farm houses and walls; planted chestnut trees, pencil pines and olive trees; and introduced the culinary traditions of their countries to the wider community. Settlers came from a range of areas, including Ticino, Piedmont, Lombardy, Veneto and Parma.

The Savoia Hotel in Hepburn Springs was named in honour of the royal family of Italy, while one of the mineral springs (Locarno) is named after a resort town in the Ticino region. A historic rendered brick and stone building in Hepburn Springs is known as Villa Parma. Built in 1864 by Fabrizzio Crippa, Villa Parma is now part of a luxury spa resort. The 20 acres of gardens at the venue feature bay trees, olive trees and herb gardens.

Many of the names of the accommodation choices in Daylesford and Hepburn Springs also reflect the Swiss-Italian heritage of the region. These names include Bella Cottage, Benessere, Finzi Contini, Genoa Country House, Grange Bellinzona, Italia Nostra Pensione, Italian Hill, Kira Villa, Perini Country House, Swiss Mount Villa, Tesoro, Trieste Villa, Tuscany on the Lake and Villa Castania.

Apart from the annual community festival, the Swiss-Italian heritage of the region has been celebrated in many ways. In 2007, the Melbourne Immigration Museum staged an exhibition entitled 'Wine, Water and Stone' that showcased the Swiss and Italian heritage of the region. Exchange visits between the twin towns and the border regions of Italy and Switzerland have also created valued cultural connections (Mulligan et al., 2006). James Milesi, one of the descendants of the Swiss-Italian migrants, was so fascinated by the story of his ancestors that he decided to study history at university then later undertake a PhD into the distinct language and culture of his ancestors. Bridget Carlson also documented the stories of 15 Swiss-Italian families in the region for a doctoral thesis. Another descendant, Maria Viola, wrote a Masters thesis on the Lucini family; while Clare Gervasoni (also a descendant) captured the remarkable stories of the Swiss and Italian settlers in the book *Bullboar, Macaroni and Mineral Water*.

Bullboar sausages are normally made from beef and/or pork (hence bull boar) and are blended with a variety of spices. The sausages are an important aspect of the Swiss-Italian culinary tradition and were named an endangered recipe by the Slow Food Movement in 2005. Gary Thomas, a local chef and President of the School Council at Daylesford Secondary College, was instrumental in organising a group of students to make traditional bullboar sausages for a national slow food competition – a 'Farm to Table Challenge'. Following a 'taste test' with the public, the students chose to use the Gervasoni and Sartori family recipes because they were the most popular. The result of the highly publicised effort was that the students and the community learned about the food heritage of their region, they presented at a Slow Food conference, were filmed by a television crew for a food documentary and also managed to win second prize in the competition. The cultural and culinary heritage and traditions of the Swiss-Italians are proudly celebrated each year with the staging of the annual community festival.

The Swiss and Italian Festa

The festival provides an opportunity for the smaller town of Hepburn Springs to display its rich heritage and traditions (see Figure 15.2). The Swiss and Italian Festa has become the largest celebration of the region's cultural heritage 'probably because it is a highly unusual heritage in Australian terms' which must 'surely rank among the best uses of stories from local history in Australia' (Mulligan et al., 2006, pp. 106–123). Of the many festivals held each year in the towns of Daylesford and Hepburn Springs, a 2006 report focusing on community celebrations and well-being found the Swiss and Italian Festa to be the most interesting as it has 'revived interest in the unique Swiss-Italian heritage of Hepburn Springs' (Mulligan et al., 2006, p. 88). Like many community festivals, it relies on the good will and commitment of a small group of volunteers.

The Festa began in 1992 as a small community event. Since then, it has evolved to become a 12-day event with a focus on heritage and culture. It incorporates a variety of activities, such as music, food, wine, the arts, heritage displays, street parades and sporting events. It has successfully managed to retain some of its most popular aspects including a community parade and candle-lit procession.

The 19th Swiss and Italian Festa held in October 2011 adopted the theme 'Unity and Individuality' in recognition of the 150th anniversary of the unification of Italy. Some of the highlights of the Festa included a Slow Food Dinner (featuring pork from Abruzzi, Ligurian pumpkin, gnocchi Milanese, Piedmont potatoes and Sardinian spinach); Dinner under the Frescoes at the Old Macaroni

Figure 15.2 The Swiss and Italian Festa logo.

Factory; the Grand Parade and Family Festa with a concert featuring Swiss Matterhorn Yodellers, Swiss Companion Singers (see Figure 15.3), Alpenrose Dancers and many other performers; an Opening Weekend Ball – La Dolce Vita; a Village Family Soiree – A Heartfelt Community Gathering of Wine, Food and Song; a Winery Wanderer Bus Tour; film screenings of Italian classics such as *La Dolce Vita*, *Cinema Paradiso* and *Il Postino*; a Descendants' Gathering; Heritage Walks; Bocce and Boccia (an indoor version of Bocce) tournaments; an indoor football match; and the popular twilight Lantern Parade and Fireworks Finale.

The 2011 Festa Programme (a professionally produced 28-page coloured glossy booklet) began with a message from the Premier of Victoria, Ted Baillieu. He stated:

> This Festival is an important celebration of the rich and diverse cultural heritage of the Hepburn Shire region. It offers locals and visitors alike the opportunity to enjoy the attractions of one of Victoria's most significant tourism, arts, food, wine and wellbeing precincts.... Festivals such as this one play a vital role in regional Victoria and help underpin the State's position as a leading tourist destination.

The programme concluded with a thank you from the Hepburn Springs Swiss and Italian Festa Committee 2011 (a group of 12 individuals). They explained:

Figure 15.3 The Swiss Companion Singers perform at the festival.

The Swiss and Italian Festa is made possible through the generous support of government funding, local sponsorship and volunteers, and the active participation of many individuals, community organizations and local schools. Without your support, the Festa would not be possible. Ringraziamenti!

Trading on tradition

In keeping with the heritage of the area, and with an eye to supporting local produce, many businesses trade on the Swiss and Italian cultural traditions. Some of the organisations that promote the cuisine heritage include Istra Small-goods, Cliffy's Emporium (offering a wide range of regional produce), Country Cuisine (makers of local jams and chutneys), Captain's Creek Organic Wines, Holgate Brewhouse, Daylesford Cider Company, Harvest Café, Gourmet Larder, Tuki Farm (a trout farm), Salute Oliva (olive growers), The Convent Gallery (a major tourist attraction and popular wedding venue), Cricket Willow (owned by one of the original Italian families of the region and a regular venue for Festa events), Farmers Arms Hotel (featuring local produce on the menu), Meredith Dairy and Holy Goat Organic Cheese.

In addition to the above companies, the formation of groups such as Dayles-ford Macedon Produce represents an emerging emphasis on local production. This regional food and wine group promotes the various wines produced in the

Macedon and Spa Country region as well as locally available food products including cheeses, processed meats, preserves and condiments. Indicative of the connection with global trends, chefs and producers in the region have participated actively in the international Slow Food Movement. Also promoting local produce is Daylesford Provenders with its slogan 'a taste of the region'. The company packages local food in gourmet hampers and sells them in selected shops in the town and online to customers around the world.

The diversity of local culinary attractions has had a positive influence on the overall popularity of the region. Some of the attractions include local wineries such as Ellender Estate, which offers wood-fired bread and pizzas, numerous fine dining restaurants; the heritage-listed hotel and restaurant Villa Parma; the Daylesford Sunday Market (where visitors buy local produce and ride on a restored tourist train); and the monthly Daylesford Farmers Market. While the continuing importance of wellness tourism remains, the celebration of food and wine-related experiences is symptomatic of the region's current and future status as a highly popular tourist destination.

As outlined in the introduction, three particular businesses worthy of further examination are: the Old Macaroni Factory, Lavandula and Lake House. The Old Macaroni Factory was built in 1859 and features frescoes painted on the walls and ceilings. Apart from making pasta, it was a place where pasta and politics met as it was the headquarters of the Hepburn Democratic Club. Lavandula is a lavender farm just out of Hepburn Springs that promotes itself as a 'Swiss-Italian Farm' and growers of lavender, olives and grapes. The farm features a collection of stone buildings from the 1860s and runs a rustic cafe called La Trattoria and a modern guest house. Finally, Lake House also trades on the European tradition of the region. It is a boutique hotel, restaurant and function centre with spa offerings, and is located next to Lake Daylesford. Lake House has been voted Australia's regional property of the year and Australia's best food and wine experience. The managers have been widely recognised for their pivotal role in re-establishing tourism in the region.

The Old Macaroni Factory

The Lucini Macaroni Factory (see Figure 15.4) is an 1859 building in Hepburn Springs that features frescoes painted on the walls and ceilings. Apart from making pasta, it was a meeting place where pasta and politics came together as it was the headquarters of the Hepburn Democratic Club. The factory has been classified by the National Trust and is listed as part of Australia's National Estate. Pietro Lucini arrived in Australia in 1854; his brother and wife arrived five years later. The artwork was painted by his brother, Giacomo Lucini, between 1862 and 1864 and displays scenes from their home town on Lake Maggiore in northern Italy. The decorative work represents some of the oldest in Australia since European settlement. The Lucini family made their fortune by striking gold and making Australia's first dried pasta (with the added ingredient of mineral water).

Figure 15.4 The Old Macaroni Factory in Hepburn Springs.

The 'Old Macaroni Factory', as it is now known, proudly claims the title of 'Australia's oldest Italian building'. Maria Viola, who restored and manages the rustic Italian building, is a direct descendant of the Lucini family. A number of events were held in 2009 to celebrate the building's 150th birthday. The factory runs functions, tours and operates as a pasta cafe. To further emphasise the Italian atmosphere, diners are encouraged to sing along to classic Italian songs such as 'That's Amore' and 'Eh Cumpari'.

Lavandula Swiss-Italian farm

Lavandula is a lavender farm just out of Hepburn Springs that promotes itself as a 'Swiss-Italian Farm' and growers of lavender, olives and grapes (see Figure 15.5). The farm features a collection of stone buildings from the 1860s, a rustic cafe named La Trattoria and guest accommodation. The Lavandula brochure displays many inviting photographs and further entices the visitor with an evocative flow of phrases: relax and hear the quiet/breathe deep/fresh air/hear the birdsong/ enjoy the space/tranquillity/views/walk in the beautiful European garden/lavender field/vineyard/climb the hill to the olive grove/play petanque/sit under the trees/find farm animals/lie on a rug by the creek.

Figure 15.5 Lavandula promotes its Swiss-Italian heritage.

During the Swiss and Italian Festa, the lavender farm hosts a celebration known as 'La Primavera' (Spring). Lavandula also hosts an 'Autumn Harvest' in May, and holds 'Music in the Park' events during weekends in January. Carol White, who began restoring the stone buildings in 1990 and manages the property, explains that 'there has been a huge push by Swiss and Italians to regain their history' over the past 15 years (O'Brien, 2007, p. 13). With a view to promoting the farm's heritage, lavender is cut in the traditional manner using a hand-held sickle.

Lake House

One of the original establishments that trades on the European tradition of the region is the boutique hotel, restaurant and function centre with spa offerings – Lake House situated on the shores of Lake Daylesford (see Figure 15.6). The 33-room boutique hotel has been voted Australia's regional property of the year and Australia's best food and wine experience. The husband and wife operating team, Alla and Alan Wolf-Tasker, have been widely recognised for their pivotal role in re-establishing the region for tourism (Lethlean, 2007).

When Lake House opened in 1984, the owners sought to make the restaurant and retreat 'a destination' since there was 'no other tourist product' in the vicinity (Ashton & Newton, 1999). When discussing the idea of opening Lake House, Alla Wolf-Tasker explains,

> It was sheer madness really – the late 1970s was not a time when people journeyed into the Australian countryside for any sort of special culinary

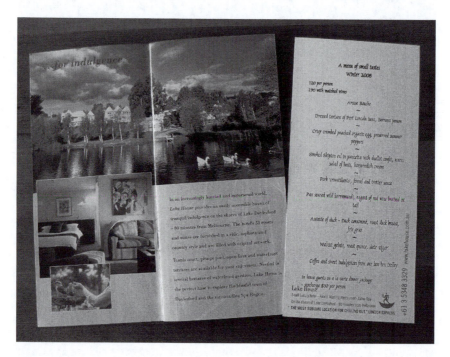

Figure 15.6 Lake House plays a key role in attracting tourists to the region.

experience. Devonshire tea or a good lunch – perhaps. But fixed-price menus with an amuse bouche to start and waiters in long white aprons in a small village that did not even boast a coffee machine – what could I have been thinking?

The restaurant has collected just about every significant national hospitality award and some international ones as well, including more than 70 *The Age* Good Food Guide hats since opening. In 2007 Alla Wolf-Tasker was made a Member of the Order of Australia for services to tourism and hospitality (Lethlean, 2007). Wolf-Tasker has also received a 'Legend' award from the Good Food Guide, and a 'Living Legend' award from the Melbourne Food and Wine Festival. *The Age* Good Food Guide was first published in 1980 and has become a vital guide for diners in Victoria. The equivalent guide for New South Wales is produced by sister-paper *The Sydney Morning Herald*. She assisted in founding Daylesford Macedon Produce, is a patron of the Daylesford Primary School Kitchen Garden project and sits on the boards of a range of organisations, including Tourism Victoria, Destination Daylesford and the Victorian Food and Wine Council.

The Lake House brand has expanded into the sale of sauces, jams and chutneys in high-end stores such as Harvey Nichols in London and the provision of their own bottled mineral water to guests (Wolf-Tasker, 2006). In keeping with the owner's culinary emphasis on regional produce, menus at the Lake House include a listing of key local producers and growers. Indicative of the revival of interest in the traditional health-giving properties of the region, Lake House has introduced 'Wellness Retreat Weeks'. The hotel and restaurant complex also offers yoga, tai chi, forest walks, spa treatments, gourmet cuisine, seminars and cooking demonstrations. The activities are promoted as providing participants with a balance for mind, body and spirit.

Lake House also hosts events such as the '50 Mile Dinner' where all ingredients are sourced within a 50-mile radius. The dinners celebrate local suppliers, organic produce and sustainable agricultural practices. The restaurant also hosts occasional special events, one being a 'Food and Drinkwiz' (merging fine food and trivia), with some of the menu items being regional antipasto, bullboar sausages (discussed earlier) with house chutney, poached tongue with horseradish cream, country terrine, cassoulet and sheep's milk pannacotta with poached quinces.

As Lake House celebrates its 30th year as a significant luxury tourist attraction in the region with more than 100 staff, its critical role in establishing the area as one of Australia's premium food and wine experiences has become evident. In many respects, the words 'Lake House' have become synonymous with 'Daylesford' and vice versa.

Conclusion

As reviewed in this chapter, the enduring Swiss and Italian story holds an important place in the heritage, culture and identity of the Daylesford and

Hepburn Springs region, and for the wider Australian community. The chapter attempted to reveal how intangible and tangible Swiss-Italian heritage is sold by business operators and experienced by locals and tourists.

Despite numerous challenges, the fact that the annual Swiss and Italian Festa has been celebrated for more than 20 years with the support of government grants, the local shire, business donations and the tireless work of dedicated volunteers, is evidence that a core group of people value and are proud to share their rich and fascinating heritage.

The Swiss-Italian heritage is a key component of Australia's national identity. When visiting Daylesford and Hepburn Springs, the heritage experience is integrated into the tourist gaze through visitors' overall interaction with tourism operators in the region. The heritage moment can be savoured by partaking in activities such as eating a Bullboar sausage, pumping water from the mineral springs, marvelling at the work of stonemasons, listening to Swiss singers and, of course, capturing some of these memories with the all-important photographs that are readily shared with friends and family via social media. Indeed, gastronomy tourism provides ample opportunities for positive reflection about the experience – often long after the initial encounter (Hall & Mitchell, 2005).

The enduring traditions of community festivals such as this one hold an important place in the heritage, culture and identity of billions of people. Focusing on just one of the many community festivals staged around the world each year, this chapter has sought to illustrate how the Swiss and Italian stories of Daylesford and Hepburn Springs might be viewed as a microcosm for the early development, diversity and tolerance of multicultural Australia.

The region's success as a tourist destination owes much to the legacy of the early Swiss and Italian settlers who had the foresight to preserve the mineral springs and fight to keep their rich traditions and culture alive. It seems likely that cuisine heritage will continue to be a source of strength for the region and its identity, and the Swiss-Italian contribution to that tradition is only likely to become stronger in the coming years.

References

Ashton, P. & Newton, G. (1999). *Sleepy hollow to boom town: A case study on the impact of tourism.* Bendigo: Video Education Australasia.

Carlson, B. (1997). *Immigrant placemaking in colonial Australia: The Italian-speaking settlers of Daylesford.* Doctoral dissertation, Victoria University, Melbourne.

Davidson, J. & Spearritt, P. (2000). *Holiday business: Tourism in Australia since 1870.* Melbourne: Miegunyah Press.

Daylesford and Macedon Ranges Tourism. (2011). *Daylesford and the Macedon Ranges official visitor guide.* Daylesford: Designscope.

Falassi, A. (1987). Festival: Definition and morphology. In A. Falassi (ed.), *Time out of time: Essays on the festival* (pp. 1–10). Albuquerque: University of New Mexico Press.

Gammon, S. (2007). Introduction: Sport, heritage and the English. An opportunity missed? In S. Gammon & G. Ramshaw (eds), *Heritage, sport and tourism: Sporting pasts – tourist futures* (pp. 1–8). Abingdon: Routledge.

Gervasoni, C. (2005). *Bullboar, macaroni and mineral water: Spa country's Swiss Italian history.* Hepburn Springs: Hepburn Springs Swiss Italian Festa Inc.

Hall, C.M. & Mitchell R. (2005). Gastronomic tourism: Comparing food and wine tourism experiences. In M. Novelli (ed.), *Niche Tourism: Contemporary issues, trends and cases* (pp. 73–88). Oxford: Elsevier.

Kurosawa, S. (2005, 10 September). Spa turns. *The Australian* (Weekend Travel section), 1.

Laing, J. & Frost, W. (2013). Food, wine … heritage, identity? Two case studies of Italian diaspora festivals in regional Victoria. *Tourism Analysis, 18*(3), 323–334.

Lethlean, J. (2007, 30 January). Gong a great honour. *The Age* (Epicure section), 3.

Mulligan, M., Humphrey, K., James, P., Scanlon, C., Smith, P. & Welch, N. (2006). *Creating community: Celebrations, arts and wellbeing within and across local communities.* Melbourne: The Globalism Institute, Royal Melbourne Institute of Technology University.

O'Brien, M. (2007, 5 June). Keeping it in the family. *The Age* (Epicure section), 13.

Robertson, K. (2008, 2 August). Time to relax. *The Age* (Domain section), 8.

Smith, L. (2006). *The uses of heritage.* Abingdon: Routledge.

Van Winkle, C., Woosnam, K. & Mohammed, A. (2013). Sense of community and festival attendance. *Event Management, 17*(2), 155–163.

Waterton, E. (2010). *Politics, policy and the discourses of heritage in Britain.* Basingstoke: Palgrave Macmillan.

Wolf-Tasker, A. (2006). *Lake house: A culinary journey in country Australia.* Prahran: Hardie Grant Books.

16 The Pozières Son et Lumière

Peace and memory after the Great War

Caroline Winter

Introduction

The small village of Pozières in northern France was the site of deadly battles in the First World War (1914–1918). The village was eventually captured by the Australians in July 1916 and they held the ridge, but at terrible cost: 23,000 casualties were suffered in a six-week period. So intense was the conflict that the village and the men who fought were blasted from the face of the earth. Not surprisingly there are relatively few cemeteries in the immediate area surrounding the village. Although there are some memorials in the village, they are not of the same monumental proportions as those at nearby Thiepval or in Ieper (Ypres) further north. The landscape is therefore difficult to interpret unless one has undertaken a significant amount of background reading. Despite the best efforts of some historians, Pozières' place in the war has been somewhat forgotten by Australians.

In 2006, on the 90th anniversary of the battle, volunteers from the area around Pozières organised a *Son et Lumière* (sound and light show), which they performed on the site of the old Tramway Trench. The performance was designed to remember the war and those who had fought, to educate young people and to welcome the citizens from all nations. Each year up to 80 people from the local area give up their time to rehearse for the two-hour-long performance, in July, and a range of other activities and entertainments accompany the show. The unique offerings of the Pozières Son et Lumière are the unpretentious village setting, the traditional village-green atmosphere, the generosity of local people and the opportunity these offer for friendship and goodwill. In addition to contributing to the local community, a global community of remembrance is also attracted to the event – British, French, Australian, Canadian and German visitors are gradually finding their way to Pozières.

This chapter describes the Son et Lumière and the way in which it offers opportunities to create and re-create memories of the war that for various reasons have faded over the past century. It examines the different communities involved, the memories that are being renewed and situates Pozières into a broader context of the First World War centenary.

There are two bases for the communities described in this chapter. The first is the notion of geography and place, and in this case, that which has been created in the village of Pozières as a result of its location during the 1916 Battle of the Somme in the First World War. The second relates to the notion of the field-interactional approach promoted by Wilkinson (1991, cited in Bessant, 2012). As Sharpley and Stone (2009) note, many communities of interest are represented at battle sites, including the nations that fought on opposing sides, local residents, tourists, military and government personnel. While the concept of place-based community has been in decline as a result of increasing urbanisation (Bessant, 2012), this chapter argues that the place that is Pozières, together with the activities of the Son et Lumière event, has the capacity to help create and link several communities into an overall community of remembrance.

This is primarily a conceptual chapter, but it is informed by several visits to Pozières by the author over the past decade, where she conducted survey work at the Son et Lumière event, on three occasions, visited many military (German, French and Commonwealth War Graves Commission) cemeteries, attended formal remembrance ceremonies, had various meetings with village officials and participated in village events. Information about the Son et Lumière was also obtained as a result of personal experience at the event, as well as from websites and newspaper items.

Research background

The importance of Pozières as place relates to the Great War of 1914–1918, when the village was a primary strategic point, and the site of massive battles, in the First Battle of the Somme, which began on 1 July 1916 and ended in November of that year. During those few months, the British suffered 432,000 casualties including 25,211 Canadians, 9,408 New Zealanders and 23,244 Australians, with German casualties amounting to 230,000 (Prior & Wilson, 2005, p. 300). The small village of Pozières is located at the southern end of the ridge towards which the British attacked, and it was here that the 1st Australian Division entered the front line on 23 July and captured the village the next day. The 2nd and 4th Australian Divisions were also sent in after the 1st Division was 'exhausted', and they too were virtually destroyed. The 23,000 casualties suffered by the Australians over the next six weeks approximate those of the eight-month campaign at Gallipoli in 1915 (Bean, 1948; Prior & Wilson, 2005). The village was quite literally blasted from the face of the earth. In terms of the casualties and the intensity of the battle, Pozières is one of Australia's most horrific battles, such that the official Australian war historian, Charles Bean (1948, p. 264), famously referred to Pozières as 'a ridge more densely sown with Australian sacrifice than any other place on earth'. During and after the war, the name Pozières was well known to Australians – it was engraved on numerous monuments and battle memorials, including the Shrine of Remembrance in Melbourne and the Australian National Memorial at Villers-Bretonneux.

The Battle of the Somme is notorious in both the history and the social memories of the First World War for the massive casualties. This is evident in the grandeur of the monuments built by Commonwealth nations on the ridge, such as the Franco-British memorial at Thiepval, which lists the names of 72,201 British and South African missing (CWGC, 2013). Close by are the Newfoundland Memorial Park with its distinctive Caribou monument and the Irish Helen's Tower. Within a few kilometres of Pozières are the Welsh Division Memorial at Mametz Wood, the South African memorial and museum at Longueval/Delville wood and the New Zealand monument to the missing at Caterpillar Valley Cemetery near Longueval.

Pozières was the 'Australian' section of the front line in July and August 1916, but in spite of these historic events, in Australia today the battle has been virtually forgotten. There are many reasons for this, not the least of which is the position attained by other battlefields, for reasons not entirely connected with the historical events. Gallipoli, for example, holds its place as the birthplace of the nation (Slade, 2003) and Fromelles is now well known because of the recent discovery of a large mass grave of Australian and British soldiers from 1916. The small village of Villers-Bretonneux was selected as the site for the Australian National Memorial, not so much because of the battles there, but because of the close links with soldiers and villagers after the war (Wade, 2010).

There are five Australian memorials in Pozières: the Australian Tank Memorial, the remains of the Gibraltar blockhouse, the 1st Division memorial obelisk, and plaques at the Windmill site and Mouquet Farm. While these memorials have profound significance, for many visitors today, they do not present the grandeur of the great Somme battlefield memorials further along the ridge. Nor are the Pozières memorials accompanied by the large visitor centres that are found at these other sites, which can generate interest through a range of visitor services such as educational and family research facilities. Similarly there are relatively few cemeteries in the immediate vicinity of Pozières. The Pozières British Cemetery just near the village holds 1,378 identified and 1,382 unidentified burials, mainly from 1916, and the memorial walls list 14,656 names of British and 300 South African troops killed and missing in the August campaign of 1918 (CWGC, 2013). The Australian missing from the Pozières battles are listed on the Australian National Memorial in Villers-Bretonneux approximately 30 km south of Pozières.

The Digger Cote 160 and the Son et Lumière in Pozières

Today, Pozières is in many ways much like it was in 1914 – a very small farming village located approximately 150 km from Paris, strung out along the D929 road between Albert and Bapaume. The population is about 250, with a school of approximately 20 students, the famous Le Tommy pub and museum, two B&Bs, the church, mairie and village hall. It has an impressive First World War 'address', being a commune in the Department of the Somme, Picardy Region, canton of Albert and Pays du Coquelicot. Even so, Carlyon (2006, p. 244) describes it as 'a dowdy farming village', and Charlton (1986, p. xi) refers to it as 'an unlovely village of undistinguished buildings'.

In 2001 a small group of residents decided to take matters of remembrance into their own hands and to re-establish the memory of their village. They formed the *Digger-Cote 160* association; 'Digger' refers to an Australian soldier and 'Cote' refers to Pozières ridge – Hill 160. The association's aims are to remember the soldiers who were killed in the war, to organise educational activities, to celebrate peace and to support exchange visits and communication between the various combatant nations (Digger Cote 160, 2013). The association has completed a number of commemorative activities since its formation, including a painting of a 'Digger' on the water tower and on signage at the entrances to the village (see Figure 16.1), hosting visitors and delegations to the town and the dedication of 'Butterworth Trench'.

The Son et Lumière is the main activity in which the association is involved, and it was first performed in 2006 to mark the 90th anniversary of the Battle of the Somme and the Australian attack by the 1st Division. It attracted 4,000 people in 2007, and it runs six performances over two weekends beginning at 10 p.m. for up to two hours. Funding is sourced through ticket sales, and is supported by a number of regional and local French government departments and organisations as well as private groups.

During the afternoon, before the show, a fair is held on the village green that is attended by local people and visitors. Entrance to the fair is free, and entertainment is provided, which has special attractions each year. These have

Figure 16.1 Entrance to Pozières (C. Winter, 2012).

included performances by the Somme Pipe Band, Morris dancers from Britain and a didgeridoo player. There is a range of food and drink stalls as well as plenty of picnic tables where people can sit to enjoy the day. A re-enactment group of approximately 30 people often attends and they set up a typical First World War army and hospital camp where they live on site for the duration of the Son et Lumière. They perform marches and other demonstrations to entertain visitors and, as for many such groups, take care with the authenticity and detail of uniforms (French, Australian, German and British), equipment and camp site. This part of the event is very quiet and understated, but precisely because of this, it allows visitors and local people to relax, to mix freely and to engage in, or attempt to engage in, French/English/German conversations. The organisers will often introduce visitors to each other and offer information about the local area.

The main show re-enacts some of the battles of the Great War with sophisticated sound and light (i.e. *son et lumière*) effects. The representation of war, however, plays a relatively small part, with greater emphasis being given to the portrayal of the war's impact on the characters involved. Short scenes depict the stories of young citizen-soldiers, their friends and families from Britain, France, Germany and Australia, their families and the townspeople of Pozières. The main language is French, but there are numerous translations in German and English. Other scenes depict the Australian Victoria Cross recipient Albert Jacka and the British artist George Butterworth. A well-known incident involving the Australian Captain Percy Cherry VC and a German soldier who encountered each other on the battlefield is also portrayed. The men fired at each other simultaneously and after the German was hit, Cherry comforted the man as he lay dying, promising to return letters to the man's wife. Cherry himself was killed the following year. Historical information relating to the war is conveyed through scenes depicting children and their teacher in a classroom. There are many smaller tableaux that evoke the emotions of war – sadness, despair and horror, and finally the joy and exuberance of peace. In the final scene, local children, dressed in black, place wooden crosses on the battlefield and then bring forward a banner that proclaims *Paix – Peace – Frieden*. Finally, there is a fireworks display that represents both peace and war: red and green flares simulate the Verey lights that once illuminated the same ground in 1916, as well as celebration for the end of the war.

The event is performed on an outdoor stage, on the site of the old Tramway Trench, with the audience seated on a tiered scaffold. On at least two occasions, the audience and the performers endured for a good part of two hours in reasonably heavy rain, and it is more often than not very cold. The 'props' include a replica of the (the original of which stood on the highest point of the ridge and which was the objective of the Australians), a horse-drawn cart and a large replica (a cut-out, drawn by a tractor) of the ship *HMAS Sydney* bringing Australian soldiers home, a classroom and dugouts. Recently a group of local retired men designed and built a plywood replica of a tank that is exhibited at the fair during the day, and later used in the show (see Figure 16.2).

Several communities, each somewhat differently defined, come together as a result of the Son et Lumière.

Figure 16.2 Replica plywood tank built by local people (C. Winter, 2012).

Multiple communities

This chapter shows how the war has created a broader range of communities in this tiny village that would not have existed in the absence of the war. While war usually presents a negative disruption to a place, Weaver (2000) argues that war can have some positive effects, especially over the long term, with the result that in some villages such as Pozières, the Great War has created touristic interest where very little would otherwise have existed. Today, part of Pozières' character is formed as much from the war as from its agricultural beginnings and contemporary interests.

Community 1: Community of the locality residents, Digger Cote and actors

The residents of Pozières and the local region are those who have long-standing links with the geographic location through family, farming and living in the place. They are the people of the village who run the pub, the mairie, the school and the farms, and are the community in the sense that Anderson (2013, p. 26) notes, they 'represent an accumulation of group experiences which comes out of the past and extends through time, even though the individuals making up the community are forever coming and going'.

Figure 16.3 Local residents (Digger Cote, 2010).

The residents involved in the Digger Cote projects are those whom Winter (2006, p. 136) refers to as 'memory activists', describing them as 'goal-directed people, with an agenda, a project, whose traces may be found in local and national archives'. This includes up to 80 people from the local area who volunteer their leisure time to organise and perform the Son et Lumière. Not all residents of the village are involved, and many are simply not interested. Even so, re-enactments are often performed by a community of actors and local people and can provide a way to link visitors and locals to develop a shared sense of place (Derrett, 2003; Gallant, Arai & Smale, 2013; Henderson, 2007). The actors at Pozières have much in common with those described by Ryan and Cave (2007) in the New Zealand town of Cambridge re-enactment, and who are involved in serious leisure, as a way to remember the men and women involved in the war and to educate younger generations. Their description of a 'mobile live action museum' (Ryan & Cave, 2007, p. 184) resonates very closely with the events in Pozières. See Figure 16.3.

Community 2: Re-enactment communities

These are the people who may come to the village from outside the immediate local area and for whom their shared interest in re-enactment bonds them together as a community. Typically, re-enactors are interested in education, historical scholarship and the detail of authentic equipment and uniforms. Their

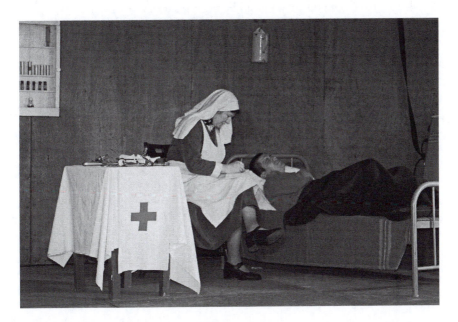

Figure 16.4 Re-enactors (Digger Cote, 2010).

primary motivation is often the comradeship of friends and family and perhaps the opportunity to escape into a past world that has appealing characteristics not easily found in contemporary life (Carnegie & McCabe, 2008; Hunt, 2004; Wilhelm & Mottner, 2005). Gallant et al. (2013, p. 332) found that 'volunteering was associated with benefits that characterize serious leisure as well as with camaraderie, a sense of connection to the community, and shared emotional connection'. For others, a personal interest in genealogy can provide some kind of personal and social identity in the face of a constantly changing world (Ryan & Cave, 2007). See Figure 16.4.

Community 3: Sacrifice, family and nation

Hutchinson (2009, p. 401) examines the way in which war 'constructs the nation as a sacred community of sacrifice' and argues that 'Wars have a sacred significance because they are linked with the foundations of the communities' (Hutchinson, 2009, p. 402). For new nations such as Australia, New Zealand, Canada and South Africa, the First World War was used to support a sense of national identity, in which battle and bloodletting was portrayed as essential to nation building. As Grant (2005, p. 510) observes for the Gettysburg battlefield, '[O]wnership of the land is conferred by the burial of the dead in it, and through them the physical landscape is transmuted into a national one'. If, as Grant (2005) and Tuan (1976) argue, the dead create a sense of sacredness and ownership, then Pozières may indeed be regarded as part of one's family home or nation, even for those who live far away in Germany, Britain, Australia, Canada and New Zealand. It can be suggested that family involvement in an on-site community, if only for a few hours, may help to address the sense of familial loss and unresolved trauma, as noted by Wilson (2009).

Lockstone-Binney, Hall and Atay (2013, p. 309) argue that Australians travelling to the Gallipoli battlefields display characteristics similar to diasporic communities in seeking an 'imagined diasporic homeland'. They support this claim by arguing for the existence of the three conditions for a diaspora (as cited in Butler, 2001). First, there has been a dispersal of the original group to two places, New Zealand and Australia; second, there is self-awareness of group identity; and, finally, links to the homeland are maintained. They also support Adamson and Demetriou (2007) in that 'collective identity is no longer constrained by traditional territorial borders' (Lockstone-Binney et al., 2013, p. 309). Visitation to Pozières by Australians may also approach the idea of an imagined diasporic community and community of sacrifice. This is to a much lesser extent than identified at Gallipoli, but for people for whom the Western Front battlefields are particularly salient, the Son et Lumière at Pozières event can potentially generate these experiences.

Community 4: Online communities – Pozières Remembered

There are many very large online communities linking historical, social and visitation interests regarding the Great War of large numbers of people who also have interests in the Pozières battlefields. The Western Front Association and the Royal British Legion are good examples, in addition to the Facebook pages and websites of hundreds of other groups. The Pozières Remembered site, based in Australia, is specifically devoted to Pozières. In addition to its online presence, the association undertakes considerable work to raise funds for the village and to support local remembrance of the Australian effort during the Great War (Pozières Remembered, 2013).

Community 5: A community of remembrance

Even though Pozières is a small village, the events of the Great War have meant that memories created here are part of the identity of a very broad range of geographically dispersed people. Pozières, as a community, can then be, as Anderson (2013, p. 26) notes, 'a place where memories are centred, both individual and "folk" memories'. Those involved in the local community who can be classed as memory activists (Halbwachs, 1992; Winter, 2006) create the Son et Lumière event by selecting certain historical events (such as Percy Cherry), omitting others, articulating them through the Son et Lumière and rehearsing the memories annually. The community of remembrance formed through these activities approaches Anderson's (2013, p. 295) idea of community as 'a behaving entity, a human aggregate having a collective experience and a collective memory'.

As a result of the activities at the Son et Lumière a number of individuals can be associated with the communities mentioned above, and in addition, to be linked into an overall community of remembrance, centred on Pozières for a short period during the event. This does not necessarily occur for everyone, and may in fact involve only a few people. Many visitors attend the performance without necessarily being involved in other activities such as the preliminary entertainment, and, in the absence of an interest in the village, may not feel or wish to be part of a remembrance community.

This community is indeed temporary and it does not fulfil many of the practical requirements of a long-lived community, such as decision-making, planning and management of local life.

Today's dynamic world is often cited as the reason for a widespread sense of loss and alienation and a need for redefinition of the meaning and perhaps relevance of community for urbanised societies. War creates even further disruption and social unrest that can persist decades later. Wilson (2009), for example, argues that unresolved trauma of the First World War still exists in British society, and it continues to motivate travel for remembrance purposes. Damousi (2005, p. 20) found that 'the psychological impact of war remains well after the event, not just for soldiers, but for those around them who also have to absorb the legacy of war'. There are numerous memorials and commemorative events on the Western Front that were designed to alleviate the grief caused by the war (Winter, 2006). Many of these are, however, very formal performances that do not allow for creativity or change by participants or the audience (Edensor, 2000), in addition to which they can be quite short with little opportunity for interaction or development of relationships. At Pozières the nature of the Son et Lumière event and the range of activities it creates, especially through the afternoon on the village green (Tramway Trench), provides such opportunities for visitors and locals, albeit for a temporary period.

As Bessant (2012) notes, the increasing social movement of people challenged the idea of functionalist place-based notions of community. In Pozières place continues to be important, ironically, because it can help to link geographically dispersed people as community. While the sense of place underlies this, ultimately community is given life through social activity, or through 'field-interaction based on social interaction and purposive action' (Bessant, 2012, p. 628). Bessant (2012, p. 641), in supporting Wilkinson's (1970) notion of social field theory of community, argues that 'The nature of its symbolic meaning(s) or place within human consciousness rests on a host of experiences, interactions, and memories'.

Ryan and Cave (2007) also observed in New Zealand that a sense of community is acted out by engaged and committed actors in serious leisure. At the Gettysburg battlefield, Chronis (2005, p. 400) found that heritage is 'coconstructed' by an interactive process involving performance at the site of the Civil War battle. He argues that 'During the performance of the story, tourists are not passive readers of the text. Rather, they're actively engaged by using their prior background, negotiating, filling gaps, and imagining'.

Some of these communities are temporary and exist only during the event itself, which would seem to put it outside the usual definitions of community. Misener and Mason (2006, p. 396), however, in discussing identity and citizenship claim that 'flexible citizenship provides one way of focusing on people's sense of place and connections to spaces, even if only temporarily, in terms of identity building'. They argue also that short-term events can offer 'meaningful sources of attachment to spaces and places for both residents and non-residents' and that a performative notion of citizenship can help develop community building and identity. These notions of flexibility, of short-term, temporary engagement can also apply to the Son et Lumière.

Conclusions

It is, then, the sense of place defined by the war, the battle and the presence of the dead in the surrounding landscape that provides the basis for community in Pozières, but the 'field' that unites them is the Son et Lumière event (Bessant, 2012). Several communities can be identified that hold an interest in Pozières, including local residents, re-enactors, visitors and online communities, and through participating at the Son et Lumière these individuals can link into a community of remembrance.

References

Adamson, F.B. & Demetriou, M. (2007). Remapping the boundaries of 'state' and 'national identity': Incorporating diasporas into IR theorizing. *European Journal of International Relations, 13*(4), 489–526.

Anderson, N. (2013). *The urban community: A world perspective*. Hoboken, NJ: Taylor & Francis.

Bean, C.E.W. (1948). *Anzac to Amiens*. Canberra: Australian War Memorial.

Bessant, K.C. (2012). The interactional community: Emergent fields of collective agency. *Sociological Inquiry, 82*(4), 628–645.

Butler, K.D. (2001). Defining diaspora, refining a discourse. *Diaspora, 10*(2) 189–219.

Carlyon, L. (2006). *The Great War*. Australia: Macmillan.

Carnegie, F. & McCabe, S. (2008). Re-enactment events and tourism: Meaning, authenticity and identity. *Current Issues in Tourism, 11*(4), 349–367.

Charlton, P. (1986). *Australians on the Somme: Pozières 1916*. North Ryde, Sydney: Methuen Haynes.

Chronis, A. (2005). Coconstructing heritage at the Gettysburg storyscape. *Annals of Tourism Research, 32*(2), 386–406.

CWGC (Commonwealth War Graves Commission). (2013, 20 November). Cemetery details. Retrieved from www.cwgc.org.au.

Damousi, J. (2005). Wartime memory and patterns of mourning in Australia. *Dialogue, 24*(3), 19–30.

Derrett, R. (2003). Making sense of how festivals demonstrate a community's sense of place. *Event Management, 8*, 49–58.

Digger Cote 160. (2013, 11 November). Retrieved from www.digger-pozieres.org.

Edensor, T. (2000). Staging tourism: Tourists as performers. *Annals of Tourism Research, 27*(2), 322–344.

Gallant, K., Arai, S. & Smale, B. (2013). Serious leisure as an avenue for nurturing community. *Leisure Sciences, 35*, 320–336.

Grant, S.-M. (2005), Raising the dead: War, memory and American national identity. *Nations and Nationalism, 11*(4), 509–529.

Halbwachs, M. (1992). *On collective memory*. Oxford: University of Chicago Press.

Henderson, J. (2007). Remembering the Second World War in Singapore: Wartime heritage as a visitor attraction. *Journal of Heritage Tourism, 2*(1), 36–52.

Hunt, S. (2004). Acting the part: 'Living History' as a serious leisure pursuit. *Leisure Studies, 23*(4), 387–403.

Hutchinson, J. (2009). Warfare and the sacralisation of nations: The meanings, rituals and politics of national remembrance. *Millennium: Journal of International Studies, 38*(2), 401–417.

Lockstone-Binney, L., Hall, J. & Atay, A. (2013). Exploring the conceptual boundaries of diaspora and battlefield tourism: Australians' travel to the Gallipoli battlefield, Turkey, as a case study. *Tourism Analysis, 18*, 297–311.

Misener, L. & Mason, D.S. (2006). Developing local citizenship through sporting events: Balancing community involvement and tourism development. *Current Issues in Tourism, 9*(4–5), 384–398.

Pozières Remembered. (2013, 26 November). Retrieved from http://pozieresremembered. com.au.

Prior, R. & Wilson, T. (2005). *The Somme*. Sydney: University of New South Wales Press.

Ryan, C. & Cave, J. (2007). Cambridge Armistice Day celebrations: Making a carnival of war and the reality of play. In C. Ryan (ed.), *Battlefield tourism: History, place and interpretation* (pp. 177–186). Amsterdam: Elsevier.

Sharpley, R. & Stone, P. (2009). *The darker side of travel: The theory and practice of dark tourism*. Clevedon: Channel View.

Slade, P. (2003). Gallipoli thanatourism: The meaning of ANZAC. *Annals of Tourism Research, 30*, 779–794.

Tuan, Y.F. (1976). Geopiety: A theme in man's attachment to nature and to place. In D. Lowenthal & M. Bowden (eds), *Geographies of the mind: Essays in historical geosophy in honor of John Kirtland Wright* (pp. 11–39). Oxford: Oxford University Press.

Wade, L. (2010). The reconstruction of Villers-Bretonneux 1918–1922. In M. Crotty & M. Larsson (eds), *Anzac legacies: Australians and the aftermath of war* (pp. 146–165). North Melbourne: Scholarly Publishing.

Weaver, D.B. (2000). The exploratory war-distorted destination life cycle. *International Journal of Tourism Research, 2*, 151–161.

Wilhelm, W.B. & Mottner, S. (2005). An empirical study of the motivations and consumption behaviors of Civil War re-enactors: Implications for re-enactment tourism. *Journal of Hospitality and Leisure Marketing, 12*(4), 27–56.

Wilkinson, K.P. (1970). The community as a social field. *Social Forces, 48*(3) 311–322.

Wilson, R.J. (2009). Memory and trauma: Narrating the Western Front 1914–1918. *Rethinking History, 13*(2), 251–267.

Winter, J. (2006). *Remembering war: The Great War between memory and history in the twentieth century*. New Haven, CT: Yale University Press.

17 End of the rainbow?

A review of community events in Liverpool

W. Gerard Ryan

Introduction

Poem for the Liverpool Community Festival 1999:

> The reds and the blues,
> The orange and the green,
> Black and white and all shades in between:
> A Liverpool Rainbow.

(McGough, 1999, p. 3)

In 1999, as a level-6 undergraduate student I paid a visit to the Liverpool Arts & Culture Unit (LA&CU) to enquire whether any placement opportunities existed. After a discussion on a number of projects with the Development Manager, an opportunity was offered to co-ordinate the Liverpool Community Festival. With the support of the LA&CU team, the event brought together 59 community organisations, 24 performance groups and performances, nine festival speakers, eight art displays, a video room, a poetry room and included a city-wide painting competition. The event was a considerable success as a means of sharing knowledge and engaging directly with local residents in one place at one time. The event was planned to continue bi-annually. However, the following year a structural review saw the disappearance of the Arts & Culture Unit and with it the Liverpool Community Festival. In 15 years a replacement has not been considered, which has prompted this review of community events in the city of Liverpool, UK.

This chapter and its discussions are the result of data obtained over the last 12 months through conversations with numerous community representatives and academics. Primary data was captured through 12 one-to-one semi-structured interviews with seven directors of community-facing events in Liverpool, three past and two present local authority managers; while secondary data derives from a review of literature related to community events. It has also been completed at a time of considerable change in the provision of arts and cultural activities that form the core of all community events. Of the festival directors approached only one refused to take part and to maintain complete anonymity, the actual participants and their relative festivals are not disclosed.

The findings of this research suggests that while the city has progressed in recent years and the number of community-facing events has increased, the communities for whom the events are meant have little influence on the decision-making process due to a lack of consultation. Moreover, some communities are actually being marginalised and are not granted any input whatsoever (Clarke & Jepson, 2011). At the same time, the process that organisers of community-facing events have to go through is creating further problems and barriers to the events' continuing existence of many events.

A sense of community is considered an invisible yet critical part of a healthy community (Derrett, 2003), and as such is the responsibility of community members themselves to maintain its well-being. Furthermore, a community of identity suggests that individuals affiliate themselves with or are categorised by others as belonging to a certain identity-based social group (Vigurs, 2009). So it could be argued that one way of assessing Derrett's (2003) healthy communities is through the events the members of these communities assume. As time passes and changes occur to the provision of community events, either through local authority regulation or the make-up of the community itself, the task of maintaining community events becomes more challenging. In some cases, community events that have existed for generations may disappear either because the make-up of the community is transformed, essential funding is removed or the realisation of the event relied on an individual who is no longer in a position to continue. Community events can also be superseded by more contemporary events that draw on present-day influences of newer communities often from distant cultures, or captivate the community with celebrity or food and drink.

In 1993, after a period of decline and in an attempt to reinvigorate the city, Liverpool's local authority, with the support of the existing cultural groups that organise community events in Liverpool, placed culture at the centre of its whole regeneration process. This allowed the various cultural organisations to improve or develop a footprint of community-facing events that would harness the inherent creativity of its people to produce future success (Taylor, 2007). It has not been without its problems or opponents (which are discussed later in the chapter), though as a result the local authority maintained it had broken the mould of traditional arts service delivery, and claimed hugely beneficial results.

City of festivals

According to Grant (2003), 100 years ago, Liverpool was Britain's only really multicultural city. It is therefore no surprise that community events exist in the city to represent just about every resident community. While not providing a 'Liverpool Community Festival', Liverpool expresses its identity through community events and festivals that are widespread across the 30 wards that make up the city. From Chinese New Year for the oldest Chinese community in the United Kindom to events that celebrate the city's music, heritage, faith, disability, food and drink, ethnicity, writings, waterfront, gender and sport, the city has quite literally become a city of festivals. One festival director pointed out that what is remarkable in Liverpool today is that these events and festivals tend to be much less about belief and much more about celebrating the art forms from where each of these communities has arrived.

Arguably, the greatest challenge for these community events is growth. When growth occurs, the event organiser is faced with a decision to consider the close involvement of the local authority. More often, this is not a choice and the local authority will become involved in the planning and/or delivery process. Reasons for this can include the application process itself, added cost, security, the need to close roads, re-routing traffic and the clean-up after the event. When growth occurs, the next decision the organisers will have to make is to determine how 'local' or community oriented the event should remain. For community-focused events, growth brings with it many new funding opportunities that are often difficult to refuse. These can lead to regeneration through international partnerships bringing with them an even greater set of demands in the planning and delivery process. However, there is a danger that the essence of the community event is left behind as the organisers focus on their wider funding requirements and embrace an international programme. The once community-based event has now shifted from local community control to an event that consists of international collaborations with international participants, often delivered by civil servants and providing a local community participation element with a much more significant tourism agenda.

Funding and adopting a business approach

While the community organisation directors interviewed remain generally optimistic about their future, they accept that the global economic downturn has affected all cultural and community-based activities. Every cultural event in the city currently receives support from any or all of the following: the Arts Council, European funding initiatives or the local authority. In an attempt to make the foreseeable future for funding sustainable, Liverpool City Council has devised a five-year plan for cultural organisations to engage with. However, the certainty of funds can never be assured. One festival director suggested that within the next 5–6 years, it is possible that no arts funding will exist, bringing a realisation of what this actually means for their own survival. Another festival director went even further and suggested:

> In the next one or two years 30–40% of the arts organisations will not be around. If they are, they will be around in a different way, or will have had to have formed alliances. Austerity forces people to work in partnerships. It is not organisations god given right to be funded and yet people really get upset when they get cut or the funding becomes limited [because they believe] they're doing really great stuff. It makes people go back to a kind of collective way of thinking and regrouping and reanalysing what your mission and purpose is.

While these comments were couched in a positive manner, in light of uncertainty over the future of funding cultural activities in the United Kingdom as a whole, community organisations may have to consider transforming their means of income. If the Arts Council were to diminish and the public sector were to have fewer funding resources to support cultural events, it is predictable that most if not all community events in the city would disappear if funding is substantially affected or stopped. In light of this, some of the more progressive community festival organisations in Liverpool are already reviewing their approach and seeking alternative funding methods by developing strategies to reduce their core funding by a considerable percentage to limit any major disturbance to their current activities.

These progressive community groups have begun to realise that a large proportion of their funding is handed over to professional organisations to provide essential services, such as food, security and equipment. Instead of holding on to a 'precious identity' of a funded community agency that finances other businesses through its grants, one director is extending the event's business activities and embracing actual commercial activities by developing micro enterprises within the organisation. These act as both a cash generator and an opportunity for employment. Examples include providing catering services for festivals and exploring merchandising opportunities that transmit the same values as the organisation. In reality, this is a contemporary approach to the 'cake' and 'bring and buy' stalls at a community fete.

In a further attempt to secure the future of community events and the organisations themselves who provide them, the setting up of alliances between a number of established groups has contributed to an improved calendar of events and a united approach. Two alliances in Liverpool create a forum of communication and help in maintaining a wide selection of community-focused events: Liverpool Arts Regeneration Consortium (LARC) is an alliance of seven of the city's major cultural organisations (including FACT (Foundation for Art and Creative Technology), Liverpool Biennial, Liverpool Everyman and Playhouse, Royal Liverpool Philharmonic, Tate Liverpool, the Bluecoat and Unity Theatre) and the Creative Organisations of Liverpool (COoL) is currently made up of around 31 arts organisations based in Liverpool who deliver collaborative work in support of its arts organisation members. As well as sharing best practice and a collective approach to safeguarding events throughout the year, both groups gain direct communication with the local authority that can provide updates on any developments that might affect the delivery of events for the community.

Community alliances such as these can also prove to be advantageous considering the emergence of cultural strategies and 'neighbourhoods' as sites for policy action and governance. Local authorities have introduced the term and use it widely as a more inclusive form of governance through community networks and in an attempt to tackle social exclusion. Neighbourhoods, it is suggested, are being used by local authorities as a means of engaging more local communities in a decision-making process (Durose, 2009). A local authority can then direct a variety of interventions towards geographical 'zones' rather than individual communities. In the outer wards of Liverpool, Neighbourhoods can have good effect as the ethnic and financial profile, (while mixed), is relatively balanced often leading to general agreement in whatever may be provided. The approach becomes much more complicated when many distinct communities within a single Neighbourhood are in existence.

A number of these exist throughout the city and the city centre is a prime example. Made up of a mix of luxury apartments, middle and low earners, student accommodation and a mix of ethnic communities, the area is less a single community and more a cosmopolitan metropolis. The implication of this is that fewer, if any, opportunities exist to provide events for, of and by the local community as the limited time and availability has been accounted for with local authority events aimed at visitors from outside the region.

The answer to this conundrum may well lie in what one festival director explained as empowering the communities themselves. The suggestion is that it is right the local authority should have a major role to play in devising and leading on cultural strategy, but it must also allow communities the opportunity to facilitate and deliver events to retain a sense of ownership and to remain independent from the political process.

Getting to where we are today

The most striking observation when talking to the directors of Liverpool community events is their deep passion for their event, the communities they now represent and the desire to advance the contribution they make to their community. Some common leitmotifs from the interviews included social justice, liberation, human rights and democracy as fundamental rationales for their existence. While these themes appear commonplace, aside from the acute deprivation that remains in some parts of the city, the actual reason for this unintentional consensus is largely unknown. One explanation could be the negative attitudes that still exist towards Liverpudlians. These are most likely to be based on erstwhile observations as many of the groups that arrived in Liverpool who chose to remain and build their own community (the Irish, for example) were heavily stigmatised as a kind of underclass, unable, unwilling or unsuited to take advantage of opportunities available to them (Belchem, 2010). The problems these small communities faced were substantial enough inside the city to lead to the formation of co-operatives such as Eldonians (1870) and the League of Well-doers (1893). It was from these community groups and latterly the co-operatives that community events began to be organised for, of and by their members highlighting living conditions and poverty and usually encompassing a message of defiance or including statements of pride with a sense of place (Allen, O'Toole, Harris & McDonnell, 2011).

Today, events in cities across the United Kingdom put considerable investment into tourism development and through this initiative commercial entities have been welcomed by local authorities into the festival sphere as sponsors and more recently as developers and producers of community events (Sharpe, 2008,

p. 220). Liverpool is no exception, and while the effect can be a raising of the profile of the city to an external target market, Jago, Chalip, Brown, Mules and Ali (2003) suggest community support and a good strategic and cultural fit with the destination are necessary. Williams, Gill and Chura (2004) propose that a city can effectively do this by capturing a market position that appeals to visitors while respecting the broader values and goals of the community. However, Jago et al. (2003) also warn that events can affect residents' perceptions of their community and that more needs to be done to examine the effects these highly sponsored events have on the community.

One local authority manager made quite clear the city's vision and direction for community-funded events in conjunction with priorities for investment in the cultural sector for the period 2014–2017:

> It is appropriate for the city to deliver fewer [community] events that will mean that some will fall off and that's just the way it is because we have a priority about job creation and economic impact, and ... there are things that we have been funding since 2009 that have not really gone anywhere and it's not a project and I think now we'll be far better off investing and it is investing as opposed to grant aiding those who are going to do that next international work for us. And it's going to be sad because some are going to drop off the end if we don't keep it high profile.

The consequence of this type of approach by the local authority is what Masterman (2007) describes as an effort to develop corporate and market awareness. Smith (2012) sums up the widespread situation by explaining that cities are forced through neo-liberal values to compete with each other for investment while the local community are forced to surrender traditional activities. There is the explicit benefit of investment and broader recognition for the city, but carrying with it corporatisation to the heart of the community and ultimately affecting the community spirit. Instead of an event that is grown out of a community and the culture of the people who make it, community events are presented as a gift from the local authority for the community as a whole. The reality is the local authority portraying an image of the city to those from outside the region. When community-facing events reach this level of control, the overarching vision portrayed by a city shifts from an inward expression of the local values of the community for its residents to an outward interpretation of higher significance over other cities to draw in visitors from outside the region. Rose (1999, p. 150) considers this approach as a modern means of doing away with out-dated methods of public management:

> In the new public management, the focus is on accountability, explicit standards and measures of performance, emphasis on outputs, not inputs, with rewards linked to performance ... and insistence on parsimony maintained by budget discipline. This required a shift from an ethic of public service to one of private management.

From a Liverpool perspective, the impact of this approach is evident through the local authority's plans to transform the local economy and to have a 'full deck of complementary and cohesive strategies in play by 2018, which will coalesce to establish a Master Plan for Liverpool Culture for 2018–25' (LiverpoolVision, 2013a). Included in this is the aim for all major events to encourage 'huge numbers of people from outside the region to visit the city and make Liverpool a truly global brand' (VisitLiverpool, 2009). The dichotomy here is underlined by the fact that the local authority is promoting a competitive business city and a beacon of enterprise (LiverpoolVision, 2012) to attract private investment while at the same time having to claim to be the most deprived local authority area in England (LCC, 2011) to draw in public funding. With a city unemployment claimant count rate of 6.7% compared to a 3.3% national average (LCC, 2012), it is possible that a large proportion of local residents cannot actually engage with the majority of the local authority-supported community events. Based on the local authority's declared vision, these residents will remain outside the local authority plans for events, raising issues of social equity and social exclusion.

The strategy of the local authority is really a full programme of city branding using the city's historical achievements as publicity to attract tourism and wider investment for events. Liverpool's rich cultural heritage is unquestioned and, as such, the city still ranks as one of the best cities in the United Kingdom for its patronage of the arts and music (Daramola-Martin, 2009). Through events such as the European Capital of Culture 2008 (ECoC, 2008), Liverpool's economy has reportedly grown faster than that of the United Kingdom (LiverpoolVision, 2013b). While ECoC 2008 was meant to be all-inclusive, there was general admission that many community groups were actually excluded from much of the celebrations. Also, a considerable amount of negative impact statements were made especially around the lack of activities for 'ordinary people' (Garcia, Melville & Cox, 2010, pp. 56–57) who, as mentioned above, become excluded from the future plans for the city.

In the Cox and O'Brien (2012) review of ECoC 2008, the 'Liverpool model' of culture-led regeneration is discussed as a policy that is demonstrated to be one that limits prospective cultural policies to a narrow vision of the possible. Unfortunately, this research has not been included in the future vision by the local authority. Instead the process is to be further narrowed, even though Cox and O'Brien (2012) suggest that the local authority are following a vision that is unlikely to be sustainable in the foreseeable future. The priorities for Culture Liverpool Investment Programme document for 2014–2017 (CLIP) is an indication of how the future of community events is to be managed.

The CLIP (2013) document is the route for community events and festival applications. The document states:

> Funding will be available to Liverpool based not for profit cultural organisations and not for profit activities produced by artistic, creative and cultural producers that can demonstrate the delivery of a high quality, innovative, creative, cultural offer and effective management and governance.
>
> (CLIP, 2013, p. 3)

Table 17.1 Application scoring summary

Assessment	Max. marks
Fit for purpose	11
Financial	15
Meeting our goals – Enterprise – People–place	44
Leadership/Collaboration/Sharing resources	5
Marketing	5
Outputs	10
Equality	10
Total	100

Source: CLIP Framework (2013).

Individuals are not excluded from applying, but must be able to prove that the skills and knowledge to produce events exists. The local authority also asks arts, creative and cultural activities to demonstrate that the event comes with value for money. The added difficulty for community-facing events is laid out in the application scoring summary as the weighting clearly favours events with a tourism and return on investment profile while remaining open, transparent, but also very controlled.

In another process of transparency, the impact of ECoC 2008 was monitored from the beginning to examine the effects and/or impacts across the city. Much of Liverpool's current cultural direction and community offering is based on the findings extracted from the Impact 08 report. While many resident communities undoubtedly were in favour of much of ECoC 2008, many reservations were also evident. For example, O'Brien (2010) researched stakeholder perceptions and discovered considerable uncertainty as to the extent to which ECoC 2008 had reached out to the geographically and socially peripheral sections of Liverpool and whether it had actually involved local people (O'Brien, 2010, p. 16). Interviewees also raised significant issues regarding the programme and delivery which can be attached to the local authority's approach to these communities ever since:

> You can see this flourish within the city centre but it's the outer communities that I think need to be developed more. I think, yeah, we're getting people in to the city and yeah, we've been very successful in that but I think now it's looking at what can we develop. What can we do to develop the residents of Liverpool?
>
> (O'Brien, 2010, p. 20)

Some other perceived impacts of ECoC 2008 suggested a great deal of reported success particularly in terms of raising the profile of the city, its arts and cultural offerings and in attracting visitors to the city (Garcia et al., 2010, p. 36). The impact of ECoC 2008 has also attracted new events that do their best to appear to be community events but are quite simply commercial entities that are loaded with commercial sponsorship and charge the public for entry. It has also given the local authority licence to remove long-standing, well-attended free events and replace them with a profile of centrally run events that are centrally initiated and organised to encourage corporate sponsorship and again charge for admission.

Corporate sponsorship at community-facing events is encouraged by the local authority and, more recently, evidence suggests the practice is becoming more widespread. If corporate sponsors are involved solely to promote major brands to those who attend, then the question must be asked, how can the event still be considered a community event? One community event director maintains that with the right approach sponsorship can work, provided the involvement is less about brand awareness and more about corporate responsibility with the community in mind. The corporate companies that engage with community events in Liverpool may have considerable profit-making responsibilities to realise, but there should also be an inherent responsibility to understand the community role being undertaken. This way the sponsor can be seen more as a social champion putting something into rather than taking something out of the community.

This particular director suggests that with the right approach, a whole range of community consultation opportunities can be created at community events that allow the sponsor to obtain something in an environment that is conducive to engagement by the festival audience. What is important from the community's point of view is that the event is enhanced by the sponsor to some degree in the interests of the community. This can range from facilitating advice or guidance opportunities such as engaging with the three emergency services, accessing limited blood stocks at a time when donors tend to be on holiday or adoption matching for minority and hard to reach groups that may normally never get the opportunity to properly engage with any of these services. A community service can then be provided through the industry in which the sponsor is based such as pharmaceuticals or the drinks industry. This is particularly significant as drink issues at one Liverpool festival led to special units and services being set up in local hospitals to support adults (parents), teenagers and even children on the problems of alcohol abuse and poisoning.

Considering the city's previous evidence of decline that for many years had an adverse influence on confidence and reputation (Trueman, Cornelius & Wallace, 2012), the local authority could take a lesson from the community reactions of the early 1980s. It is pertinent that this chapter largely discusses the scarcity of 'genuine' community events considering festivals' long association with resistance, social emancipation and social protest (Sharpe, 2008). Rioting against the police and the local authority may be uncommon in the region, but many similarities to events a generation ago are evident. A recession hit the United Kingdom at the turn of 1980s, employment was a major concern for a considerable proportion of residents and officially controlled community events, while still very popular (including Larks in the Park and the Liverpool Show), had local authority support removed.

The years of abject misery in the region that came and continued up to the 1990s can be likened to what Gilmore (2002) described as doubting the abilities of the people governing the area and a loss of pride in the community. Brand (2013) suggests that 'people for the first time in a generation are aware of massive corporate and economic exploitation', and the review of grass-roots activities in favour of events that must 'provide real authenticity and a strong sense of identity to the Liverpool brand' (CLIP, 2013) is a direct example of this.

Post ECoC 2008

As discussed, the local authority is using evidence from the ECoC 2008 report as the main driver in the future of the city's cultural offering. This is unfortunate because the report is evidently not particularly positive from a local community perspective. What is even more unfortunate is that the people in key positions at the local authority in the run-up to ECoC 2008, who understood the importance of community events as incubators for bigger things and ultimately their significance to the local community, have either left the local authority or retired. The year 2008 will undoubtedly become a seminal moment in the history of Liverpool and much of the fundamental effort that was built up in previous years that led to ECoC 2008 will be lost to history. The well-deserved credit is more likely to be attributed to people who in reality did little to make it happen.

For any meaningful community event to take place in Liverpool before 2017, an application through the new CLIP programme should have been undertaken before the application process closed mid-2013. Consequently, any new ideas will have to wait some time to apply. The guidance for applications articulates a clear and transparent agenda of exclusion by its process and by doing so risks losing the commitment of even more sections of the community. Regrettably, the local authority's mantra of a return on investment from public events is measured by economic impacts and not the intangible social and cultural impacts on the community that can affect the long-term profile and positioning of a tourist destination (Bowdin, Allen, O'Toole, Harris & McDonnell, 2011, p. 657). Decisions to support events are largely based on visitor numbers to the city and hotel performance figures during each particular event. However, a recent study (Ryan, 2014) of the new Liverpool International Music Festival (LIMF), which in 2013, due to attendee behaviour and policing issues, replaced the 20-year-old Mathew St Festival (MSF), provides evidence that the intended influx of visitors did not actually happen.

In preparation for visitors to the city for LIMF, the City Council, Arriva and Stagecoach agreed to provide a shuttle service between the city centre and Sefton Park to ensure direct access for tourists in and out of the principal free event of the festival. The event was a major success, though not as an event attended by tourists, but as an event attended by local people. The empty shuttle service buses needed to be redirected onto domestic routes where the demand existed. The audience was made up of local people, many of whom would normally travel to the city centre for the MSF. While parts of the city centre, including Liverpool One and Albert Dock, received a regular bank holiday trade, the lack of tourism was further evidenced by the fact that hotel numbers were down on like-for-like figures during the same weekend. Large parts of the city within the boundary of the 2012 MSF footprint were deserted during the August Bank Holiday, when the event was usually held, seriously affecting the local authority's intended economic return on investment.

When funds are 'invested' in certain events and tighter controls are imposed on community events, resentment inevitably begins to increase. The community leaders' efforts to build a community spirit is tested and stretched to the limit and often broken by a lack of local authority support and communication. One community manager summed the situation up in Liverpool as follows:

> Community spirit is not dead, it is very much alive and you know you can see that with Hillsborough – the Justice Campaign you know, you can see it when any tragedy happens in our city as in all other cities, the community comes together. But, when the community want to do something for themselves, then they're faced with barriers and constraints.

Certain community leaders and managers feel they are portrayed as being angry because they believe that support for community events that can break down barriers between social groups (Evans, 2005; Newman, Curtis & Stephens, 2003) and improve educational engagement (Carter, 2013) should be widely accessible and not restricted. Instead they are frustrated that events such as Royal de Luxe's parading of giants through the city centre at a cost of £1.5 million (Coslett, 2012) are prioritised ahead of community events. The myopic view suggested by one local authority manager that these large-scale events create a wealthy environment and bring benefits for the entire city and its inhabitants is fundamentally flawed and, more importantly, lacks community consultation. They assume far too much engagement from a large proportion of the community who do not have a disposable income and do not engage with the tourism-led events. It also assumes that local authority-supported events will attract visitors from outside the region; in some cases this is yet to be fully proven. LIMF may have removed the problems of MSF, but time will demonstrate whether these issues have merely been relocated. It is right that the local authority should seek broader investment both for and from tourism, but not to the detriment of local community events.

Conclusions

It can be generally accepted that community events bring people together to convey ideas, ideals and traditions and while a model community event does not exist as a point of reference, many events will continue to be presented to residents as community events. The model community event, after being free to enter, should include three core considerations: it is presented 'for' the community, the focus and/or content is characteristically 'of' the community and the event is delivered 'by' the community. Many of the now so-called community events in Liverpool will fall far short of meeting all three, but through alliances, legacy and certain individuals, Liverpool has created a robust arrangement that will – funding provided – guarantee the future of numerous events for a very long time. Whether they reach the mood and indeed the heart of the local community is less certain.

In cities today, the ability to deliver an event for the community is no longer a simple idea or combined effort of a few local residents. It was suggested by Quinn (2009, p. 9) that community festivals emerge as small-scale, localised endeavours founded by people in placed-based communities who are interested in celebrating something. If Quinn's (ibid.) people were to attempt to plan a community event today, they would have to be in possession of a number of skills that would equal those of a professional event manager. In situations where the knowledge, workforce and desire exist, the proposed event may still become unstuck if it does not meet the policies and cultural direction of the local authority. For existing community events, a combination of these difficulties have led to and will continue to contribute to the disappearance of popular community events in favour of centrally controlled tourism-led regeneration and the local authority's programme to ensure a return on *their* investment. To suggest that a 'community participation element' in every event that is held in Liverpool makes it 'for the community' is utterly disrespectful to the community.

The Liverpool Community Festival of 1999 did not meet the full criteria for what is explained to be the ultimate community event. It was funded by the local authority and included corporate sponsorship. However, the corporate sponsors were putting a considerable amount into the community and the local authority facilitated the needs of the community organisations. Therefore, both managed to meet with basic community event values. However, if a level-6 student had not walked in off the street and offered their time and effort for free, the 1999 Liverpool Community Festival would never have taken place. With the extent of scrutiny and control that exists for community events today, the same scenario is completely unimaginable.

References

Allen, J., O'Toole, W., Harris, R. & McDonnell, I. (2011). *Festival and special event management*, Milton, Qld: John Wiley & Sons.

Belchem, J. (2010). Hub and diaspora: Liverpool and transnational labour. *Labour History Review, 75*, 20–29.

Bowdin, G., Allen, J., O'Toole, W., Harris, R. & McDonnell, I. (2011). *Events management* (3rd edn). London: Elsevier.

Brand, R. (2013). *Newsnight: Paxman vs Brand – full interview*. Retrieved from www.youtube.com/watch?v=3YR4CseY9pk.

Carter, D. (2013). Urban regeneration, digital development strategies and the knowledge economy: Manchester case study. *Journal of the Knowldege Economy, 4*, 169–189.

Clarke, A. & Jepson, A. (2011). Power and hegemony in a community festival. *International Journal of Events and Festival Management, 2*(1), 7–19.

CLIP. (2013). *Culture Liverpool Investment Programme 2014–17*. Retrieved from http:// liverpool.gov.uk/business/finance-funding-and-grants/arts-and-culture-sector-grants/ culture-liverpool-investment-programme-grants.

Coslett, P. (2012). *Sea Odyssey giants capture Liverpool's heart*. Retrieved from www. bbc.co.uk/news/uk-england-merseyside-17806029.

Cox, T. & O'Brien, D. (2012). The 'scouse wedding' and other myths: Reflections on the evolution of a 'Liverpool model' for culture-led urban regeneration. *Cultural Trends, 21*, 93–101.

Daramola-Martin, A. (2009). Liverpool One and the transformation of a city: Place branding, marketing and the catalytic effects of regeneration and culture on repositioning Liverpool. *Place Branding & Public Diplomacy, 5*, 301–311.

Derrett, R. (2003). Making sense of how festivals demonstrate a community's sense of place. *Event Management, 8*, 49–58.

Durose, C. (2009). Front-line workers and 'local knowledge': Neighbourhood stories in contemporary UK local governance. *Public Administration, 87*, 35–49.

Evans, G. (2005). Measure for measure: Evaluating the evidence of culture's contribution to regeneration. *Urban Studies, 42*, 959–983.

Garcia, B., Melville, R. & Cox, T. (2010). Creating an impact: Liverpool's experience as European Capital of Culture. Impacts '08 European Capital of Culture Research Programme. *Impacts 08*. Liverpool: University of Liverpool and John Moores University.

Gilmore, F. (2002). A country: Can it be repositioned? Spain: The success story of country branding. *Journal of Brand Management, 9*, 281–293.

Grant, L. (2003). History broke Liverpool, and it broke my heart. *Guardian* G2, 2.

Jago, L., Chalip, L., Brown, G., Mules, T. & Ali, S. (2003). Building events into destination branding: Insights from experts. *Event Management, 8*, 3–14.

LCC. (2011). *The index of multiple deprivation 2010: A Liverpool analysis*. Liverpool: Liverpool City Council.

LCC. (2012). *Liverpool labour market update – October 2012*. Liverpool: Liverpool City Council.

LiverpoolVision. (2012). *People place & prosperity an economic prospectus Liverpool 2024*. Liverpool: Liverpool City Council.

LiverpoolVision. (2013a). *International festival for business 2014*. Liverpool: Liverpool City Council.

LiverpoolVision. (2013b). *Liverpool culture action plan 2014–2018*. Liverpool: Liverpool City Council.

Masterman, G.R. (2007). A strategic approach for the use of sponsorship in the events industry: In search of a return on investment. In I. Yeoman, M. Robertson, J. Ali-Knight, S. Drummond & U. McMahon-Beattie (eds), *Festival and events management: An international arts and culture perspective*. Oxford: Elsevier.

McGough, R. (1999). *A Liverpool Rainbow*. Liverpool: Liverpool Community Festival.

Newman, T., Curtis, K. & Stephens, J. (2003). Do community-based arts projects result in social gains? A review of the literature. *Community Development Journal, 38*, 310–322.

O'Brien, D. (2010). Liverpool on the map again: Liverpool stakeholders' reflections on the Liverpool European Capital of Culture. *Impacts 08 – European Capital of Culture Research Programme*. Liverpool: University of Liverpool and John Moores University.

Quinn, B. (2009). Festivals, events and tourism. In T. Jamal & M. Robinson (eds), *The SAGE handbook of tourism studies*. London: Sage.

Rose, N. (1999). *Powers of freedom: Reframing political thought*. Cambridge: Cambridge University Press.

Ryan, W.G. (2014). *A review of the Liverpool International Music Festival 2013*. Manuscript in preparation.

Sharpe, E.K. (2008). Festivals and social change: Intersections of pleasure and politics at a community music festival. *Leisure Sciences, 30*, 217–234.

Smith, A. (2012). *Events and urban regeneration: The strategic use of events to revitalise cities*. Abingdon: Routledge.

Taylor, P. (2007). Liverpool arts: A world turned upside down. *NALGAO Magazine*, Winter.

Trueman, M., Cornelius, N. & Wallace, J. (2012). Building brand value online: Exploring relationships between company and city brands. *European Journal of Marketing, 46*, 1013–1031.

Vigurs, K. (2009). Reconceptualising conflict and consensus within partnerships: The role of overlapping communities and dynamic social ties. Unpublished doctoral thesis, Staffordshire University.

VisitLiverpool. (2009). *Liverpool city region visitor economy strategy to 2020: A summary*. Liverpool: The Mersey Partnership.

Williams, P.W., Gill, A.M. & Chura, N. (2004). Branding mountain destinations: The Battle for 'Peacefulness'. *Tourism Review, 59*, 6–15.

18　Back to the future

Allan Jepson and Alan Clarke

If you have read the book from beginning to end, let us thank you for your attention and you are welcome to the conclusions, after what we trust will have been a fascinating journey through a series of challenging chapters, drawing on multi-disciplinary methods and a truly international selection of examples. If you have come here first or via some other shortcut, we urge you to go back and look more thoroughly at what you have missed. It will be time well spent, even if you cannot see the direct relevance of the individual chapter to what you are interested in right now.

The chapters we have brought together in this book have provided a wide-ranging view of communities, a vast array of festivals and events linked in many different ways to those communities, presented from a variety of research perspectives and with a variety of foci. There are many synergies within the book that appear to us, both between the chapters and with our previous work that, as we explained in the Introduction, helped to frame the context of the book. The joy of being the editors is that we have not just read the chapters but we have worked with the narratives and come to know the subjects in a much more detailed way than a simple reading would have given us. In many ways we have come to see our contributors as a part of our new community and our editing has involved reinforcing rituals and conventions fostering a definitive sense of those community relations.

We have seen a respectful acknowledgement of the amount of work that has been undertaken in this field before but no one has expressed a sense of contentment with that previous research. We believe that the chapters collected here have broadened our critical understandings of the specificities of communities and their festivals and events. There are many contributors who have proposed new avenues for further research and we would look forward to seeing where these ideas can be taken.

There is a potentially huge agenda addressing the role and importance of the history of the community festival and events. Looking backwards has shown how the discourses that we experience in the present were also living in the past and helped to shape our presents as they were played out. Our ideas of nationality, identity and sense of place have been shown to be deeply rooted in the specific experiences of our communities. Also we recognise the power that the whole idea of identifying the festivity within communities and their festivals and events brings to our analyses. We can no longer see any tenable position that holds to a monocultural account of our sense of place as we have seen that discourses of home and identity are both multifaceted and dynamic.

We are also impressed by the weight this adds to the case for ensuring that research into communities' festivals and events needs to be multidisciplinary in order to grasp the complexities of these phenomena. There will still be a place for studies that emerge from a single discipline and questions that can be answered through these disciplinary discourses. However, we believe that the research presented here demonstrates the validity and justifies further research into community festivals and events utilising multidisciplinary approaches. The quest for understanding by working with the meanings that are embedded in the communities and these productions of experiences necessitates multidisciplinary sensitivities. We have been bogged down in searching for single interpretations of difficult concepts when we might be better encouraged to explore a variety of constructions and recognise the multiversity of these settings and experiences.

The narratives presented here have urged us to recognise the value of cultural meanings within the communities and their festivals and events. This recognition is not a call for our research to focus on value in a narrow functional sense of its economic return. This is one element in our understanding, but not enough to provide any real understanding of the festivals and events. What the contributions have shown is that we need to inform our research from the surrounding fields of study, including history, sociology, psychology, anthropology, ethnography and policy analysis if not politics. Our future lies in finding our way through this multidisciplinary matrix to fully grasp the holistic picture of the communities and their festivals and events.

We also feel that bringing the book together has demonstrated the value of the mutual benefit of bringing communities and culture together. The chapters clearly demonstrate how communities value and need their cultures, while also reinforcing how those communities themselves are rooted in their cultures. It is the expression of these senses of cultures, their meanings and values that allow communities to identify themselves and allow people to claim belonging to those communities. The analyses of these situations draws us back to the complexity of the power relations and the play of discourses involved in the way people come to define themselves or to recognise others.

We have seen that there are serious debates to be engaged in around these identities and the senses of place that are generated in the communities and their festivals and events. We have seen how communities can make use of their cultures from previous places of residence and how the sense of home can be reinterpreted. The chapters have offered revelations about how communities, even when separated from home territories, seek out familiar cultures to unite themselves and others around them to provide links to their homeland. It may also be possible to see these claims to a sense of homecoming from those who may not have any strict claim to the sense of national inheritance, as the Irish have noted with the 'plastic paddies' who emerge around St Patrick's Day

(17 March). The communities, with more or less fixity, demonstrate the inter-linkages with the values and meanings of the play of the cultures.

The other contribution that we believe emerges from this volume is the importance of adopting an international perspective. The 16 chapters we have included come from nine different countries but even more importantly they have not come from simple representations of those nations. The negotiation of the sense of place and the idea of home, expressed readily in terms of the belonging to football, in memories around peace and war, and even in Dowson's notion of churched and dechurched, is central to the understanding of communities that emerges from these complex narratives. There are significant similarities to be found in events from around the world but the accounts also reveal the necessity of specificity as the differences can be as significant as the similarities.

We believe that this book shows the way forward for event research as multi-disciplinary and presents a call for internationally coordinated research into festivals and events. The validity of multidisciplinary research into community festivals is demonstrated by the multiplicity of viewpoints articulated through the chapter contributions. This book cannot be and should not be the final word in this field of studies. We need to continue to interrogate and critically evaluate constantly what is happening in our communities and how they are working with or being reworked by their or other people's festivals and events. Ownership and direction become significant elements in the future and we neglect them at our peril. Narratives of culture, heritage, identity and place have powers that may be intangible but nonetheless shape the communities we live in and those we visit.

Communities will benefit from involvement in festivals and events as they build skills and competences in the context of the festival. This involves new discourses of power and recognising new claims to legitimacy and opening the organisation to new stakeholders and their voices with possibilities of other ways of thinking about what is important in the festival. Analyses of the community relations between the different actors will deepen the exploration of the ways in which a range of voices come to be heard or not heard within the development processes. Therefore studies of the community relations involved should also explore those situations where these communities may even feel marginalised and disenfranchised from these processes. This has been demonstrated in their lack of desire to participate even in shaping the agendas of what could have become their own communities' festivals.

We foresee further research into the constructions of the agendas and content of community festivals. Our investigations suggest that the decision-making processes have demonstrated that the agenda of community festivals has been shaped by the powerful stakeholders rather than the powerless. Hegemonic decisions have constrained the elements that have been showcased, marginalising other minority cultures in the development of the festivals. From the perspective of exploring communities and gaining a holistic understanding, the future will demand research concerning involvement and capacity development that must approach these terms from a consideration that these processes are neutral. Considerations of relations within communities show that involvement is a site of negotiation and even contestation over what and who can be involved in which roles and places. Similarly, claims that festivals empower local communities require studies of the power relations involved in the creation, production and consumption of the festivals. The range of skills and competences that the festivals and events can support are only realised if there is full involvement by the communities in the processes involved in the festivals. Cultural diversity within local cultural festivals and events can only achieved through an integrated and inclusive event planning process.

We think the research agenda should encompass further studies of communities illuminating the patterns of decision-making processes employed within and around local cultural festivals and events. This would explore the way in which festivals construct images of the communities and unpack how we have come to see so many mono-ethnic events and placeless festivals. Empowerment would help to ensure that festivals fully represent the multicultural nature of the communities and represent the full complex dimensions of the places that give support to those festivals. This would mean seeing the communities directly involved in funding decisions and event planning, not just performance.

The implications for the involvement of the local communities in the event industry based upon the present evidence suggest that organisers must become more aware of and sensitive to the wide range of stakeholders potentially involved in community festivals. They will have to look beyond the readily identifiable lists of the great and the good to uncover the dynamics within the communities themselves. Power has been revealed as a pervasive and constructive set of forces that are both enabling and disenfranchising.

Further analyses of community relationships are necessary to unpack the ways in which the events and festivals are put together, consumed and experienced. This will involve exploring the ways in which the positions of power are constructed, challenged and reinforced both within the management of the festivals and events and within the diverse cultures and heritages that could be involved. It will become necessary to identify those who maintain and reinforce dominant positions within these processes and how they shape the involvement and exclusion of other stakeholders from the development of festivals.

Communities must be seen as multifaceted and shifting. Stakeholders can build and contest positions based upon the construction and reconstruction of discursive practices. These arguments are pertinent in the evolution of community festivals as the key players develop power from a number of different sources; the traditional bases of the established community may not equate to those in the local communities. The community's values can suggest other ways of thinking and seeing the shape of the festivals in ways that recognise the meanings that are important within those communities.

Index

Page numbers in *italics* denote tables, those in **bold** denote figures.